HITLER'S
IRISHMEN

HITLER'S IRISHMEN

TERENCE O'REILLY

MERCIER PRESS

WHAT YOU NEED TO READ

MERCIER PRESS
Cork
www.mercierpress.ie

Trade enquiries to:

CMD,
55a Spruce Avenue, Stillorgan Industrial Park,
Blackrock, County Dublin.

ISBN: 978 1 85635 589 6

10 9 8 7 6 5 4 3 2

Mercier Press receives financial assistance from
the Arts Council/An Chomhairle Ealaíon

Printed and bound in the EU.

Contents

Prologue

By September 1946, the euphoria that had swept Britain in the wake of the victory over Germany was a fading memory. Strict rationing was still in force. Most of Britain's merchant fleet, once the largest in the world, had been lost to German U-boats during the war. Many of the 'demobbed' servicemen returning from the battlefields had no homes to return to – more than half a million British homes had been destroyed by Luftwaffe bombs and V-1 and V-2 missiles. Britain's first postwar parliament, held in July 1945, had to be held in the smaller House of Lords, the House of Commons itself having suffered bomb damage. Just two months after Winston Churchill's triumphant victory speech as Britain's wartime prime minister, he had been banished to the opposition benches in the wake of the Labour party's general election victory. The British working class, after so many years of sacrifice, had higher expectations of what the postwar years should bring, as indeed had many subjects of Britain's severely weakened empire. In the face of Russia and the United States' opposition to colonialism, the disintegration of the British empire was already beginning in India and the Middle East. Clement Attlee's new government quickly instituted sweeping reforms, nationalising vital industries and creating new social programmes, including the National Health Service. With these new measures came higher taxes. By 1947, Britain was approaching bankruptcy.

Already the first serious strains in the alliance between Soviet Russia and her western allies were becoming apparent. In 1946, Joseph Stalin was consolidating his gains in eastern Europe and had ordered the communist parties of the western nations onto the offensive. Already civil war was raging in Greece between American and British-backed government forces and communist guerrillas. The United States in turn initiated a policy of 'containment' of communism worldwide. In March 1946, in Missouri, Churchill made his famous speech in which he declared that an 'iron curtain' had descended across the continent of Europe.

By 1946, the flow of liberated prisoners-of-war returning to Britain from Europe, and subsequently Asia, had all but ceased. During the war, most of those who had made the difficult 'home run' from a POW camp in occupied Europe back to Britain had been directed to the Great Central Hotel in Marylebone, London. This building, commandeered by the British War Office after the outbreak of war, was designated the 'London transit camp' where former POWs were debriefed on the second floor by MI-9, the secret service which was set up early in the war to aid escape attempts from German POW camps. Many intriguing stories came to light in the hotel's once luxurious surroundings, but few were as strange as the one that emerged on the morning of 24 September 1946, when a tall young Irishman who had been flown in from occupied Germany three days earlier was escorted to one of the hotel rooms where he was met by two men in civilian dress sitting behind a trestle table. These were not members of MI-9, however – that organisation had been disbanded at the end of the war. They were in fact members of a special unit set up after the outbreak of the war to investigate serious crimes committed by members of the British Army.

One spoke: 'I am a Sergeant in the Special Investigation Branch, Corps of Military Police. I am making enquiries with regard to your activities whilst a prisoner-of-war in Germany.'

The addressee nodded. 'I've been expecting this.' A little later, he was asked to display a tattoo under his left armpit.

It was a small, simple marking, consisting of no more than the letter 'A', but its import was far more serious. The practice of tattooing a blood group in this manner was generally associated with membership of the SS.

At 10.45 a.m., with Sergeant Cash dictating, the Irishman began a lengthy statement.

'Start at the beginning,' Cash instructed. 'Where were you born?'

'My name is James Brady. I was born on 20 May 1920, Co. Roscommon, Ireland of Irish-born parents.'[1]

Of the handful of Irishmen who worked for Nazi Germany during the Second World War, only a few are known to have served the notorious SS, and of these only two are known to have worn the uniform of the organisation's military wing, the Waffen-SS. These two men, James Brady and his friend, Frank Stringer, are unique in a few respects, not least the fact that only a very few Irishmen have served any military force of Germany or its predecessors. Irish soldiers served in their thousands and with distinction in the Irish legions of France, Spain and Austria, and eventually in the Irish regiments of the British Army, to mention only the largest contingents. Many armies have boasted Irish units; on occasion these Irishmen having fought on opposite sides, as for example during the American Civil War and the Boer War. One Irishman, Marshal Peter de Lacey, commanded the Russian Army of Catherine the Great, while individual Irishmen made a significant contribution to the independence movement in South America in the early nineteenth century. But there was hardly any tradition of Irish service in the Germanic armies; while the Irish served the Catholic kingdoms of Europe in their thousands, examples of Irishmen who have opted to serve the post-Reformation German states or the post-1870 unified Germany have been few and far between. Germany and Ireland are heirs to proud military heritages, which have remained largely separated. The Germanic reputation for military excellence was firmly established in AD 9 with the annihilation of three Roman legions in the Teutonburger Wald. It was particularly enhanced by Frederick William I, who ruled Prussia as the 'soldier's king' from 1713 to 1740, establishing a country with a population of just two million as a major military power in Europe. The fierce disciplinary code of his 80,000-strong army, in which floggings and executions were commonplace, combined with such technical innovations as an iron musket ramrod which considerably increased infantry firepower, resulted in the most formidable force on a European battlefield.

Despite the introduction of new tactics, such as bringing three lines of fast-firing infantry against the enemy, bayonet charges still remained important, and tall grenadiers were considered the most effective in this type of fighting. From this, Frederick William is said to have developed the obsession with the battalion of freakishly tall grenadiers that became the only ceremonial unit in his army. The king sent agents all over Europe to find recruits for this unit, no expense spared; given the exceedingly harsh regime of the Prussian army, volunteers were unsurprisingly rare, and most enlistees were, quite literally, kidnap victims. This was the only endeavour on which the normally miserly Frederick William was willing to spend money freely, although he did not spend state revenue, instead establishing a special fund to which anyone seeking favour might contribute.

One of the few concessions to the welfare of these 'Potsdam Grenadiers' was the appointment of a chaplain, Fr Raymond Bruns of the Dominican order, to administer to the Catholics among them. Fr Bruns' account of his service in Potsdam mentions at least two Irishmen, James Kirkland and Grenadier 'Macdoll' (probably MacDowell). The former had been inveigled, at the age of twenty, into the service of Herr von Borcke, a Prussian envoy in London, ostensibly as a footman, following which he had been sent to Hamburg on an 'errand'. He soon found himself on the barrack square at

Potsdam, learning the straight-legged goosestep and 180 different rifle exercises, any mistakes being swiftly 'corrected' by the sticks of the Prussian drill sergeants. Due to his height of 6'8" he was appointed file-leader and served thus from 1734 to 1739.

Grenadier 'Macdoll' apparently came into Frederick William's good graces. Fr Bruns tells a tale in which the king, out riding, met a pretty girl and, deciding that she would make a good wife for the Irishman, ordered her to deliver a message to the commander at Potsdam, which detailed him to marry 'the bearer' to 'Macdoll' without delay! The girl, however, astutely passed the message to an old woman, resulting in a 'stormy' marriage ceremony which was annulled by the king the following day, Fr Bruns evidently not having been consulted on either occasion. This might not be entirely far-fetched: in later years the Potsdam Grenadiers became the king's personal bodyguard, and the tale is certainly in keeping with the king's personality.[2]

After Frederick William's death and succession by his son, Frederick the Great in 1741, a new royal bodyguard was formed in the shape of the Lieb-Husaren regiment, which adopted the Totenkopf (death's head) motif along with a black uniform. Frederick also acquired some Irishmen for his army; after the Battle of Pirna in 1756, the commander of the Prussian Infantry Regiment No. 19 'persuaded' several Irish prisoners who had been fighting for the Saxons to join his force.[3]

German troops, in service with the British Army, were deployed in Ireland during the 1798 rebellion, when the 5th Battalion of the 60th Foot (Hesse-Darmstadt Legion) under the command of Major von Verna was deployed in the Wicklow area, taking part in the British General Moore's operation in the Glen of Imaal area in mid-July of that year. As in the American War of Independence, these Hessian soldiers quickly gained a reputation for brutality, no mean feat given the standards of that conflict. Already disgusted by the 'dreadful' conduct of the Germans, and perturbed by the fear which they inspired among the local populace, General Moore expressed no sympathy when several Hessians on a pillaging expedition were ambushed and massacred by locals and took the opportunity to tighten control over them.[4]

Even within the British Army of the time, there was an obvious animosity between Irishmen and Germans. When an infantry battalion and a Hussar squadron of the King's German Legion were based in the Irish town of Tullamore in 1806, they were involved in a bloody clash with Irish militiamen, in which firearms, bayonets and cavalry sabres were used freely. Although the causes of the clash owed more to rivalry for the attentions of local females rather than politics, 'years later it was yet evident that the Irish and Germans in King George's service were far from friends'.[5]

Following the crushing of the 1798 rebellion, the Prussian Army expressed an interest in finding recruits among the many Irish rebels who were now being held prisoner. In March 1799, Lord Castlereagh, the British chief secretary in Ireland, received a letter from Captain Schouler of the Struckwitz Infantry Regiment proposing the general terms for the recruitment of such prisoners. Subsequently, Captain Schouler selected 318 prospective recruits from the rebel prisoners being held at New Geneva Barracks in Waterford, and in September 1799 they were transported to Emden. The Prussian Army apparently distributed them among several regiments rather than forming any 'Irish Brigade', and in peacetime they were used as slave workers in the mines. In 1806, Napoleon's armies inflicted a heavy defeat on the Prussian Army at Jena, and thousands of Prussian soldiers were taken prisoner. When Napoleon's Irish Legion arrived in Mainz, they were greatly surprised to encounter Irishmen among the Prussian prisoners there, many of whom quickly joined their countrymen in the French Army. Captain Miles Byrne of the Irish Legion was delighted to welcome several fellow Wexfordmen whom he had fought alongside in the

1798 rebellion. Another former rebel and Prussian conscript named Molony subsequently became a sergeant-major in Napoleon's Irish Legion, and afterward a captain in an Irish regiment of the Spanish Army. Few of the conscripts from New Geneva Barracks ever saw Ireland again.[6]

The Prussian Army's rank list of 1873 includes a 'Second Lieutenant O'Grady', holder of the Iron Cross second class, probably awarded during the Franco-Prussian War of 1870. This same officer, as a colonel, served in the First World War, responsible for emplacements on the eastern front. A Lieutenant O'Grady is recorded as having served with the German field artillery before 1914. Oberst and Leutnant O'Grady, however, are thought to have been Irish by descent rather than birth.[7]

The outbreak of the First World War seemed to present Irish republicans with an opportunity to further their cause, and to this end, Sir Roger Casement, noted human rights activist, was sent to Germany to elicit aid. In November 1914 he claimed to the German foreign ministry that he could convince significant numbers of Irishmen, members of the British Army being held in POW camps in Germany, to defect to a German-organised Irish brigade. An agreement was drawn up which stated: 'With a view to securing the national freedom of Ireland, with the moral and material assistance of the Imperial German Government, an Irish Brigade shall be formed from among the Irish soldiers or other natives of Ireland now prisoners of war in Germany.' Germany would supply arms and equipment 'as a free gift to aid the cause of Irish independence'. The Irish brigade, however, was not to be 'employed or directed to any German end'. It was also to have its own distinctive uniform.

The Irish POWs were concentrated in a camp at Limburg, near Frankfurt. These were all volunteer soldiers, many of whom had served in the Irish regiments of the British Army for some years and who had been captured by the Germans in the first year of war. Casement's first address to them in December 1914 inspired only shock; his second provoked outright hostility. His early efforts provided only two recruits, a Sergeant Keogh and Corporal Quinlisk. They struck Casement as 'rogues', and this estimation would certainly prove correct of the latter.

By April 1916, there were no more than fifty-three members of the 'brigade'. An Irish officer was added to the establishment when Robert Monteith, a former warrant officer in the British Army, arrived in Germany and was commissioned into the German Army. Despite its modest numbers, the establishment of the 'brigade' included two senior NCOs (Quinlisk and Keogh), three sergeants and three corporals. The uniform worn by 'Casement's brigade' was the standard German feldgrau worn with a brown leather belt carrying the famous 'GOTT MIT UNS' buckle of the German Army. NCOs' insignia were a combination of British and German; prominent chevrons on the upper arm and distinctive piping on the collar. Some distinctively Irish insignia was also worn, for example a harp on the headgear and shamrock on the buttons.

The 'brigade' was not an effective force. Drinking and fighting were rife; when the Irishmen were based in the German Army barracks at Sossen, the commander is ruefully said to have remarked that the fifty Irishmen caused him more trouble than the 17,000 Germans also based there.

Despairing of his efforts, and contemptuous of the German government whose only eventual contribution to the imminent Irish rebellion was the dispatch of a ship covertly carrying weapons, Casement prevailed on the Germans to return him to Ireland by U-boat, in an apparent attempt to call the rebellion off. Two members of his 'brigade', Robert Monteith, and Daniel Bailey, the latter travelling under the name 'Sergeant Beverly', accompanied him. In April 1916, after a long and difficult submarine voyage to the south-west of Ireland, the three were landed on the Kerry coast. Casement was soon captured by two members of the Royal Irish

Constabulary, one of them called Constable Reilly. Bailey was apprehended shortly afterwards. The German boat, the *Aud*, was captured by the Royal Navy and scuttled by the German crew in Cork harbour.[8]

On Easter Monday 1916, the Irish Volunteers and the Irish Citizen Army seized key posts throughout Dublin and declared an Irish Republic. A proclamation was read which claimed that the rebellion had the support of 'our gallant allies in Europe', which the landing of Casement and the capture of the *Aud* seemed to lend credence to. The British reaction was vicious; reinforcements were rushed in from England and artillery shelled the rebel positions. The lightly armed rebels were soon outnumbered and the rebellion was crushed within the week, devastating central Dublin in the process. Irish public opinion, indifferent to republicanism before the Rising, was strongly influenced by the British Army's execution of thirteen of the rebel leaders, was further disturbed by the mass internment of Irish people who had no involvement in the rebellion and was finally incensed by the British government's threat to introduce conscription in Ireland. The 1916 rebels, reviled by Dubliners as they went into British captivity, received a hero's welcome on their release. In the general election of December 1918, the Sinn Féin republican party, formally moderate nationalists, won seventy-five of 105 seats in Ireland. Refusing to take their seats in Westminster, the Sinn Féin party declared an independent Irish parliament (Dáil Éireann) in January 1919; that month also saw the first shots fired by Sinn Féin's military wing (the Irish Republican Army) in a guerrilla war known in Ireland as the War of Independence.

It would seem that two of the most famous members of Casement's 'brigade' were loyal to no other cause than their own self-interest. When Casement went on trial for treason, resulting in his eventual conviction and execution, Daniel Bailey gave evidence against him.

In 1919, one of Casement's first recruits, Timothy Quinlisk, introduced himself to Michael Collins, the *de facto* leader of the newly organised Irish Republican Army (IRA). Believing that Quinlisk's military experience and knowledge of German could be useful, Collins supplied him with accommodation and money. In November 1919, Quinlisk secretly contacted the British authorities with an offer to provide them with information regarding Collins. Unfortunately for him, Collins' extensive list of contacts included detectives in the Dublin Metropolitan Police's 'G' (political) division. Quinlisk was manipulated and fed disinformation by the IRA until January 1920, when a price of £10,000 was placed on Collins' head. Acting on (false) information, Quinlisk sent the Royal Irish Constabulary to a hotel in Cork, to which he travelled with unseemly haste to ensure his bounty. His corpse was found in a ditch shortly afterwards.[9]

The guerrilla war between the IRA and British forces continued with increasing bitterness and was greatly intensified by the deployment of the notorious 'Black and Tans', a force intended to reinforce the beleaguered Royal Irish Constabulary but whose brutality to the civil populace greatly reinforced resentment against the British government. A truce in the summer of 1921 led to negotiations between the two sides, and the signing of an Anglo-Irish Treaty in December of that year established the Irish Free State. Although ratified by Dáil Éireann and a national vote, a large portion of the IRA opposed aspects of the treaty and a civil war erupted in July 1922. The anti-treaty faction faced defeat by May 1923, and many members eventually chose to support a constitutional political party, Fianna Fáil, led by Éamon de Valera.

It was a time of political upheaval throughout Europe. Italy's participation in the First World War had brought about the postwar collapse of its economy and democratic politics. By 1920 left-wing agitation had reached a point where revolution seemed imminent. War veteran and former socialist Benito Mussolini seized the opportunity to emerge as the champion of the right, organising groups of disgruntled ex-servicemen into squads of black-shirted 'fasci' to oppose socialist groups in increasingly bloody clashes. While the word 'fasci' meant 'groups', the 'fasces' also referred to the Roman axe carried as a symbol of unity and authority, hence naming a new political movement: fascism. While Mussolini was able to claim that he had defeated socialism in Italy by mid-1921, in October 1922 he orchestrated an effective *coup d'etat* by ordering his Blackshirts to march on Rome, bringing him to power and establishing the first European fascist state.

In Germany, fascism was represented by the Nazi party (NSDAP – *Nationalsozialistische Deutsche Abeiterpartei*), now led by war veteran Adolf Hitler. Its political muscle was provided by thousands of members of the Sturm Abteilung (SA), who chose a brown shirt as their uniform. Although the famous air ace, Hermann Goering, was officially appointed commander, the driving force behind the organisation remained former army captain, Ernst Roehm. There were many undesirable elements among the ranks of the SA, however, and in March 1923 Hitler ordered the formation of a personal bodyguard, the 100-strong Stosstrupp Adolf Hitler, which adopted a totenkopf (death's head) as its distinctive symbol. The death's head motif was originally carried by Frederick the Great's Lieb-Husaren regiments, and this, along with the black uniform, was subsequently associated with the famous Death's Head Hussars. The totenkopf was carried by several crack units of the German Army during the First World War and became synonymous with loyalty and self-sacrifice. It was thus eagerly seized upon as a symbol by the Stosstrupp Adolf Hitler in 1923. When the German Army founded an armoured corps (the Panzerwaffe), they too adopted a death's head motif (worn on the collar) along with a black uniform. Following the liberation of the concentration camps in 1945, and the revelations of the SS engineering of the Holocaust, the SS totenkopf would take on an awful new significance.

On 9 November 1923, Hitler attempted to seize power in

Bavaria, in the 'beerhall putsch' in Munich. Groups of Brown-shirts seized government buildings in the city, and were besieged by government forces. When Ernst Roehm's group was trapped in the War Ministry, a relief column of 2,000 Brownshirts led by Hitler (surrounded by his bodyguards) and the famous General Ludendorff marched to their aid. Armed police opened fire on the column, killing sixteen Nazis. The putsch collapsed and Hitler spent a year in Landsburg prison during which he wrote *Mein Kampf*. After his release, Hitler formed a new bodyguard, originally named the 'Schutzkommando', but in November 1925 renamed the 'Schutzstaffel' – the SS. This may have been a suggestion by Hermann Goering as an allusion to a fighter escort, or 'protection squadron'. Unlike the SA, which took any applicant, the SS introduced selective entry criteria. The SS, however, was still subordinate to the SA, and tended to be assigned menial tasks by local Brownshirt commanders. When a bespectacled young agriculturalist by the name of Heinrich Himmler was appointed to the lofty sounding post of 'Reichsführer der SS' in January 1929, SS membership stood at less than 300. From such humble beginnings Himmler was eventually to build his new power base into the most powerful organisation in Nazi Germany.

By the time Hitler came to power in Germany in 1933, SS strength stood at 50,000. In March that year, Himmler was appointed police president of Munich, and opened the first SS concentration camp at Dachau. In the same month, Hitler ordered the formation of an SS armed guard for the protection of the Reichschancellory. An elite force, originally 117 strong, was organised and soon took up duties, wearing a distinctive black uniform and setting new standards in ceremonial drill. Prospective recruits to this showpiece force had to satisfy increasingly higher physical standards (even a filled tooth merited disqualification) and had to prove German ancestry back to the year 1800.

One of the most humiliating stipulations of the Treaty of

Versailles which had ended the First World War had been the order that all German military academies were to be abolished. This included the Lichterfelde Kaserne at Berlin, Germany's equivalent to Sandhurst or West Point. On 10 March 1920, the date of the academy's closure, the last class of cadets staged a defiant parade through Berlin, led by a score of senior officers, former cadets in years past. These included General Ludendorff, who hinted to the cadets that the closure of their school might prove temporary. When the Nazis gained power in 1933, however, the barracks at Lichterfelde was not returned to the German Army, but became the home of Hitler's SS bodyguards. On 9 November 1933, Hitler granted the new force, now 835 strong, the title of Leibstandarte SS Adolf Hitler.

By June 1934, the increasingly unruly SA were posing a threat to Hitler's position. On the 'Night of the Long Knives' the SS proved its loyalty by killing several Brownshirts and other political opponents of Hitler. A Leibstandarte firing squad carried out several executions in Lichterfelde. The SS was rewarded by being finally removed from SA jurisdiction. The SA, although allowed to continue in existence as an impotent paramilitary force, was reduced in strength from four million to one million. Himmler did some purging of his own, dismissing some 60,000 undesirables from the ranks of the SS in his continuing quest to establish his organisation as a knightly elite. Items such as ceremonial rings and daggers were authorised, and Wewelsburg Castle was established as an SS 'Camelot', complete with a round table for Himmler and his twelve most favoured senior SS officers.

The military aspirations of the SS were becoming increasingly apparent, to the concern of the Wehrmacht, the regular German armed forces. Apart from the Leibstandarte, now organised into two motorised battalions, the SS formed the SS-Vergungstruppe (SS-VT), armed 'internal security' troops, and the armed SS-Totenkopfverbande, which although originally formed to administer the SS concentration

camp system, eventually formed the notorious 'Totenkopf'
division of the Waffen-SS. The Wehrmacht were undergoing a much-welcomed expansion under Hitler's rule. An armoured corps and an air force (Luftwaffe) were established
and the Heer (army) was growing far greater than 100,000
troops, all of which had been forbidden by the Treaty of Versailles. The pre-Nazi German Army (Reichswehr) had kept
their officer corps to no greater than 4,000, keeping the 'one
officer to twenty men' ratio that was the hallmark of many of
history's best fighting forces. Ironically, in view of the Heer's
contempt for the SS (whom they referred to as 'asphalt soldiers' in a reference to their parade ground abilities), this very
select corps would provide several senior officers for the SS
military wing.[10]

In February 1932, the Fianna Fáil party was elected to power
in Ireland, an event which naturally caused some dismay
among members of the Irish Free State's army and police
who had, after all, been fighting members of the new government ten years earlier. The only attempt to oppose the new
regime, however, was by garda (police) Commissioner Eoin
O'Duffy, who had approached garda and army officers before
the election to establish support for a proposed *coup d'etat*.
Although O'Duffy had been confident enough to print
several copies of a proclamation to explain to Irish citizens
why the democratic process had been abandoned, almost
all of these officers reacted angrily against the proposal, the
Army's Chief of Staff threatening to have O'Duffy arrested.
After the election of Fianna Fáil, O'Duffy was removed from
his post.

In July 1933, O'Duffy accepted the leadership of the Army
Comrades Association, founded the previous October, ostensibly as a Free State Army veterans association, but evidently
to add some political 'muscle' to the opposition parties, who
were facing intimidation from the remnants of the IRA. The
organisation had already adopted a blue shirt as its uniform,

and its manifestly right-wing antecedents naturally led to
comparisons with the similarly attired fascist organisations
in Italy and Germany. O'Duffy announced that he intended
to lead a march on government buildings in Dublin, ostensibly to lay wreaths at a memorial to dead Free State leaders. Comparing O'Duffy's proposed action with Mussolini's
march on Rome, De Valera banned both the march and
the National Guard. While the Blueshirts abandoned their
march, they simply renamed their organisation the 'Young
Ireland Association', which in turn was banned and quickly
renamed the 'League of Youth'. The organisation adopted the
straight-armed Nazi salute, and became heavily involved in
nationwide political violence. A new opposition party, Fine
Gael, was formed with O'Duffy in charge, but performed
badly in the local government elections of 1934. Moderates
in the new party began voicing concerns about O'Duffy and
his methods, and in September that year a split within the
League of Youth sent O'Duffy into the political wilderness.
Under new leadership, the Fine Gael party concentrated on
democratic politics, while the Blueshirts dissolved within
a year. Once the true nature of European fascism became
clear, a certain stigma became attached to membership of the
Blueshirts. The term 'Blueshirt' became a popular insult, and
to this day very few of the original blue shirt garments are
known to remain in existence.

On 17 July 1936, a group of Spanish army officers launched
an armed rebellion against their democratically elected
government. This started the Spanish Civil War, which split
the country into supporters of the leftist Popular Front ruling
party and of the right-wing rebels. Italy and Germany soon
began sending military aid to their fellow fascist, nationalist
General Franco, while the Soviet Union eventually supported
the republican government forces.

While the Spanish Civil War tends to be viewed today as
broadly a struggle between fascist and democratic forces, this
division was not so apparent in 1936. In Spain, the Catholic

Church tended to be identified with the nationalists, while the republic's supporters included fanatical communists and anarchists. In Ireland, public opinion was galvanised by press reports and newsreel footage of atrocities against Catholic churches and clergy by Spanish republican forces. Within three weeks, Eoin O'Duffy announced his intention to raise an Irish brigade to fight for the nationalists. This was the genesis of O'Duffy's 'fascist' battalion which, according to popular ballad, 'sailed under the swastika to Spain'. Like the Blueshirts, O'Duffy's battalion, equipped with German uniforms and weapons, was certainly fascist by appearance. While the leadership was certainly pro-fascist, the main motivation for the rank and file were their devout Catholicism, and an earnest desire to fight 'Bolshevism'. While 300 of this unit's eventual seven hundred members had prior military experience, mostly with the Irish Free State Army, relatively few of these 'crusaders' could be classed as military adventurers. Two of this category had already served in the Spanish Foreign Legion, one having also served in the French Foreign Legion while the other had served in the Royal Navy and the US Navy. Whatever their actual intentions, the members of O'Duffy's battalion would end up serving a fascist cause, but not very effectively.

On a perhaps significant date, namely Friday 13 November 1936, an advance party of ten of O'Duffy's volunteers sailed from Ireland to Spain. Other groups followed, the largest of which left Galway on the *Dún Aengus* ferry on a stormy night in December to rendezvous with a larger German vessel, the SS *Urundi*. There followed a hazardous transfer of several hundred personnel between the two ships in gale-force conditions, after which they were transported to El Ferrol in north-west Spain aboard the *Urundi*. By Christmas, the 700 volunteers were assembled in the town of Cacares, the men accommodated in purpose-built barracks, the officers in a nearby hotel. By the new year, the men received German uniforms of the First World War issue, no doubt an irony to some members of the battalion who had served in the British Army during that conflict. A harp insignia was worn on the tunic lapels. Obsolete rifles of various designs were originally issued but were replaced by German weapons. It was announced that the Irish volunteers would form the XV Bandera (battalion) of the elite Spanish Foreign Legion, an indication of the Spanish nationalists' high expectations for the unit. Eoin O'Duffy was appointed to general officer rank (outranking Colonel Yague, the Legion's commander) since it was anticipated that more Irish units would be formed. Enough Irishmen in fact volunteered to form another bandera, but this group was left stranded in Ireland in early 1937.

The XV Bandera, organised into four companies, began six weeks of basic training, and evidently made a good impression on ceremonial occasions. O'Duffy spent most of this time attending various functions held in his honour. He was absent in early February 1937 when General Franco himself made a surprise visit with orders for the Irish bandera to participate in an offensive on the Jarama valley south of Madrid. On 17 February 1937, the bandera left Cacares for the front line. Two days later they engaged in combat for the first time.[11]

As they approached the village of Ciempozuelos, the lead company observed a group of forty troops moving towards them. As they were approaching the front, the company prudently deployed into defensive positions. After a short time Captain Beauvais, a Spanish liaison officer, decided that the other group were nationalist troops and he led a small party forward to meet them. Beauvais stopped a short distance from the other group, saluted the officer in charge and announced 'Bandera Irlandaise del Tercio'. Instantly the other group opened fire, killing both Beauvais and a Spanish interpreter. The Irish company opened fire and in the following fire fight two Irish were killed as well as twenty of the opposing party. It later transpired that the 'enemy' were fellow nationalists, Falange militiamen from the Canary Islands,

who had apparently mistaken the Irish unit for members of
the republican international brigades.

The XV Bandera dug in, under republican artillery fire, at
Ciempozuelos and established a frontline routine. At the request of the German General von Thoma, who in 1943 would
succeed Erwin Rommel as commander of the Afrika Korps,
an Irish platoon was supplied to guard a German artillery
position. The Irish found the Germans to be 'cold and aloof'
but enjoyed their coffee. At about this time, the Irish may
have been involved in other 'friendly fire' incidents. An Irish
journalist meeting some Spanish Foreign Legion officers ten
years later was told: 'Although the Legion admires the fighting qualities of these Irish volunteers, it thinks little of their
discipline. Apparently a certain incident during one battle
left a bad taste in their mouths, when, they alleged, the Irish
troops fired into the Legion ranks – they were fighting on
the same front, a few miles away from each other.' Certainly
there were accusations of alcohol-related problems at Ciempozuelos.[12]

On 12 March 1937, the Irish received orders to capture the
village of Titulca on the heights opposite their position. This
village, not a particularly important objective, was on the
crest of a high cliff and defended by crack republican troops
liberally equipped with machine guns and with strong artillery
support. The XV Bandera attacked the next day, across a mile
of valley floor in torrential rain over a canal and the Jarama
river itself, under heavy and accurate artillery fire. Few, if
any, made it across the river and the assault was called off by
nightfall. Casualties were lighter than expected (four dead, six
wounded) due to the worst of the shelling being absorbed by
the rain-soaked ground. O'Duffy declined to obey an order
to mount another attack and claimed to have had this refusal
sanctioned by his immediate superior and by Franco himself.
On 17 March Franco paid a surprise visit to the bandera, and
talked at length with the bandera's Spanish liaison officers.

O'Duffy was absent; it is unlikely to be coincidental that this was the feast day of St Patrick. On 23 March the XV Bandera was transferred to La Maronosa, a quieter sector of the front apart from occasional air attacks. The following day, Colonel Yague visited; O'Duffy was naturally absent for this. Yague interviewed the liaison officers and subsequently recommended to Franco that the XV Bandera be disbanded. There was no doubt that the unit was suffering from internal problems and that O'Duffy's leadership left a great deal to be desired. Although a gifted if authoritarian administrator in earlier years, these talents seemed to have deserted O'Duffy by 1937. Particularly resented by the frontline troops in the bandera was O'Duffy's entourage of non-combatant staff-captains with which he spent most of his time sightseeing and socialising. One of this 'elite' was O'Duffy's *aide-de-camp* Tom Gunning, who had been assistant general secretary of O'Duffy's 'League of Youth' movement. He made his own particular contribution to the decline of the bandera's morale by his strict censorship of the men's mail home to the extent of halting it altogether. Yague's recommendation may have also been influenced by the bloody ethos of the Spanish Foreign Legion; while O'Duffy's refusal to launch a second attack on Titulca might have saved many unnecessary casualties, this would have been anathema to the legion, who were often referred to as the 'bridegrooms of death' and who typically suffered 50 per cent battle casualties throughout the civil war. O'Duffy could be credited for at least avoiding such casualties on this scale among his command.

The XV Bandera remained in the line for another two months, suffering many privations which caused another four fatalities. Discipline and morale collapsed, water was in short supply, the men's German uniforms had all but disintegrated, and infighting between the officers was reaching a point where injuries were being inflicted. In early April, General Franco announced the dissolution of the XV Bandera and by the end of the month they were withdrawn from the line.

While the men handed in their weapons, the officers retained their pistols after a request by O'Duffy which suggested that their safety might be in doubt. A poll was taken in which 654 men voted to return home, only nine electing to stay.[13]

The Irishmen were eventually repatriated in June 1937, arriving in Dublin on the twentieth of that month. Gardaí searched all baggage thoroughly and confiscated the officers' pistols. O'Duffy, whose smart uniform and considerable baggage contrasted with the ragged appearance of most of his men, formed up his troops for the march into town but only half complied, the rest making their way to the city's pubs. O'Duffy's group was met by cheering crowds and a reception from Dublin Corporation; at this time they were still broadly perceived as Catholic 'crusaders', and one Irish newspaper, the *Irish Independent*, carried wildly exaggerated claims of their prowess on the battlefield. They were soon to face ridicule, a popular claim being that they returned with more troops than they left with! They would also be regarded with contempt as the true nature of the fascist cause that they had served, however naively, became all too evident.[14]

Five years later, after the German invasion of Soviet Russia, O'Duffy covertly sent several messages to the German legation in Dublin to indicate his willingness to raise a division in Ireland 'to fight against Bolshevism'. The Germans demurred, not least due to 'O'Duffy's lamentable performance in the Spanish Civil War'.[15]

The performance of O'Duffy's bandera was to compare poorly with the fighting spirit of the Irishmen who had fought for the opposing side. In early December 1936, while O'Duffy's men were assembling in Cacares, about eighty Irishmen were slipping across the Pyrenees in small groups to volunteer for the International Brigades being formed to fight for the Spanish Republic. These men included Frank Ryan, a Dublin journalist and former IRA activist. It had been hoped to form an Irish unit, but operational necessity obliged them to combine with about 200 Britons to form a

'British battalion' at Madrigueras. A great degree of friction between the two groups soon became apparent: the Britons were led largely by former British Army officers while most of the Irishmen were ardent Irish republicans, several having been members of the IRA. On Christmas Day, a company of a hundred men, including forty Irishmen and led by Englishman George Nathan, were sent into action near Andujar, at a heavily defended part of the nationalist front. Although losses were heavy (eight of the Irish were killed) Nathan proved himself a genuine leader of men and earned the trust of the Irishmen in his command.

Despite a new year's appeal from Frank Ryan to the Irish at Madrigueras to fight alongside the Britons in a common struggle against fascism, trouble continued to brew between the two groups. Any hopes that Nathan's proven leadership qualities might have helped were dashed when it was revealed that he had been a member of the notorious Black and Tans during Ireland's struggle for independence. Although he was transferred to a post on the brigade staff (where Ryan was also serving) and replaced by Irishman Kit Conway, his removal caused further resentment among the Britons, who had elected the popular Nathan to officer rank on the battalion's formation. Things came to a head when a small group of the Irishmen broke away and joined the 'Lincoln' battalion of American volunteers.

In February 1937, the British battalion, now six hundred strong, was deployed to the Jarama valley for one of the most vicious battles of the Spanish Civil War – 17,000 were killed in a month's fighting. Most of the British battalion were lost in the first day of fighting, in which it held out against a determined assault by elite nationalist troops. After three days of savage fighting, the battalion was reduced to less than 200 men and began to withdraw. At this moment, Frank Ryan courageously rallied the demoralised troops and led them back to the front, being shot and wounded twice in the process. Assuming that Ryan's group were republican reinforcements, their enemy withdrew.[16]

In March 1937, Frank Ryan returned to Ireland to recover, making a brief but unsuccessful return to politics. Despite his personal doubts about the Spanish Republic's chances of survival, Ryan returned to Spain in June.

Of the original eighty Irish members of the British battalion, thirty were killed at Jarama and nearly as many badly wounded. More Irish volunteers continued to arrive, and in July the battalion performed superbly at Brunete but at terrible cost, being reduced to less then a hundred men. The Irish contribution to the battalion was recognised with the appointment of two Irishmen, Peter Daly and Paddy O'Daire, to be the unit's commanding officer and adjutant respectively. Daly was mortally wounded that August when the battalion took part in the offensive on Aragon, again holding out against elite nationalist troops and suffering grievous losses in the process. By the end of the year, when the battalion was committed to the fighting at Tereul, only one hundred and fifty members of the battalion were English speakers; a third of the battalion was lost in a month's fighting under appalling winter conditions.[17]

The following March, the British battalion (to which staff Major Frank Ryan was attached) was deployed to the Aragon front in a desperate attempt to stop a nationalist offensive. On a night march to their assigned positions at Calaceite, the lead company stumbled into a nationalist tank unit and over one hundred men, including Ryan, were taken prisoner. They were fortunate in that they were taken by the Italians, who did not summarily execute their prisoners, as was the case with Franco's Spaniards.

Ryan was brought to Zaragoza for execution but was saved when he was recognised by a foreign journalist, and was sent to rejoin his fellow prisoners at a prison camp near Burgos. By all accounts, he proved himself a troublesome prisoner to his captors while providing an inspiration to his fellow prisoners, and in June he was court-martialled and sentenced to death. He was transferred to Burgos prison to await execution, but his life was saved by a well-orchestrated campaign for his freedom organised in Britain, Ireland (where petitions were signed in both the Dáil and the House of Commons) and the United States. Although Ryan's death sentence was commuted to thirty years' imprisonment in late 1939, the two years that he eventually spent in the dreadful conditions of Burgos prison destroyed his health and shortened his life expectancy to just a few more years.[18]

In July 1938 the British battalion, by now reduced to two hundred men, took part in the battle of the Ebro river, the last republican offensive of the war. Initially meeting with some success, the republicans were gradually forced back through August. In November, the republicans disbanded their international brigades and fifteen Irishmen were present at their final parade in Barcelona that month.

1

GUERNSEY

On 2 December 1938, a young Irishman who gave his name as 'James Brady' entered a recruiting centre in Liverpool and volunteered his services for the British Army. When he gave his birthplace as Co. Roscommon and his date of birth as 20 May 1920, he was evidently not asked to produce a birth certificate as proof. This was not unusual at the time. Although some 35,902 volunteers had joined the British Army by November that year, this still represented an annual shortfall of 21,000 men, and prospective recruits were unlikely to be questioned too closely. Brady's given date of birth made him very slightly older than eighteen years of age, the minimum age necessary to join the army without parental consent. Subsequent events suggest that Brady might have originated from a more privileged background than the simple farmer's son he claimed to be. A later acquaintance described Brady as 'well-mannered and considerate, about 5'11" in height, well-built, fresh complexion, blue eyes and brownish fair hair'. The same man also noted: 'His people [i.e. his family] did not know that he had joined the Army.'[1]

Brady's entry to the British Army was preceded by a few days by that of Frank Stringer, a thin dark-haired young man born in Ballinamore, Co. Leitrim on 24 July 1920. Stringer's father, a 'fitter's mate', was dead, and Stringer had a minor criminal record, having been arrested for stealing turf at the age of fifteen. While Brady apparently followed the traditional Irish emigrant route of the 'boat train' from Dublin to Liverpool, Stringer signed up in Scotland Yard, London, having served a short stint in the Royal Navy, from which he was discharged for reasons not stated by him.[2]

Leitrim is traditionally the poorest and most sparsely populated county in Ireland, a rural society which was particularly hard hit by the worldwide economic depression of the 1930s. Even the soil of the region is too heavy to sustain significant agriculture. Conditions were scarcely better in Brady's native Roscommon, which borders Leitrim. Options for any young man growing up in the area were minimal, particularly one whose family had been deprived of its breadwinner. For those of an adventurous bent, service in the particularly well-travelled British Army had obvious attractions.

Brady and Stringer both swore the British Army's oath of allegiance and proceeded separately to Borden Camp in Hampshire, Stringer from London and Brady from Liverpool, to begin their basic training. Both had been assigned to the Royal Irish Fusiliers, 'that most Irish of the Irish regiments', commonly known as the 'Faughs' after the regiment's Gaelic battle-cry, the *polite* translation of which is 'clear the way'. This regiment traced its origins back to the raising of the 87th and 89th Regiments of Foot in Ireland in 1793, the latter regiment being heavily involved in the putting down of the Irish rebellion of 1798. The 89th Regiment subsequently fought the French in Egypt, the Dutch in Java and the Americans in Canada in 1813. The 87th Regiment fought at Montevideo in 1807 and later at the fierce battle of Talavera in Portugal. Later, at the Battle of Barossa Hill in Spain in 1811, part of this regiment routed the elite 8th Demi-Brigade of the French Army, capturing their prized eagle standard. This was the first such standard to be captured in battle by the British Army, earning the regiment and its descendant the sobriquet of 'the eagle-takers'. The outbreak of the Crimean War in 1854 saw the 89th fighting at Sebastopol. Both regiments were involved in putting down the Indian mutiny in 1857 and the 87th fought in the China War in 1860. The 89th returned to Ireland in 1867 to deal with another Irish rebellion, this time the abortive Fenian rising. In 1881, the 87th and 89th Regiments of Foot were amalgamated to become Princess Victoria's Royal Irish Fusiliers, with their depot in Armagh. A battalion was deployed to Egypt the following year, winning the regiment's first battle honour. The regiments' two battalions suffered heavy losses in the Boer War from 1899 to 1902, the second battalion relieving the siege of Ladysmith.

In the First World War, the Royal Irish Fusiliers were expanded to fourteen battalions, fighting on the western front and in the Middle East, two members winning Victoria Crosses. Following Irish independence in 1922, most of the Irish regiments of the British Army were disbanded, the Royal Irish Fusiliers only surviving by the generosity of a sister regiment, the Royal Inniskilling Fusiliers, who sacrificed one of their two allotted battalions to allow the 'Faughs' room on the British Army establishment.[3]

In May 1937, the regimental depot of the Royal Irish Fusiliers moved from Omagh in Northern Ireland to Borden Camp in Hampshire, thereby breaking the link with their benefactors, the Royal Inniskilling Fusiliers. Stringer and Brady arrived here at about the same time in early December 1938, receiving consecutive army numbers (7043206 and 7043207 respectively). Both young men were of the same age, from the same region of the west of Ireland, and both had suffered the bereavement of a close relative; Brady's mother was deceased, as was Stringer's father. It is not surprising that the pair appear to have become friends. It was common practice in the British Army at the time to accommodate individual recruits in a depot until there was a sufficient number to form a training unit; 'the normal number of recruits in a squad will be 30, and training will commence on the first Monday after the squad is complete', to quote the training manual. Since their recruit training commenced in January 1939, it is likely that Brady and Stringer spent the Christmas period together in Borden Camp, the first of several such Christmases together.

Construction of Borden Camp, near the huge British Army camp in Aldershot, had begun in 1903. Originally an artillery barracks, it was expanded in 1906 by the mammoth task of transferring nearly seventy large huts by a purpose-built railway from the nearby infantry camp at Longmoor. By 1937, the camp had expanded into several barracks complexes. The Royal Irish Fusiliers moved to Guadalope barracks, named after a battle, not due to any misapprehension regarding the local climate. The 'South African' model huts in which Brady and Stringer were accommodated were constructed of heavy corrugated iron. These tended to be noisy during heavy rain, and the hut's solid-fuel 'pot-belly' stoves often proved not to be equal to the demands of the Hampshire winter.

For a typical British Army recruit of 1939, the day began with a bugle call at 6 a.m. After a short run, the men assembled at the cookhouse with knife, fork, spoon and a tin plate and mug. Breakfast consisted of porridge (usually too watery or too lumpy) washed down with strong tea. After a morning inspection of uniform and quarters, the morning was usually spent in intensive 'square-bashing' (foot drill) on the parade ground. There was a lunch parade at midday at the cookhouse, consisting of meat, vegetables and 'duff' or tart to follow, again with strong tea. The quality of the food depended very much on the cook. Afternoon training sessions were usually physical training or classroom lessons, for example military discipline or map reading. After an evening meal of tea, meatloaf, bread and jam, there was little free time for a recruit. The issued 'ammunition boots' had to be kept highly polished, from the toecaps to the studs. The newly-issued 1938 pattern webbing, consisting of belt, yoke, ammunition pouches, bayonet 'frog' (holder) and waterbottle container had to be thoroughly 'blancoed' and the brass buckles polished with Brasso. This was an awkward business, as any spillage of the latter would result in an obvious and hard to remove stain. For the same reason, the use of Brasso on the brass buttons and badges of the recruit's uniform required infinite care; any neglect would result in the incurring of a training NCO's wrath. The rest of the recruit's kit (most items of which were marked with his number to prevent theft), from his rifle to his eating utensils, had to be kept in immaculate condition, as had the recruit's barrack rooms, from the windows to the floor. The latter was typically scrubbed four times daily.

Some elements of this regime may have seemed nonsensical. Many other armies insisted on their soldiers' boots being coated in dubbin rather than being highly polished, which although looking smart on the parade ground actually decreased the boot's waterproof qualities. Likewise in early 1939, the new recruit had to wind on 'putties', long lengths of serge cloth to be wound tightly and symmetrically from the ankle to the knee, with the fastening to be placed on the outside. This was difficult at the best of times, and a nightmarish proposition when rushing to be on a morning parade. If not wound tightly, the puttee would unwind on the parade ground, tripping the recruit or a colleague and provoking the rage of a superior. On the other hand, when puttees were wound tightly enough, they restricted circulation for soldiers involved in long route marches and sentry duty and were frequently the cause of varicose veins in later life. There did not seem to be any readily discernible logic to some aspects of this regime, other than an apparent belief that any cause of discomfort for the troops was somehow good for discipline. The hated puttees began to be phased out in 1939 with the introduction of a new battledress. This consisted of 'an overall made of khaki serge with large patch pockets; the trousers of the same design as skiing trousers and are of full-length, being secured round the ankle by a short canvas gaiter'. The new battledress was not issued to the Royal Irish Fusiliers until just before their deployment to France in October 1939, by which time Brady and Stringer were unable to avail of its relative benefits.[4]

Other aspects, such as the insistence on high standards of hygiene, and on keeping the soldier's rifle and kit in good order, assumed an obvious importance on the battlefield. Some of the apparently more mindless methods of instilling discipline actually served certain purposes – making a group of individuals undergo various discomforts and indignities together was a proven method of instilling team spirit and camaraderie.

The British Army was famous for insisting on a high standard of foot drill as a means of instilling discipline and group cohesion. Physical training assumed great importance for any army and for an infantry regiment in particular, but in 1939 a particular problem had to be addressed; many of the recruits inducted at this time were in poor physical condition due to the low standards of nutrition in the working class of the 1930s. The American journalist William Schirer would, in 1940, unfavourably contrast the bad teeth and skinny physique of British soldiers taken prisoner with the fine physical condition of their German captors.[5]

'Anti-gas training', in which recruits were taught how to don a respirator and experience the discomfort of wearing this awkward item for long periods, was to prove, in the Second World War, a wise but mercifully unnecessary precaution.

Brady and Stringer would not have been issued with weapons until after at least two weeks' training on the parade ground. The British Army's standard rifle was the ubiquitous Lee-Enfield, a bolt-action rifle with a reputation for reliability and accuracy that had been firmly established in the trench warfare of the First World War. The army prided itself on a high standard of marksmanship, and the two young Irishmen would have become thoroughly familiar with their Lee-Enfields through long hours of arms drills on the parade ground, followed by a minimum of sixty hours of classroom sessions culminating with several practice sessions on the nearby rifle ranges, just south of Borden Camp.

Relatively little time, especially when compared to training later in the Second World War, was devoted to actual combat training, such as camouflage training or 'fire and manoeuvre' tactics. This was probably a legacy of the crude tactics employed by the British infantry throughout the First World War. The commander of an infantry division in France in 1939, Major-General (later Field-Marshal) Bernard Montgomery observed that the British Army had not carried out any realistic large-scale manoeuvres for several years.

Contact between officers and men was discouraged in the British Army of 1939. Rather than learning skills that might be useful in a possible war, young officers were required to learn a bewildering array of officers' mess etiquette and social rules. A new officer being posted to a new regiment, for example, was required to introduce himself to all married officers by presenting an engraved card, printed cards being unacceptable. Young officers joining the Royal Irish Fusiliers were expected to learn Irish dancing.

Brady and Stringer would also have received training in the 'Bren' light machine gun. This superb weapon's designation referred to its place of design (Brno, in Czechoslovakia) and its place of manufacture (Enfield, in England). Firing the same .303-inch calibre round as the Lee-Enfield rifle, the Bren was to prove a reliable and popular weapon throughout the Second World War. On 15 March 1939, as the regiment was preparing to celebrate the feast of the patron saint of Ireland, the Brno weapons plants fell into the hands of the Nazis as Germany annexed the remaining part of Czechoslovakia that had not been granted it under the Munich agreement the previous year. Neville Chamberlain, British prime minister, announced a rapid expansion of the British Army without consulting his defence chiefs.

In that month the British Army re-introduced conscription. Brady and Stringer would have trained with one of the last all-volunteer recruit platoons before the outbreak of war.

As Brady and Stringer's training continued, the strict regime may have been alleviated by access to a NAAFI (Navy Army Air Force Institute) which stocked such items as Brasso, polish and soap at cheap prices, and where a recruit

might enjoy tea and buns in the evening. In March 1939 it
is likely that the pair may have been allowed to participate to
some degree in the Royal Irish Fusiliers' two most sacred days,
the enthusiastically celebrated Barossa Day (5 March) and of
course St Patrick's Day on 17 March.

Following completion of their basic training in May 1939,
Brady and Stringer transferred to Guernsey where the 1st
Battalion Royal Irish Fusiliers had been based since November 1938. Guernsey, the second largest of the Channel Islands, was situated thirty miles off the Normandy coast and
was regarded as a particularly pleasant posting. The Channel
Islands were the holiday destination of choice for Britons in
the 1930s, in much the same way that package holidays in
Spain and Greece are today. The climate of Guernsey is semi-
tropical, and was no doubt a welcome contrast to Hampshire
in winter. In 1939, Guernsey was dotted with glasshouses for
the cultivation of tomatoes, which, along with tourism, represented the main source of income for the island's 40,000 inhabitants.

Guernsey, although a British dependency, maintained its
own system of government. The office of Bailiff combined the
duties of prime minister and chief justice, and since 1935 had
been held by the elderly Victor Carey. The king of England's
representative on the island was the Lieutenant Governor,
who sat to the Bailiff's right when the States of Deliberation (Guernsey's parliament) were in session, and was usually a position held by a serving major-general of the British
Army.

Brady and Stringer's new commanding officer was the
benevolent old warrior Lieutenant-Colonel The O'Donohue
('the' indicating his position as the senior member of the Irish
O'Donohue clan.) A native of west Cork, Lt-Col O'Donohue
had fought on the western front throughout most of the First
World War, notably at Ypres and the Somme, being awarded
the Military Cross in 1917. He was badly wounded at the
Battle of Cambrai in November that year, suffering serious

head and arm injuries and losing an eye. Popularly known among his troops as 'Red Ned', something of his style of leadership might be ascertained by the many visits he received from his former fusiliers while in postwar retirement in Co. Cork.[6]

Brady and Stringer were not to enjoy the more pleasant aspects of their posting to Guernsey for very long. On the night of Friday 9 June 1939, the pair entered a public house in St Sampson wearing British Army uniform and were refused service, the landlady reckoning that they had had enough to drink already. Both used strong language and one smashed a large plate glass on the premises while leaving. The pair then made their way through the town, leaving a trail of broken windows in cars, houses and greenhouses. A passing motorist drove to the house of a sergeant of the Guernsey police, and together they drove around the town searching for the two errant fusiliers. When the two found Brady and Stringer, they had discarded their tunics and headgear, and were being followed by a small crowd. This group were keeping a prudent distance, because Brady was now carrying a wooden club and Stringer a spade. When Police Sergeant Charles le Lievre approached them, the pair first threatened him, and then attacked. Stringer swung his spade at Sergeant le Lievre's head; the policeman successfully blocked the first blow, but the second struck him on the shoulder blade, injuring his arm. Le Lievre then took the offensive, knocking Stringer to the ground, but Brady intervened, striking the policeman across the head with his club repeatedly and with such force that the club broke, after which Brady began to punch le Lievre with his bare fist. A special constable (part-time policeman) then arrived on the scene, helping the sergeant, now bleeding from a head injury, to subdue and handcuff Stringer. Brady attempted to escape through a hedge and across a nearby field, but two civilians gave chase and captured him. In handcuffs, Brady and Stringer were driven to the police station, allegedly shouting such choice epithets as 'Up the IRA' and 'F- the king'.

On 12 June 1939, both men were charged with the attempted murder of Sergeant le Lievre in Guernsey police court.[7]

By the time the pair appeared in Guernsey crown court on 23 June, Sergeant le Lievre had been back on duty for a week, although not for any apparent lack of effort on the part of Brady and Stringer. The crown court brought lesser charges of 'feloniously and with force and violence assaulting a police officer in the execution of his duty; concerned in the breaking of windows and panes of glass in various premises to the values as follows: £15; 18/-; 30/-; £1/19/7d; £2/7/6d'.[8]

To put the latter charge in context, it should be remembered that the soldier's pay of each individual amounted to less than twenty shillings per week. James Brady and Frank Stringer pleaded guilty to the charges, and were sentenced to eighteen months and twenty-one months respectively, both sentences to be served with hard labour.

Years later, neither man recalled the whole sorry episode with much enthusiasm. Stringer remembered: 'In June 1939, I and a soldier named James Brady got involved in a disturbance and as a result I was arrested and sentenced to 21 months' imprisonment for assaulting the civilian police.' Brady's recollection was that 'with another soldier, named Frank Stringer, I got drunk in June 1939, and we assaulted a civilian policeman, although I cannot remember much about it because I was too drunk.' Although the pair's behaviour on this night was inexcusable, it might be borne in mind that at the time of the incident both were young men of just under nineteen years of age and that there was not any recorded repeat of this kind of misbehaviour.[9]

Recognition of Sergeant le Lievre's courage in tackling the two men came in January 1940 with the announcement by the *London Gazette* that he had been awarded the King's Police Medal. He had been nominated for this prestigious decoration, awarded for acts of 'conspicuous gallantry' and exceptional courage by a police officer in the course of his duty, by Inspector Sculper, the senior police officer on Guernsey, and the proposal had been approved by the Bailiff, Victor Carey, and the island's Lieutenant Governor. In peacetime, Sergeant le Lievre would have received the medal from King George in a ceremony at Buckingham Palace. The exigencies of wartime were to prevent this, however, and so le Lievre received the King's Police Medal in a small ceremony after a sitting of the 'States', the island's parliament.[10]

Hard labour in any prison of the 1930s was hardly a convivial experience, and the windowless Victorian-era Guernsey prison, conveniently located near to the courthouse, was known for being particularly cold, even in midsummer. Neither Irishman was dismissed from the British Army, as would normally have been the case with a serious criminal conviction, and they would both apparently have returned to their regiments having served their sentences. This was probably due to the intercession of Colonel O'Donohue, and was very much in keeping with his character. In time, however, Brady and Stringer would have cause to regret that they were not so discharged, as their continuing status as British soldiers caused them to face charges in relation to their subsequent actions. The two men probably received occasional visits from their fellow fusiliers through the summer of 1939, but on 1 September Germany invaded Poland, and Britain and France declared war on Germany two days later. The 1st Battalion Royal Irish Fusiliers was quickly withdrawn to England, leaving Brady and Stringer behind. After a brief period 'under canvas' in Oxfordshire, the battalion moved to Aldershot where the business of mobilising, calling up reservists and issuing of kit could be completed. On 3 October 1939, the battalion sailed for France where it was incorporated into the British Expeditionary Force. They were to spend the bitterly cold winter of 1939 in a 'pioneer' capacity, however, digging trenches and building fortifications which would prove ultimately to be of dubious value.

Towards the end of 1939, Brady and Stringer volunteered

to be returned to their unit. The Lieutenant Governor of the island, Major-General A. P. D. Telfer-Smollett, apparently approved the two men's request and forwarded their application to the British Home Office whose agreement however, was not forthcoming. As Europe uneasily settled into a winter of 'phoney war', the two continued to languish in Guernsey prison.

While the French Army settled into an apathetic routine, having concentrated their resources on the defensive Maginot Line between France and Germany, the Germans were already plotting the invasion of western Europe. Their eastern frontier was secure, thanks to a non-aggression pact between Nazi Germany and Soviet Russia. The Russians had participated in the invasion of Poland in September 1939, and felt themselves safe enough to occupy the Baltic states and to launch an invasion of Finland on 30 November 1939. Against all expectations, the Finns heroically held off the vastly superior Russian force throughout the winter, inflicting heavy casualties. The Russians' initial failures were due mostly to poor leadership and lack of preparation for the savage arctic winter. These faults, however, were addressed by February 1940, when a new offensive under the command of Marshal Timoshenko defeated the Finns by March. Over 16,000 square miles of Finnish territory was ceded to Russia. Aid from western democracies had not been significant. In the early final phases of the war, the Finnish had been willing to accept foreign volunteers, but unrealistic stipulations, such as a requirement that these men should only come from certain specified nationalities and that they should arrive in organised groups with their own officers and weapons, proved impossible to fulfil. These requirements were rescinded in mid-January and untrained individuals were declared acceptable, but few foreign volunteers reached the front line before the end of hostilities. A few Irishmen were evidently among these volunteers, as in Spain choosing to serve with a unit composed mainly of Britons, but this unit did not reach the front line before the end of hostilities.[11]

Although nominally still a member of the Commonwealth, Ireland had declared itself neutral on the outbreak of war. This was tacitly recognised by the British, who appointed Sir John Maffey as a *de facto* ambassador shortly afterwards. The most immediate threat to Ireland's neutrality was the IRA, which in 1938 had come under the leadership of Seán Russell, a proponent of a bombing campaign in England. In January 1939, Lord Halifax, the British foreign secretary, received an ultimatum from the IRA, demanding the withdrawal of all British forces from Northern Ireland. On the expiration of a four-day period, the IRA detonated several large bombs in power stations and electrical installations in London, Manchester and Birmingham. By July, one hundred and twenty IRA bombs had detonated throughout England, causing over one hundred casualties. The S-Plan, as the IRA labelled their bombing campaign, was the brainchild of an electrician and explosives expert, Seamas O'Donovan. The S-Plan had in fact been opposed by several hardliners within the IRA; Frank Ryan in particular, still in a Spanish prison, is said to have been appalled by news of the terrorist campaign. Things came to a head about a week before the outbreak of the Second World War, when an IRA bomb in Coventry killed five people and injured sixty. This was a particularly controversial bombing, for which two IRA men were later hanged.

The bombing campaign had attracted the attention of the Abwehr (German military intelligence), and as early as February 1939 an Abwehr agent was dispatched to Dublin to contact the IRA. Although badly briefed, he succeeded in meeting the IRA leadership and invited them to send a representative to Germany to discuss possible cooperation. Seamas O'Donovan was selected and made at least three visits to Germany before the outbreak of war.

On 9 September 1939, a series of garda raids around the country netted a large number of IRA men, including most of the IRA's 'headquarters staff' and $8,000, most of the organisation's finances. The IRA continued to pose a serious threat to state security, however, and shortly before Christmas 1939 carried out a well organised raid on the Irish Army's main magazine, netting a million rounds of small arms ammunition. A massive search operation by the Irish Army soon recovered not only all of the stolen ammunition but some of the IRA's as well. At the end of December 1939, the gardaí seized an IRA transmitter in Rathgar, Dublin. This was the end of 'Irene', the code name for the radio link between the IRA and the Abwehr. In October, the Abwehr had received the first of several weekly messages, broadcast in four-letter groups. 'Reception was poor, and the Irish WT operator was so unskilled that Abwehr could at least be certain that the code had not fallen into enemy hands.' Nothing of any importance, in the Abwehr's view, was broadcast. 'From the IRA side messages were sent asking for delivery of arms and supplies, and a good deal of what Abwehr considered frivolous messages; for example, a message of congratulation to the Führer on the occasion of the sinking of the *Royal Oak*.' The British battleship *Royal Oak* had been sunk at anchor by a German U-boat on the night of 13 October 1939 with the loss of 833 lives. Abwehr replies were 'short and brief', requesting that the IRA begin sabotage attacks on British military targets. 'After two months, Irene went off the air. Nothing more was heard of it for the rest of the war, except for a few garbled messages which were later dispatched by Görtz (see Chapter Two). Apart from weekly broadcasts to Germany, the IRA had been using their transmitter to broadcast propaganda locally, allowing the gardaí to pinpoint its location.[12]

By early 1940, with the introduction of military tribunals and mass internment of suspects, the IRA's capacity to cause further trouble had been crippled, but certainly not vanquished. Their abilities, however, were rather outweighed by their ambition. In early 1940, an IRA courier named Stephen Held reached Germany with a grandiose scheme hatched by an IRA amateur strategist, in which the Germans were expected to land 50,000 troops in Northern Ireland. The IRA plan, later known as 'Plan Kathleen' was a work of fantasy, envisaging the union of the Irish Army and the IRA (bitter enemies since the vicious civil war of 1922–3) at the head of a popular uprising which would sweep the IRA to power:

> The IRA suggested a joint IRA–German military operation for the conquest of Northern Ireland. In particular there was mention of an Irish lake (Carlingford Lough?) suitable for landing troop-carrying flying boats. Three or four other strategic points for airborne operations were also mentioned, from which British garrisons and military targets could also be conveniently attacked. Quantities of weapons and men were to be supplied to the IRA (Held was somewhat airy about the means of doing this) and it was anticipated that some of the Éire army would make common cause with the IRA. If there was sufficient German support, the IRA anticipated that the Irish people as a whole would rise to a 'people's war', so that the first impetus of military insurrection would be carried to a successful military conclusion. The popular uprising would imply that the IRA would take over political power for the whole of Ireland. The IRA proposal was greeted with dismay. It seemed to show the IRA as unpractical [sic] dreamers with an obstinate single-mindedness. Plainly they had disregarded the agreement reached in Aug 1939 in Berlin and would not get down to hard work and concentrate on minor military targets within the scope of Abw II. Yet they were still potentially valuable allies and must not be bluntly refused. Held was given a non-committal answer and told that his plan would be considered. The Held proposition was forwarded without comment through routine channels to Abt Landesverteidung [planning department] of the General Staff, where it was promptly turned down.[13]

It is amazing to relate that in January 1941 General Kurt Student, as commander of German airborne forces, proposed the dropping of 20,000 paratroopers and 12,000 airborne troops by night into Northern Ireland, capturing RAF airfields from which German fighter aircraft would operate. It was not a practical scheme: even if the Luftwaffe had a significant number of transport aircraft, or indeed any fighter aircraft, with the range to reach Northern Ireland (which it had not), the dropping of such a large force so far behind enemy lines without hope of reinforcement or resupply would have been an effective death sentence for most involved. Hitler himself gave the plan some consideration, even suggesting the twenty-fifth anniversary of the 1916 Rising as a possible date. It might be facetious to point out that Student was still recovering from a serious head wound, having been accidentally shot by the Waffen-SS during the fighting in Holland. It should be noted that at this time, German airborne forces were flushed with success following their victories in western Europe, and it was not yet appreciated just how vulnerable air-landed forces were if they were not quickly reinforced. The Fallschirmjager (German paratroops) learned this lesson the hard way during the invasion of Crete.[14]

The Abwehr continued attempts to establish links with the IRA. In early February 1940, Abwehr courier Ernst Weber-Drohl was brought by U-boat to the west coast of Ireland where he was to contact the IRA. His mission started badly, when a radio transmitter he had brought to enable contact between the IRA and the Abwehr was lost while rowing ashore. He succeeded in contacting Jim O'Donovan and delivered over £14,000 and instructions from the Abwehr which included a request to continue with the S-Plan in England and to dispatch an IRA agent to Germany to liaise on such matters as weapons supplies. Weber-Drohl, a sixty-year-old weightlifter, was eventually arrested and interned for the duration of the war.

On 9 April 1940, the 'phoney war' ended abruptly with the German invasion of Denmark, followed quickly by the invasion of Norway.

In the early hours of 5 May 1940, a black Heinkel He-111 bomber took off from the Luftwaffe airbase at Fritzlar, near Cassel and set course for Ireland. At the controls were Oberleutnant Edmund Gartenfeld, a pilot of near-legendary ability who was selected to fly several Abwehr agents to Britain and one more to Ireland. His 'cargo' was Hauptmann

Hermann Görtz, a fifty-year-old lawyer and First World War veteran. Görtz was arguably the most famous German spy in Britain, having been arrested for spying on RAF installations in 1935 and serving three years in prison.

Shortly after Görtz's aircraft had taken off from Fritzlar, a car from Berlin arrived at the Luftwaffe base, carrying Abwehr officer Kurt Haller and IRA leader Seán Russell. Russell had arrived in Italy a few days earlier, having travelled from New York aboard an American liner under an alias. He had been accorded VIP status, having been issued with a German passport and immediately transported to Berlin where he was accommodated first at a hotel and later in a villa at Berlin's Grunewald. The day after his arrival, a conference took place between Russell and Abwehr officials in the presence of SS-Standartenführer Dr Edmund Veesenmayer, an SS officer attached to the German Foreign Office. It was suggested that Russell should meet Görtz before his Irish mission, and Veesenmayer ordered a fast car from the foreign office to transport Russell to Cassell immediately. An urgent message to the local Abwehr sub-office failed to arrive, however, and the meeting between Russell and Görtz did not occur.[15]

Oberleutnant Gartenfeld's task was not an easy one. Navigating an aircraft by night was a primitive science in early 1940. The only reliable method would have been to plot stars with a sextant; this would have required the pilot to fly straight and level for a distance, not advisable in hostile airspace. The weather forecast had been wrong, and a heavy cloud had blanketed Britain and the Irish sea, leaving Gartenfeld blind for most of the journey. Görtz, wearing Luftwaffe uniform, jumped from the belly of the Heinkel at 5,000 feet over Co. Meath before dawn. This was an unusually high altitude for a static line jump, whereby the parachute is opened automatically by means of a thick webbing strap, because of Gartenfeld's reluctance to fly any lower due to the mountains in the vicinity. This resulted in the loss of Görtz's radio which had been dropped on a separate parachute. Although Görtz was subsequently evasive as to the location of his intended drop zone, having landed he set out on an epic 80-mile trek to Laragh in the Wicklow mountains. There he presented himself at the house of Iseult Stuart, wife of the Irish writer Francis Stuart who had been resident in Berlin since the previous January. Mrs Stuart arranged for Görtz to be moved to the house of Jim O'Donovan, after which he was transferred to the home of Stephen Held, which was anything but a safe house. This man, who had a German stepfather, had travelled to Germany as an IRA courier only the previous month. A short time later, the house was raided by the gardaí, who discovered Görtz's medals, Luftwaffe insignia, his parachute and $20,000 in cash for the IRA, conclusive proof of German links with a terrorist organisation dedicated to overthrowing the Irish government. At about this time, the Irish government drew up a secret defence plan with the British in case of German invasion of Ireland. Although neutral, Ireland continued to adopt an increasingly pro-Allied stance as the war continued. Görtz evaded arrest and remained 'on the run' for some eighteen months, but without any hope of contacting Germany.[16]

Just before dawn on the morning of 10 May 1940, three Dutch sentries on the eastern end of the important Gennep railway bridge, just two miles from the German border, observed a small group of men approach their position. Two were wearing Dutch military police uniform, and they seemed to have four prisoners, all wearing raincoats. The Dutch hesitated, and within minutes had been overpowered by the six men, who in fact were German soldiers. After reinforcements had reached their position, the two 'military policemen' brought their 'prisoners' to the Dutch position in the middle of the bridge and handed them over to the Dutch sentries there. Within minutes, a German troop train which had crossed the border earlier arrived at the bridge, and the 'prisoners' produced concealed weapons and overwhelmed their Dutch 'captors'. The vital Gennep bridge thus fell into German hands without any loss to them.[17]

The Germans that carried out this raid were members of 'Bau-Lehr battalion z.b.v. Nr. 800', which were to become more famously known as the 'Brandenburgers'. Germany was an early innovator in the field of special forces, and a particular characteristic of the Brandenburgers was their willingness to adopt civilian dress or enemy uniform to approach their objectives. This did not actually contravene international law, as long as the soldiers involved did not engage in combat while wearing enemy uniform.

Just after sunrise, waves of German aircraft swept across the skies of Belgium, Holland and Luxembourg. Fallschirmjager jumped from JU-52 transport aircraft onto targets in Holland in the first large-scale use of airborne troops. Just over forty JU-52s, each towing a DFS-230 glider carrying a squad of crack airborne troops, slipped across the German border and released their loads twelve miles from their targets. While most of these German glider-borne troops began capturing vital points on the Albert canal, nine gliders swooped onto the roof of the vital Belgian fortress of Eben Emael. A small force of eighty highly trained combat engineers disembarked and deployed another new secret weapon; the hollow charge warhead. This concentrated an explosive charge through a small area that blasted holes through steel and concrete. Flamethrowers and more explosive charges were brought into play and, although not immediately captured, the Belgian fortress was rendered ineffective. The German Army Group B, comprising thirty divisions, then drove across a 200-mile front into the low countries, overrunning Holland in five days.

On 4 May 1940, the 1st Battalion Royal Irish Fusiliers moved forward to Amiens, and along with the 7th Battalion of the Queen's Regiment and the 2nd Battalion of the Essex Regiment, formed the 25th Brigade of the British 50th Division. A new battalion commander, Lieutenant-Colonel

G.F. Gough MC, had taken command. When the Wehrmacht swept into Holland and Belgium, the British and
French Armies began to execute Plan D, which involved a
cumbersome move into Belgium intended to set up a defensive line in front of the Germans, a strategy perhaps feasible
in the previous world war. The Royal Irish Fusiliers, then in
the middle of last-minute combat training, moved to Arras
to test all weapons. The battalion's stock of support weapons
was depressingly deficient. One of the battalion's two 3-inch
'heavy' mortars was unserviceable, and there was no high explosive ammunition available for the 2-inch mortars. To deal
with German panzers, the fusiliers were equipped with the
Boyes anti-tank rifle. Although a laudable attempt to provide each infantry platoon with an anti-tank capacity, this
weapon's drawbacks were many. With a weight of 35 pounds
it was a heavy weapon for an infantryman to carry, and its
recoil was so fearsome that operators were warned: 'Always
press the right cheek close against the rifle well forward on
the cheek rest – making sure that the cheek is clear of the
spade grip and shoulder piece so as to prevent possible bruis-
ing and broken bones to the firer.' At 300 metres, point-blank
range against an armoured vehicle, its .55-inch projectile was
capable only of penetrating 21 millimetres of armour, useless
against all but the lightest German armoured vehicles.

When the British Expeditionary Force moved forward
into Belgium, the 25th Brigade remained in reserve. When
the bulk of Allied forces were deployed to face the German
Army Group B, the Germans deployed their main force;
Rundstedt's army group A, comprising 45 divisions which included the bulk of the Wehrmacht's armour and mechanised
infantry. This massive force drove through the Ardennes forest (thought by the Allies to be impassable), across the rear
of the Allied forces, and had reached the French coast in ten
days.

Divided among the German Army groups were three
divisions and the Leibstandarte regiment of the newly estab-

lished Waffen-SS, which combined the armed elements of
the SS into a military force. Some of the new force distinguished themselves in battle, but were also responsible for
the most serious war crimes committed during the German
campaign in the west by the massacre of nearly 200 captured
British soldiers at Le Paradis and Wormhoudt.

On 17 May, the British 25th Brigade moved forward
into Belgium and deployed along the river Dendre to cover
the Allied armies' withdrawal, the 'Faughs' taking position
at Meerbeke. After a clash with the Germans, the battalion
pulled back to Oudenarde, where they were shelled, suffering
sixty casualties. On 21 May, the Fusiliers moved to occupy a
defensive line along the Bethune-La Basee canal. They had to
struggle against a constant flow of refugees, and were eventually forced to push the unfortunate civilians off the road
in order to advance. Taking up positions along an 11,000-
yard front, the battalion fought off a series of attacks over the
next few days, with no artillery support. They were, however,
joined by some French troops and two French tanks, the latter
the only survivors of a regiment that had been involved in a
counter-attack near Arras. At Bethune, the 'Faughs' found
themselves facing elements of the 7th Panzer Division, commanded by Major-General Erwin Rommel, later famous as
'the Desert Fox' when he commanded the Afrika Korps.[18]

On 25 May, the battalion was finally provided with artillery support and a re-supply of ammunition. After they fought
off another enemy attack, the Fusiliers were withdrawn, the
Lancashire Fusiliers that replaced them being overwhelmed
by Rommel's main assault the next day. By this time, the two
German Army Groups had linked up, forcing the Allied force
into a small pocket in northwest Belgium.

Some miles to the north-west of Bethune, another battalion of the British 2nd Division, the 1st Battalion of the Royal
Welch Fusiliers, was holding the little town of St Venant,
with a detached company holding the nearby town of Rebecq. The following day, the Germans surrounded the latter

town and both towns were attacked on the morning of 27 May. When the Welshmen received the order to withdraw to the river Lys, they had to fight their way through the German lines. Few of the company holding Rebecq were able to avoid capture. Among those captured was an Irishman, Corporal John Codd. He would later feature prominently in Brady and Stringer's story.[19]

The Royal Irish Fusiliers in the meantime, were deployed to another area, to hold a defensive line along the Canal de Lawe near Vielle Chapelle. The scale of the disaster that was overtaking the BEF was brought home to Lieutenant-Colonel Gough when he received an order to send a nucleus of officers and warrant officers straight back to England. This was to provide a cadre from which the regiment could be re-built if the battalion was unable to reach the evacuation beach at Dunkirk. In the event, the battalion was in fact able to fight its way through to the coast by 29 May, and nearly 600 officers and men were brought back to safety across the English Channel after nearly two weeks of unrelenting combat. The battle honour 'Bethune-Le Basee' was added to the regimental colours.

In 1939, it had been considered unthinkable that the Germans could ever threaten the Channel Islands. The British Army had established a technical school on Jersey, and anxious English parents sought to enrol their children in the apparent safety of Elisabeth College on Guernsey. As late as March 1940 an advertisement in a British newspaper had advertised Jersey as an ideal holiday resort for the summer.

After Dunkirk, and the subsequent German advance across France, the Channel Islands suddenly became acutely aware of the danger posed to them. Road signs were removed, and Austrian and German nationals were interned. It was in this atmosphere of grave crisis that the change-over of Lieutenant Governor of Guernsey took place, when Major-General A.P.D. Telfer-Smollett handed over to Major-General

Minshull-Ford. The former, it will be remembered, had been willing to free James Brady and Frank Stringer from prison to return to the British Army. Subsequent events suggest that perhaps he had forgotten to mention their circumstances to his successor, or that Minshull-Ford, in the face of an impending German invasion, had in turn forgotten the two Irishmen. The two would have had a great deal to discuss, not least an impending German attack.

After Friday 14 June 1940, and the Wehrmacht's crossing of the river Seine, the British War Office decided to defend the islands, and dispatched troops and RAF aircraft to them. By the end of the weekend, the British cabinet, acting on the advice of their chiefs of staff, decided instead to demilitarise the islands. As a serving military officer, this included the new Lieutenant Governor. Major-General Minshull-Ford subsequently received an order from Alexander Maxwell (Permanent Under-Secretary at the Home Office) directing that in the event of his recall to England, the duties of Lieutenant Governor were to be discharged by Baliff Victor Carey, who was to remain on the island. Maxwell had been involved in plans to evacuate the Channel Islands, and had been informed by the Ministry of Shipping that there were ships ready for this purpose.

The demilitarisation of the islands was confirmed by the British cabinet on 19 June, on the advice of the Admiralty, who warned that the islands were indefensible with the Germans occupying Brest and Cherbourg, and the RAF aircraft were flown back to England. The Royal Guernsey Militia, a part-time defence force, was demobilised. All uniforms and weapons held by its members were ordered to be handed in at the town arsenal, and all privately held firearms were ordered to be handed in to the police.[20]

On that morning the Germans entered Cherbourg, and the noise of explosions could be clearly heard on Guernsey, even in the prison where Brady and Stringer were still incarcerated. Realising that Guernsey was in imminent danger of invasion and that they could fall into German captivity, both again applied to be transferred back to the British Army. However, Major-General Minshull-Ford, had already been ordered back to England, and at 4 a.m. on 20 June 1940, along with the last remaining British troops on the island, he embarked on the SS *Biarritz* in St Peter's Port and returned home. Later that day the Bailiff, Victor Carey, was sworn in as Lieutenant Governor. Carey by now was a man of seventy, considered 'vague' for his years.

Brady and Stringer's application for transfer was apparently refused. James Brady later bitterly claimed: 'The Sheriff [*sic*] in charge of the Police said that he was afraid to release us in case he got into trouble with the Germans and was himself shot.' If Brady were referring to Victor Carey (the island's Bailiff) it would not appear to have been a particularly selfless decision on his part, although it should be noted that there was a genuine terror of the Germans on the Channel Islands at this time. French refugees had brought tales of atrocities rather similar to those told of the Kaiser's troops in 1914, including the amputation of children's hands with bayonets. It might also be noted that Carey might not have been particularly well-disposed toward the two Irishmen, having after all personally sentenced them for their vicious attack on one of his policemen the previous year. It should also be remembered that there is only James Brady's word that he and Stringer were abandoned on Guernsey deliberately rather than accidentally, and that when he made this allegation (in 1946) he was facing serious charges. In the absence of any conclusive investigation, it is impossible to say whether the two Irishmen were left behind by accident or design.[21]

Throughout the day, the evacuation of Guernsey's civilians got underway, beginning with the children, and by the following morning 5,000 had sailed from St Peter's Port. Carey and his Attorney-General, Ambrose Sherwill, who had won the Military Cross in the First World War, decided on a policy where each adult would decide for themselves whether to

leave or to stay (except obviously Brady and Stringer). When
the last two evacuation ships returned to England (almost
empty), about half of Guernsey's 40,000-strong population
had been evacuated.

An uneasy calm reigned over Guernsey as the inhabitants
awaited the Germans. Cargo ships were still carrying consign-
ments of tomatoes to England and when a Luftwaffe reconnaissance aircraft flew over the island, the trucks carrying the
crop at the quays were apparently mistaken for ammunition
trucks, the demilitarisation of the Channel Islands not having
been communicated to the Germans. On the warm evening
of 29 June 1940, at 6.54 p.m., three Luftwaffe bombers swept
over St Peter's Port, strafing and bombing the trucks. The
bombers then attacked random targets, including the clearly
marked Guernsey lifeboat, killing a crewman. Twenty-nine
civilians were killed in Guernsey, and nine in a similar attack
on Jersey. The worst fears about the Germans appeared to be
confirmed. That night the BBC announced that the Channel
Islands had been demilitarised.

At about 1 p.m. the following day (30 June) it was reported that a German aircraft had landed on the island's airfield.
Several members of the island's police, including Inspector
Sculper, set off for the airfield, but by the time they arrived
the Germans had already left in such a hurry that the pilot
had left his pistol behind. Later that evening, four Junkers
JU-52 transport aircraft had landed. This time they stayed,
and while German troops unloaded motorcycles from the
aircraft, Inspector Sculper escorted the senior German officer to the Royal Hotel in St Peter's Port to meet Carey
and Sherwill. The island's newspapers soon carried an order
from Victor Carey warning that 'no resistance whatever' was
to be offered to the Germans. This was simple pragmatism
as any attempt at resistance would have been suicidal on a
30-mile square island with open terrain, no safe havens and
a civilian population that was fearfully vulnerable to reprisal.
In fact, the same newspapers carried a German threat to

bomb St Peter's Port 'should anyone attempt to cause the least trouble'.[22]

Ironically, virtually the only resistance offered to the German occupation of the Channel Islands occurred the following day on the neighbouring island of Jersey, when an Irishman punched an overbearing German soldier in a café. The island's civil court was obliged to sentence him to a month's imprisonment, although it might be noted that a German court-martial would undoubtedly have imposed a much heavier sentence.

Only a fifth of the population of Jersey had been evacuated, apparently due to the closer proximity of the island to the German-held coast. Among those left behind were 90 British servicemen, who the Germans interned in the camp which had previously been occupied by British and Italian civilians, before sending them on to Germany. A number of Irish civilians were also trapped on the island for the duration of the war, seasonal workers who had been stranded there by the German invasion. Many of these were quite happy to collaborate with the German occupiers; one of these, John Kenny, even volunteered to join the Wehrmacht. His offer was declined, largely due to 'language difficulties', although the Germans initially employed him as a waiter. Another, John O'Reilly, began working for the Germans at the airfield, now being prepared for use as a Luftwaffe base. Both returned to Ireland in late 1943 as German-trained spies.[23]

On 8 August 1940, the first meeting of the States of Guernsey was convened since the German occupation, but sitting to Bailiff Carey's right, instead of the king's Lieutenant Governor, was a uniformed major of the German Army. The Attorney-General made a long speech which ended with a call for strict conformity with German orders and the call: 'May this occupation be a model to the world.' In mid-August, the Germans established 'Feldkommandanteur 515', responsible for the civil administration of the Channel Islands, with its headquarters in Victoria College House on

Jersey, with the Guernsey branch established at the Grand
Lodge Hotel.

With time off for good behaviour, James Brady was eligible for parole in the third week of September 1940, while
Stringer had a slightly longer sentence to serve. Whether the
Germans would have allowed them to go free if they had
been dismissed from the British Army after their sentencing
is a matter of conjecture, but shortly before Brady's release
date the pair received a visit from a German officer who had
learned of the presence of two British soldiers in Guernsey
prison. Stringer was released with Brady, and the Guernsey
police, whose distinctive British 'bobby' uniform had already featured in several propaganda photographs alongside
German servicemen, were obliged to quietly escort the two
Irishmen from the prison building to the port, where they
were delivered into the custody of the German Wehrmacht.
Given prison practices of the time, it is almost certain that
they were wearing British Army uniform. They were placed
on a German transport ship and brought to the prisoner of
war camp near St-Lo, near Cherbourg, where they were to
remain until December, the camp population consisting of
'about forty British soldiers and ten thousand Frenchmen'. To
aid with administration and delivery of mail, the Germans issued Brady and Stringer with POW numbers 7815 and 7816
respectively.[24]

2

FRIESACK

At about the same time that Brady and Stringer were being transported to the coast of France, a battered French fishing boat, the *Anni Braz-Bihen*, came limping into port at Brest after an epic, but futile, voyage to the west coast of Ireland. It was an ignominious end to Operation Lobster II, an ambitious attempt by the Brandenburg regiment to land two of its men on the coast of Sligo, in an attempt to enter England covertly and prepare the way for a Brandenburger assault on Dover. This raid (for which the Brandenburgers would have worn British uniform) would only have taken place in the event of Operation Sealion, the projected German invasion of Britain, being initiated. The Brandenburgers were based in Westende in Belgium for such an eventuality. The two individuals in question were the young Obergefreiter Bruno Reiger, whose skill as a radio operator apparently owed something to his ability as a musician, and another NCO, Helmut Clissmann. The latter had intimate Irish connections; before the war he had studied at Trinity College Dublin, and he was even married to an Irishwoman, Elizabeth Mulcahy. Christian Nissen who most ably skippered the vessel was better known in international ocean racing circles as 'Hein Mueck', after another legendary sailor. Even he knew Ireland and the Irish well; the British had interned him in Tipperary and Meath during the First World War. Although burdened by an inexperienced crew, Nissen sailed the *Anni Braz-Bihen* to the west coast of Ireland without incident. It was there that he discovered, shortly before the onset of a force ten gale, that the boat's French owners from whom the vessel had been commandeered at short notice had sabotaged the engine and pump. Landing the pair on the treacherous Sligo coast was now out of the question and Nissen was left with no alternative but to return to France under extremely difficult circumstances.[1]

This was only the latest in a series of Abwehr fiascos relating to Ireland. Abwehr attempts to carry out missions in Ireland assumed such a farcical nature that they provided the basis for a television comedy drama some forty years after their occurrence (RTÉ's *Caught in a Free State*). In June 1940, former ship's captain Walter Simon was landed by U-boat in Dingle bay. He walked to the town of Dingle where he had intended to catch a train, only to discover that the local passenger service had ceased some years previously. In Dingle, he availed of the famous local hospitality and by the time he had reached Tralee railway station (by bus) he was heavily intoxicated. There, he made the acquaintance of two plain clothes detectives who accompanied him on his train journey to Dublin and arrested him on arrival. He was soon identified as the same Walter Simon who had been deported from Britain for espionage the previous year.[2]

In July 1940, Christian Nissen had been tasked with implementing 'Lobster I', a plan to land three Abwehr agents on the south coast of Ireland. Having competed twice in the famous Admiral's Cup race from Cowes to the Fastnet Rock (he had many friends in London's Royal Ocean Yacht Club), Nissen had an intimate knowledge of the west Cork coast, and it was here that he decided to land the trio. Despite not having an engine aboard his requisitioned French yacht, the *Solzic*, he successfully brought his three charges to the Baltimore area, landed them safely and returned to Brest. The three agents, however, were arrested within hours of their landing. Two were ethnic Germans born in German southwest Africa (now Namibia) while the third, Henri Obed, was of obviously Indian heritage and was of rather conspicuous appearance in the west Cork of 1940. The trio were carrying concealed explosives for sabotage missions in England, as an apparent precursor to the projected German invasion of Britain.[3]

IRA leader Seán Russell, according to the account of an Abwehr officer, was 'practically a prisoner during his stay in Germany, which was kept a close secret'. Only a small and select group of people were allowed contact with him, all Abwehr personnel with one exception: Dr Edmund Veesenmayer. Born in 1904, Veesenmayer received his doctorate in political science in 1928, was an early member of the Nazi party, and joined the SS in 1934. After Hitler's assumption of power, he was appointed to the German Foreign Office, the Auswartige Amt. According to a German account:

> When Ribbentrop in May 40 invited Seán Russell to Germany, he entrusted Veesenmayer with the handling of the IRA as the only FO man versed in conspiratorial technique. Ribbentrop gave orders to Canaris that in future all Abw operations from or against Ireland required Veesenmayer's consent. Veesenmayer held many interviews with the IRA leader, but was 'disappointed by the scope of Russell's knowledge about the IRA. His lengthy absence from the country had left him out of touch with current events, and while he could give general information about the IRA set-up and leading personalities, he lacked detailed knowledge of the org.' Worse, Russell was still advocating the IRA's fantastic plan for a mass German landing in Northern Ireland and was 'anxious to persuade the German government to give him a definite promise to help'. Russell 'displayed an obstinacy and narrowmindedness, which made him unable to see the Abw preference for sabotage. No details of this nature could be discussed with him. He was even more vague when it came to facts.
>
> Nevertheless, the Germans still hoped to make use of the IRA leader. Operation Taube – a scheme to send Seán Russell, the IRA leader, to Éire to foment unrest and lead the IRA in revolt against Northern Ireland – was controlled wholly by the Ausw Amt (Veesenmayer), Abw II being merely responsible for arranging facilities.[4]

The Abwehr war diary records that on 20 May 1940, Russell commenced instruction in sabotage materials at the Abwehr training facility at Quentzgut. On one visit, he was taken to watch a military exercise by the Brandenburg regiment. There, he was recognised by a Brandenburg officer, Dr Jupp Hoven. This officer had studied anthropology in Ireland before the war, under the offices of Helmut Clissmann's German Academic Exchange Service. There was more to this 'student' than met the eye; in 1937 he had accompanied the then IRA leader Tom Barry on a visit to Germany.[5] Hoven managed to speak privately with Russell, much to the distress of Veesenmayer, who ordered an official enquiry into the security arrangements surrounding the IRA leader. Before the war, Hoven had been good friends with Frank Ryan and was to be instrumental in organising Ryan's release from his Spanish prison. Although it took some time for Hoven to convince the Abwehr of Ryan's potential usefulness to them, discreet contacts were soon made with Ryan's lawyer in Spain and the Spanish secret police. An 'escape' for Ryan was engineered, and in mid-July 1940 he was handed over at the border between Spain and recently conquered France to Abwehr Sonderführer Kurt Haller. Haller was shocked at Ryan's physical appearance; the Irishman was emaciated and was so deaf that Haller had to shout at him to make himself understood. The confused and disorientated Ryan was driven to Paris where he spent several days staying at a country house and being fed at expensive hotels. In early August he was transferred to Berlin and reunited with fellow IRA man Seán Russell. Any doubt that the Germans had about the pair's willingness to cooperate were dispelled when the pair 'embraced one another like brothers':[6]

Veesenmayer found RYAN an able politician and a fervent Irish nationalist. He was favourably impressed by his strong personality and political acumen, which was much above that of Russell and what was known of the other IRA leaders. On the other hand Ryan had been away from Éire since 1936 and had made enemies among the right-wing clique in the IRA. He was, however, the only Irishman of sufficient stature available.

To this day, opinions are fiercely divided on the extent of Russell's collaboration with the Nazis. Supporters of Russell tend to describe him as 'a fool rather than a knave', a physical-force republican whose lack of interest in politics made him willing to request help for the IRA from any available source. Opponents sometimes compare him to Vidkun Quisling, the puppet leader of Nazi-occupied Norway, whose very name became a synonym for 'traitor'. Those holding such a view could point to the fact that Russell's arrival in Germany occurred after the German invasion of Denmark and Norway, and that he continued to work for the Germans even after the Nazis had further demonstrated their contempt for the small nations of Europe by their invasion of Belgium, Holland and Luxembourg. The Germans themselves evidently did not regard Russell as wholly reliable, or at least less so than Frank Ryan:

> It was left to the discretion of Russell whether or not he took Ryan with him on his mission. After some hesitation (Ryan and Russell had formerly belonged to opposite camps within the IRA), he consented. The German motive for sending Ryan was that Russell throughout his stay in Germany had shown considerable reticence towards the Germans and plainly did not regard himself as a German agent.[7]

Whatever the truth of the motives of Seán Russell, he was actively seeking a course of action that would have resulted in the involvement of Irish affairs of a particularly dangerous individual. Dr Edmund Veesenmayer is usually described as Ribbentrop's 'coup d'état specialist'. He had played a significant role in the German annexation of Austria in 1938, and later organised the Nazi seizure of power in Croatia and Serbia in 1941, Slovenia in 1943 and Hungary in 1944. In the postwar estimation of British intelligence:

He was the 'political agent' on the grand scale, the man of mystery operating in the murky twilight of Balkan politics. Patiently he plotted to disrupt the stability and integrity of Germany's neighbours, so that when the Wehrmacht struck, a government would crumble more easily, an army surrender more quickly, a general desert to the other side, and a new government of 'honourable men' be in office before the dazed people had had time to express their indignation.

The Germans had noted that Russell 'had no clear picture of the future government of Ireland, except that it was to be in the hands of the IRA or their sympathisers'. It is not difficult to imagine Veesenmayer exploiting such a power vacuum for Germany's best advantage. Such an outcome would have dire consequences for Ireland's Jewish population in particular. Veesenmayer has also been justifiably described (by Francis Stuart) as a 'Jew exterminator'. As German ambassador to Hungary in 1944, he worked alongside Adolf Eichmann to engineer the deaths of 450,000 Hungarian Jews, for which he received a 20-year sentence at the Nuremburg trials. It is disturbing to note that IRA literature at this time was displaying nakedly anti-Semitic sentiment.[8]

By early August 1940, preparations for Operation Taube were complete. A submarine, the *U-65*, was standing by at the German naval base in Wilhelmshaven to bring Russell and Ryan to Ireland along with a German radio set to re-establish the 'Irene' link between the IRA and the Abwehr, for which the Auswartige Amt had prepared a special code. On the morning of 8 August, the two Irishmen left Wilhelmshaven aboard the *U-65*, intending a landing on the coast of Kerry. Russell soon began complaining of crippling stomach pains and died, apparently of a burst gastric ulcer, on 15 August. He was buried at sea, and although offered the option of landing in Ireland alone, Ryan chose to return to Lorient with the U-boat, a course of action his supporters do not find easy to justify. According to Haller, 'Russell's death on the U-boat came as a shock to Veesenmayer. Apart from the end of Operation Taube, Veesenmayer knew that Russell's death might well be regarded with suspicion by the IRA.' After an investigation, the IRA were eventually advised of Russell's death through covert channels. Frank Ryan was still willing to work with the Germans 'and after his return from Lorient in August 1940 Veesenmayer began to groom him for his role as leader of Operation Taube II, the proposed sequel to the Russell mission'.

In the summer of 1940, following Nazi Germany's victory over western Europe, Abwehr II, the German intelligence division responsible for sabotage, subversion and minorities, with the cooperation of the Kriegsgefangenwasen OKW (POW directorate), began to segregate national minorities among its many prisoners-of-war into special camps. This was in the hope of establishing a pool from which the Abwehr could recruit agents and saboteurs. Flemings were separated from Belgians, Bretons from French, and Irish from British. The Abwehr III (counter-espionage division) officer attached to each POW camp selected potentially suitable candidates who were later be interviewed by recruiting officers from Abwehr II.

According to Dr Kurt Haller, 'the formation of an Irish Brigade from these men was near to the hearts of the staff of the Irish section of Abwehr II.' Haller was to feature in several German intelligence operations involving Ireland. Born in 1913, he had studied law at Konigsberg and Berlin, during which time he had been involved in nationalistic student movements. Through these, he had been introduced to Abwehr Major Voss, and in 1935, while an exchange student in France, had compiled a report on Breton nationalists. In 1937, he joined the Nazi party, but after the war claimed that he 'took no active part' in its activities. From early 1938, while studying for his doctorate, he periodically underwent short training sessions with the Abwehr, and just before the outbreak of war he was called up to Abwehr II's Office I 'West' as a Hilfsoffizier, 'responsible mainly for handling Irish affairs'. In March 1940, he was appointed a Sonderführer, a German rank equivalent to warrant officer, awarded to certain civilian specialists. Considered 'intelligent and highly adaptable' by British intelligence, Haller was a somewhat thickset individual who spoke English slowly and who wore an orthopaedic boot due to a club foot. He appeared to have been somewhat sensitive about this ailment, some acquaintances presuming that his severe limp was due to a prosthetic lower leg.

Abwehr II's Irish section originally was optimistic for their 'Irish brigade', which, strangely, appears to have been inspired by Casement's futile attempts to raise a similar unit during the First World War. 'They envisaged a highly trained body of men, comparable in standard to the Brandenburg Regt, keen and reliable, which could be committed, either alone or with German troops, in a national war for the liberation of Ireland, or later, as defenders of Ireland against British aggression.' Major Marwede and Major Astor of Abwehr II, however, considered the plan too ambitious, and pointed out that the formation of such a large force fell outside Abwehr II's sphere of operations.

A special POW camp for potential Irish recruits was established at Friesack in Brandenburg, 35 miles west of Berlin. Known to the Abwehr as Damm 1, its official designation was Stalag XX A (301). A Stalag (Stammlager, camp for POWs of non-commissioned rank) number normally indicated the Wehrkreis (German military district) that administered it; however Wehrkreis XX was actually located in occupied Poland, and Stalag XX was a POW camp at Thorn. This was evidently to ease the transfer of Irish POWs from other camps, and to conceal Friesack's true purpose. Contrary to Abwehr intentions, conditions in Friesack were harsh. For example, a British POW could normally expect to have the meagre camp diet of watery soup and black bread alleviated by Red Cross parcels. Sanctioned by the Geneva convention, these contained such items as tinned food, butter, chocolate and even cigarettes. Due to the need for secrecy, however, no Red Cross parcels were distributed at Friesack. Abwehr's protests to the Kriegsgefangenwasen OKW, 'that Damm I was more of a penal camp than a special POW camp, had little effect'.

Two recruiters, a German and an Irish civilian, began to tour the POW camps, to interview candidates thought to be suitable by the camp's Abwehr officers. The Irishman was Francis Stuart, a writer with IRA connections who had arrived in Germany in January 1940 to accept a teaching post in Berlin University, but was initially willing to work with the Abwehr. The German civilian was Franz Fromme, often referred to as 'professor', a small thin man with spectacles who often displayed an eccentric streak. He had been a frequent visitor to Ireland before the war, had written a book on the Irish independence movement, and had briefed Görtz and another agent before their missions in Ireland. Ironically, given his current activities in the POW camps, he was said to be something of an expert on the life of Sir Roger Casement. Fromme and Stuart had first met in Dublin in 1939, and Fromme had thereafter vouched for Stuart when he presented himself to the Abwehr in Berlin in January 1940. That April he had introduced him to Hermann Görtz shortly before his departure on his Irish mission, and Stuart had given Görtz his wife's address as a safe house, which the German availed of after his landing in Ireland. In May 1940, Fromme had escorted IRA leader Seán Russell from Genoa to Berlin and thereafter had acted as his interpreter.[9]

It soon became obvious that any hopes of raising anything like a brigade from the Irish POWs were to prove greatly ambitious. All of these Irishmen had, after all, volunteered to join the British Army, and even those who had joined from economic necessity were not favourably inclined to Nazi Germany. They were even less so following the treatment meted out to them after their capture by the Germans. Two hundred British soldiers had been massacred after their capture by the

Waffen-SS. Those members of the British Expeditionary
Force who had not made it to the beaches of Dunkirk in
time had begun their captivity being marched across France
at an average rate of over twenty miles a day in the heat of
summer. They were issued with almost no rations and were
prevented from drinking water and milk set out by French
villagers. Eventually, a column of over 20,000 Allied POWs
were assembled at Cambrai and were force-marched across
the Belgian border, through the Ardennes and Luxembourg,
to Trier in Germany. Here they received a hot meal for the
first time since capture and were loaded onto goods wagons
at the railway sidings, where they were given eight loaves of
bread and one milk churn of water between every sixty prisoners, arriving at their final destination after three days, most
suffering from dysentery and malnutrition.[10]

Eventually, some 180 Irishmen found themselves at Friesack. Apparently the only criteria for their transfer here was
anyone who had not rejected the German proposals outright.
These included a group of men who in fact were overtly hostile to the German recruiting effort. They had been transferred
to Friesack in error when the elderly Fromme had accidentally 'mixed up the lists of rejected and selected candidates
from one camp'. For reasons of security, it was not possible
to return them to their former camp, and so they remained at
Friesack, adding to the Germans' difficulties.

Fromme 'proved unequal to the job', and was soon transferred to the German military government in Belgium.
Stuart, 'pleading his academic duties', returned to Berlin.
He had been disillusioned by the poor quality of the few
Irishmen that did volunteer, but he had also witnessed
something of the uglier side of Hitler's Reich. While tour-
ing POW camps in Poland, he had witnessed Polish civilians being ill-treated by German occupation forces, and he
later claimed that this left a lasting impression. Nonethe-
less, Stuart agreed to broadcast propaganda on German radio from March 1942.

To replace Fromme and Stuart, Rittmeister von Stauffen-berg (Abwehr II's Liaison Officer to Kriegsgefangenwasen OKW) appointed Brockmann ten Brock, a German actor of Dutch ancestry. Apart from having a good command of English, he had the advantage of having visited Ireland be-fore the war. He was to select the majority of the Irishmen sent to Friesack.[11]

In December 1940, James Brady and Frank Stringer, along with the entire population of the temporary POW camp at St-Lo, were transferred to the huge camp at Luckenwalde in Germany, which was actually also being used as a transit camp for Irish POWs on their way to Friesack. At this time, back in Ireland, a curious little saga was unfolding.

A middle-aged farmer who lived in Co. Roscommon received official notification from an address in Edinburgh (later forgotten by him) that 7043207 Fusilier James Brady had been reported 'missing'. About a week later, a letter ar-rived from the same address that stated that Fusilier Brady was a prisoner-of-war in Germany and had been taken pris-oner in the Channel Islands. The Roscommon farmer was baffled. He had never heard of James Brady in his life. Sus-pecting a delivery to the wrong address, the farmer enquired among neighbours who shared the name of Brady, and con-tacted the local garda, but his investigation drew a blank. The mystery would resurface in time.[12]

It would appear that at some stage James Brady falsely gave the name of this Roscommon farmer as his next-of-kin, whose correct address he must have known (possibly from personal acquaintance), probably on his enlistment in the British Army. The puzzle is why this 'next-of-kin' was not notified that Brady was missing until nearly six months after he had fallen into German captivity. While it is possible that Brady might have named the farmer to the Red Cross having become a POW, the fact that most subsequent communica-tions regarding him originated from Britain suggests that it is more likely that the British Army had the falsely-given name on their files. If the latter was the case, the six-month delay in notifying the given next-of-kin would not appear to do great credit to the person responsible.

Apart from interview, another method used by Abwehr II to screen prospective Irish recruits in Luckenwalde was an Arbeitskommando, a work party of POWs which were detailed to work on roads near the village of Schonbone. This Arbeitskommando eventually comprised nearly 60 Irishmen from various British Army regiments, and in May 1941 over thirty of these, including Brady and Stringer, were told that they were being transferred to 'an Irish camp', and soon found themselves at Stalag XX A (301). Conditions in the camp had improved by then, and Friesack even included a canteen that supplied beer and cigarettes, unheard of in most POW camps. Frank Stringer quickly obtained a position in this canteen, where he first encountered Corporal John Codd, formerly of the Royal Welch Fusiliers. Codd, who introduced himself to Stringer as 'Juan', had been born near the Slieve Bloom mountains of Co. Laois in 1912, his father and older brother also having served in the British Army. In the estimation of Kurt Haller, he was 'a strong character: self-centred, stubborn and very shrewd'. Although of limited education, Codd was intelligent and a gifted linguist; he already spoke Spanish, with a working knowledge of some Asian languages. Later, he would also master French and German. He was a well-travelled individual, having emigrated to Canada for a short time in 1929 before travelling to Wales to enlist in the British Army in 1931. He was later posted to Gibraltar, and to Hong Kong in 1937. In contravention of British Army regulations, he secretly qualified as a civilian instructor of 'physical culture' and helped a civilian friend to manage a gym in his spare time. Codd was involved in the evacuation of civilians from Shanghai in 1938. He returned to Britain with his regiment in 1939 and left the British Army in April. He later claimed to the Germans that he had worked for the IRA at this time. Codd's spell in 'civvy street' was short-lived and he was recalled to his battalion in August 1939. After the outbreak of war, the 1st Battalion Royal Welch Fusiliers were deployed to France, and on 11 May 1940 advanced into Belgium as part of the British Expeditionary Force. The battalion was overrun by the Germans at St-Venant on 27 May and Codd, suffering a wounded foot, was captured.

Codd was hospitalised and his big toe amputated, and he spent until November being transferred between various hospitals, including Lille and Enghien. He was registered as a POW at Heumarr near Düsseldorf before being transferred to the Stalag at Luckenwalde. In Luckenwalde, Codd was interviewed by a German Sonderführer who was known to the other POWs as 'American Joe'. This may have been Oskar Lange, an intelligent man who spoke good English with an American accent, learned having spent many years as a longshoreman in New York. Codd was quizzed on his political views: 'he expressed sympathy with any movement working against England', and also claimed that he approved of the IRA's bombing campaign against English civilians in 1939. 'American Joe' was apparently happy with these answers, and told Codd that he was being sent to a camp 'with other Irishmen'. At the end of January 1941, he was sent to the stalag at Luckenwalde, then containing French POWs and some British POWs in transit, and arrived at Friesack camp in mid-February. Soon after his arrival, he was interviewed again by Brockmann ten Brock, who questioned Codd on his language skills, the countries he had visited and his opinion on the partition of Ireland. He finished by asking Codd whether he would work with Germany against England. Codd claims that he expressed a preference to discuss such matters with another Irishman. It was clear that the Abwehr was already taking a keen interest in Corporal Codd.

Codd's subsequent claim that he had 'more or less established himself by forceful means as the leader of the camp' would appear to reveal more of his own personality than the actual course of events. Codd was already a deeply unpopular figure in the camp, and in fact the leader of the prisoners was Lieutenant Bissel, the senior British officer (SBO) at Friesach. The senior non-commissioned rank in Friesack was Sergeant-Major Whelan, a Corkman with twenty-two years' service with the British Army. He was soon to warn Codd against 'trucking with the Germans', and a mutual animosity between the two men would continue to grow.

The camp interpreter was Obergefreiter (Corporal) Bruggemann, formerly a reception clerk in a hotel. Originally from the Rhineland, he spoke good English and was on good terms with several of the prisoners. Before joining the army, he had been a member of the Sturm Abteilung, the brown-shirted street brawlers that had provided the Nazis with their muscle before their fall from grace in 1934, when Hitler had several troublesome members eliminated in 'The Night of the Long Knives'.[13]

The Abwehr eventually decided that, although he had picked most of the Friesack Irishmen, 'Brockmann ten Brock lacked the finesse to undertake the final selection of PW at Damm 1'. By the time Brady and Stringer arrived at Friesack, Dr Jupp Hoven, who had persuaded the Abwehr to engineer the release of Frank Ryan from his Spanish prison, had replaced him. Hoven introduced himself to the Irish POWs as 'Lieutenant Rainers', and was quickly nicknamed by them as 'Gestapo Joe', although he was not a member of that organisation. It is of interest that while Brady and Stringer continued to know him (phonetically) throughout the war as 'Rheinhorst' or 'Rheinherst', Codd was aware of his true identity.

It was by now abundantly clear that there was no hope of forming a significant Irish military unit for the Wehrmacht. Hoven, however, saw other possibilities for the Friesack Irishmen, for example as spies or saboteurs in the United Kingdom or even as guides in the event of any German invasion of Britain. He set about his new task with enthusiasm. 'Hoven was left in complete charge of the Abw side of the camp, and spent a good deal of time there. He controlled all propaganda, and he took some trouble over this. He had frequent and long talks with small groups of PW or individual men, during which he tested and strengthened their anti-British feelings; he also obtained certain literature and films from the Wehrmacht Propaganda Dept.' Hoven interviewed the prisoners more carefully than ten Brock and seemed to find Codd of particular interest when Codd hinted to him that he was willing to 'fight for Ireland' and work with the Germans against England. Two weeks after their arrival in camp in May 1941, Hoven interviewed Stringer and Brady. Stringer was questioned about his political views and Irish background, while Brady was asked if he was a member of the IRA. Stringer, working in the camp canteen with Codd, was very much taking the older man as an example, to the extent that it was uncharitably suggested in the camp that the pair were having a homosexual affair, although this is more likely to reflect their growing unpopularity than anything else. Stringer had travelled little in his twenty-one years, fifteen months of it spent in prison, while Codd was very much a man of the world. Stringer did not go into any detail when informing Codd of the true reasons for his imprisonment in Guernsey, mentioning to Codd only that they had 'attempted to set a petrol tank on fire and were arrested, convicted and imprisoned by members of the local authorities'.

James Brady, however, was to fall under the influence of a very different individual. Soon after Brady and Stringer had arrived in Friesack, Dr Hoven had Lt Bissel, the SBO, removed from the camp. Typically, Codd claimed that this was because he was young with 'not much sense', and had become a 'laughing stock' after drinking in the canteen with private soldiers. In fact, according to Haller, 'Hoven had Bissell removed from the camp because Cushing informed him that he was leader of an escape party.' It would not be the last apparent act of treachery by Thomas 'Red' Cushing (named for hair colour rather than political beliefs). Cushing had a

colourful background. He claimed to have been a teenage
scout for the republicans during the Irish Civil War and had
served in the United States Army from 1926 to 1936. He also
claimed to have joined the republican forces in the Spanish
Civil War, after which he had joined the Royal Inniskilling
Fusiliers of the British Army in November 1938. His 1962
autobiography, however, reads more as a series of drunken
escapades than military deeds, and his career in both US and
British Armies was characterised by a series of promotions
followed by demotions. He freely admitted (postwar) that he
had taken advantage of the chaotic Stalag administration to
promote himself to sergeant, the rank he held in Friesack.[14]

Lieutenant Bissel's replacement as SBO was Lieutenant-
Colonel John McGrath, Royal Engineers, who had been
transferred from the Oflag (officer's camp) at Luckenwalde.
Cushing claimed, not implausibly, that McGrath had been
detailed to investigate the Friesack camp by Major General
Fortune, the highest-ranking British POW held by the Germans. On arrival at Friesack, McGrath was wearing a Major's
rank insignia, suggesting that his rank was the result of a field
promotion shortly before capture. Accounts of the Friesack
camp tend to speak very highly of his conduct there; Codd's
and Haller's are exceptions. Codd's account reveals more of
his own character than of McGrath's, while Haller was evidently not prepared to be magnanimous to a man who would
do more than any individual to subvert the Abwehr's scheme
to recruit Irish POWs.

McGrath later recalled:

It was the most difficult situation I have ever been called upon to
face. From the hour I entered the place I knew it meant trouble.
After consultation with my NCOs, I decided on a definite plan
of action that had for its foundation that we should stand firm
against all odds and undertake nothing that would be against
the best interests of Ireland and England. From that position
we never moved. It was a difficult time in 1941 and 1942, when
I had to convince everybody that, no matter how black things
looked – and they were black – that Germany would, in time,

lose the war. I often had doubts myself of the result in those dark days, but nobody under me ever knew that. However, I always felt that the German idea of what would really influence the Irishmen was very misguided, and its general effect on the Irish boys was absolutely nil. [15]

McGrath, who before the war had been manager of Dublin's Theatre Royal, was, like James Brady, a Roscommon man. Not only, according to a reliable source, was Brady's family well known to McGrath, but that 'some relative ... wrote to the Lieut Colonel asking him to look after Brady'.

When Brady made his statement in London in late 1946, he claimed that 'I do not know where my father is because I have had nothing to do with them [*sic*] for over five years', which might suggest that he had had some contact with him in 1941.

The Germans attempted to 'wine and dine' Colonel McGrath. Jupp Hoven brought him to Berlin for a few days where he was entertained and introduced to Helmut Clissmann. Although Hoven was hopeful that McGrath would cooperate with the Germans, Clissmann was more sceptical. Hoven brought McGrath to Berlin on subsequent occasions, including one where the pair had lunch with Clissmann, Kurt Haller, and Dr Hoffmann, a senior Abwehr II officer. According to Haller, the conversation was 'of a general nature', largely concerning theatrical affairs, the Germans being aware that McGrath was the manager of 'a Dublin music hall'. [16]

On 22 August 1941, Hitler unleashed Operation Barbarossa, the German invasion of Russia. After a dawn attack by the Luftwaffe had decimated forward units of the Red air force, over 120 divisions drove into the Soviet Union. Although the Russian forces were numerically impressive, much of their combat equipment was obsolete, and Stalin's pre-war purges of the Soviet officer corps ensured that incompetent lackeys such as Semyon Budyenny and Klimenti Vorishilov held high rank, and continued to do so even after their shortcomings were exposed. Once again, German forces seemed invincible, driving deep into Russia. Smolensk was captured within the month, and Leningrad placed under siege by the end of September. Throughout the Reich, even in POW camps, Goebbels' propaganda ministry poured forth a stream of triumphant radio bulletins throughout the summer and autumn of 1941. Each Sondermeldung (special announcement) was preceded by a trumpet fanfare and would announce the capture of yet another Russian town or city.

About a month after his arrival at the Friesack camp, Frank Stringer was working with John Codd in the camp canteen, when he received a summons for an interview with Hoven. He later claimed that Haller was also present but the account of Codd and Haller both refute this. At this interview, Hoven invited Stringer 'to leave the camp and go for a course of training in radio and sabotage by explosives with the object of being sent to England or Ireland as an agent'. Stringer wholeheartedly agreed with this proposition and Hoven promised that they would discuss the matter further. Stringer returned to the canteen, and John Codd left to be interviewed himself.

'When he returned,' according to Stringer, 'we discussed the proposals which Rheinhorst and Haller had made to us. Cod[d] said that he was to be the "boss" and I was to be his assistant. He did not say why he had agreed to work for the Germans nor did I tell him why I had.' To Haller, 'Hoven reported that two of the camp inmates, Cpl Codd and Fus Stringer, were in his opinion thoroughly co-operative and ready for sabotage training.' In July 1941, Haller appeared at Friesack and with Jupp Hoven, interviewed the pair, 'and they both enthusiastically agreed to work for Abw. It was made clear at the time that they would be required to undertake sabotage operations against the UK. Codd was much the stronger personality of the two; Stringer was younger and inexperienced, and lacked the initiative which Codd showed to a marked degree. He was therefore regarded as Codd's 'mate', and figured in Abw files as 'Gehilfe' [assistant], while Codd was referred to as 'Gastwirt' [innkeeper].'

Although Haller had noticed Codd's 'stubborn' nature, the Abwehr rather naively considered that 'his obstinacy was a point in his favour, because it was thought he would be able to work on his own'. Codd was already showing great interest in the financial aspects of the deal, in particular the sum of £8,000 that had been suggested to finance his mission. Haller recalled that 'this sum was mentioned by Codd and [Haller] brushed it aside by saying that they would be unlikely to quarrel over financial matters', adding petulantly 'but they did'.

The next item discussed, according to Codd, was how the pair could leave the camp 'without causing suspicion', and it was agreed that Codd and Stringer 'should get drunk, smash up the canteen and get arrested by the German guards' who would take them away, a course of action which even Hoven later described as a 'comedy'. Codd also claimed that Haller had informed him that they would meet 'an unnamed Irishman' later.[17]

After the outbreak of war, the Irish Army had established a series of observation posts around the Irish coast, whose diligent crews of coast watchers were able to observe and report aircraft straying into Irish airspace through a remarkably effective telephone system. In the early hours of the foggy morning of 18 July 1941, a Heinkel He-111 bomber slipped over the south Irish coast and was heard circling for some time in the vicinity of Youghal, Co. Cork. It then flew northwards and headed inland over Co. Tipperary. Its progress was monitored carefully by the Irish Air Corps central control set up near Dublin in the seclusion of a Clondalkin monastery, linked to a network of ground observers. The previous May, such an aircraft had dropped its bombs onto Dublin, killing thirty-four civilians. The Heinkel continued inland until it reached Summerhill, north-west of Dublin. It then turned south and flew over Maynooth to Naas (not far from Clondalkin), overflew the military base at the Curragh Camp, and continued south until it passed over the Wexford coast and out of Irish airspace.

Unseen by anyone on the ground, a parachutist had jumped from the belly of the Heinkel over Summerhill and had made a safe landing. Joseph Lenihan, the first Irish agent to be dispatched by the Germans, had come home. Lenihan, a member of a famous Irish political family, had travelled to the Channel Islands for seasonal work in 1940, and had been stranded in Jersey by the invasion along with several other Irishmen. On the night of 9 November 1940, he staged a daring escape attempt, stealing a motorboat from the harbour intending to sail across the English Channel. The engine flooded, however, and Lenihan ended up being washed ashore near Soudainville on the French coast. Quickly captured by the Germans, he was brought to the local Kommandanteur where after several days in custody a German officer in civilian dress interviewed him. This officer, who spoke perfect English, 'knew a great deal about the Irish problem', and despite the fact that Lenihan had proved himself not particularly willing to be a subject of the Third Reich, invited him to work for Germany in Ireland. Lenihan assented, outwardly at least, and soon commenced a six-week course in radio at 22 Avenue de Versailles in Paris, after which he was sent to The Hague. He later claimed to have been offered a course of parachute training, but declined, intriguingly claiming to the Germans that he had already gained parachuting experience in the United States.

By mid-January, Lenihan was told that the Germans had decided to send him on a mission. 'He would be flown to Ireland, dropped in some suitable spot and was to make his way to Sligo, and to establish himself there to send weather information. On the night of 29 January 1941, Lenihan claimed he was flown out of Schipol in Holland en route for Ireland by flying across England. Over Norwich, by his account, the aircraft's 'heating apparatus' malfunctioned and had to return to Schipol, all four crewmen and Lenihan suffering frostbite.

On the night of 18 July, Lenihan boarded a Heinkel He-111 bomber at Brest, carrying a radio, £500 sterling and such spy paraphernalia as invisible ink powder. He jumped successfully over Summerhill and, having landed, concealed his parachute, a jump-suit and a small spade. These were discovered four days later by a farmer who alerted the local gardaí, and soon the security forces were on the hunt for the mystery parachutist, newspapers having been prevented from carrying reports on the incident by government censors. Lenihan, however, had a head start adequate for his purposes. Having bought clothes and other personal effects in Dublin, he opened an account with the Ulster Bank and deposited £370 of unspent money in it. He then took a train to Dundalk, where he booked a room in the Lorne Hotel. When the gardaí raided this room on 24 July 1941 they found Lenihan's radio, spying equipment and his bank book. Lenihan, however, had left on the train to Belfast two days earlier. After the train had crossed into Northern Ireland, Lenihan approached a policeman of the Royal Ulster Constabulary who was checking identity papers, and informed him that he had important information. On his arrival in Belfast, a police car brought him straight to RUC headquarters where he was interrogated by police and military intelligence officers.

The same day he was flown to England, where he was soon being debriefed by MI5. A former medical student and civil servant, Lenihan had 'a phenomenal memory for facts and faces' and provided MI5 with much valuable data on the Abwehr in France and Holland. Lenihan remained in England for the rest of the war, with full freedom of movement.[18]

By September 1941, Corporal John Codd was the most hated man in Friesack camp. He himself blamed Colonel McGrath for this, making the very dubious claim that McGrath was 'giving money to groups within the camp to buy drink and to incite them against Codd, and to win them over to himself'. A far more likely reason, apart from the interest the Germans were taking in him, was alluded to by Codd himself when he was discussing Sergeant Collins of the Royal Engineers. According to Codd: 'Collins strung Hoven and the German authorities along for quite a time. Codd warned Hoven about him, but Hoven would not be influenced by Codd's opinion at times'. According to Haller, 'Codd, of all the Irish PWs, was the most enthusiastic collaborator.' One observer considered Codd's life to be in danger. He himself admitted that there were several people 'after him' in the camp.

With the assistance of Gefreiter Bruggemann, a 'rough house' was organised in the canteen in mid-September 1941, in which evidently quite a number of the POWs ended up participating! As planned, Codd and Stringer were 'arrested', and that night were taken to Berlin. There they were introduced to a German called Harold Lechtweiss, who was to be their 'guardian and interpreter'. Codd, who claimed to have already met Lechtweiss before leaving Friesack, believed him to be a former soldier who Bruggemann claimed to be an ex-priest. In fact, according to Haller, Lechtweiss was a Gefreiter in the Brandenburger regiment and an old friend of Jupp Hoven. The two Irishmen changed into civilian clothing for the first time in over a year; for two years in Stringer's case.

This would have been a psychologically important moment, the donning of comparatively light and comfortable clothing emphasising their new freedom. Lechtweiss brought them to a restaurant in Berlin, where they were joined by Hoven. After their meal, they left the restaurant and in the street met Helmut Clissmann, 'Dr Schreiber' and 'another man'. Haller later suggested that 'Dr Schreiber' may have been an alias for a man called Schofer, another member of the Brandenburgers who had accompanied Clissmann on his abortive attempt to land in Ireland the previous September. The extent to which pseudonyms were used when introducing Codd and Stringer to Abwehr and Brandenburg regiment personnel would strongly suggest that the Germans were not willing to take the two Irishmen into their confidence completely.

The group then made their way to 'Allotrie's', a bar on the fashionable Kurfuerstendamm, where they were joined by Kurt Haller. After they had sat down, Hoven called to a man who was sitting on a high stool at the bar. 'He came over to the table and was introduced to Codd and Stringer as Frank Richards. The German said something about his fighting in Spain and he and Codd got into conversation in Spanish, about things and conditions in Spain.' This was the first time that Codd met Frank Ryan, who usually used the name 'Frank Richards' in Germany. Codd genuinely never appears to have learned Ryan's real name, or ever to have even heard of him. It should be noted that at the time that Ryan's imprisonment was a *cause celèbre* in Ireland, Codd was serving in the Far East with the British Army.

At the end of the night, Lechtweiss brought Codd and Stringer to their accommodation in Berlin, a flat on the first floor of Number 8, Ludwigskirstrasse. According to Haller, 'This house was used by Abw II for meeting their agents, and occasionally agents were housed there for a time.' The two Irishmen spent the night here, as did Lechtweiss. At all times the Irishmen would be accompanied by him or a deputy ('Dr Schreiber', according to Stringer).[19]

The next morning, Lechtweiss gave the pair 200 marks each 'as pocket money'. For the next two weeks, they 'did nothing but sight-seeing in Berlin, always accompanied by Lechtweiss'. For anyone that would truly have chosen to throw their lot in with Germany, the spectacle of Berlin in September 1941 would have been a powerful vindication of such a decision. The city was the heart of an empire 'victorious on all fronts', stretching from Norway to North Africa, and from the coast of the English Channel to the steppes of Russia.

Grandiose plans were being made to rebuild Berlin in the style befitting an imperial city. Renamed Germania, the new city of ten million people would be the heart of the German Reich. Its centrepiece was to be the 'Prachtstrasse', the 'Street of Splendour.' Under Hitler's direction, his chief architect, Albert Speer, had designed a three-mile long boulevard, a 100-foot scale model of which had been assembled in the exhibition room of the Berlin Academy of Arts. To its north would tower the 1,000-foot-high dome of the 'Kupferhalle', which with a diameter of over 800 feet would hold standing room for over a 150,000 people. To the south of the avenue, lined with eleven separate ministry buildings, would rise the 'Triumhbogen', an arch of triumph rising to four times the height of its Parisian equivalent. South of the arch would be built the central railroad station (larger than Grand Central Station in New York) and in late 1941 Hitler added the detail of lining its 1,000-foot plaza with weapons captured by his victorious armies. Speer, after the war, claimed that, in retrospect, he considered the entire Prachtstrasse to be regimented and lacking any sense of proportion. He also realised that the body heat generated by the huge crowds in the Kupferhalle would have risen to the cold copper dome, generating small clouds and eventually rainfall inside the hall!

In late 1941, although the patrons of the cafés along the Kurfuersterdamm sipped bitter 'ersatzkaffee' (coffee substitute) and some rationing was in force, so too were Berlin's shops stocked with goods sequestered from Germany's occupied territories. A blackout was in force at night, but RAF raids were ineffectual as yet. Berlin even had its own television service, inaugurated in 1935 and heavily involved in broadcasting the 1936 Berlin Olympics. By 1940 several public service receivers displayed a six-hour daily schedule of feature films, documentaries, exercise programmes, news and sports, some of the material live. Near to Berlin's most famous landmark, the long enduring Brandenburg Gate, could be seen the old Reichstag, an arson attack upon which had provided the Nazis with the pretext to seize power in 1933. A walk down Wilhelmstrasse would have been of interest. The

British Embassy was closed and its windows shuttered, as was the Russian Embassy. The US Embassy, for now, was still open. The two Irishmen might have joined the crowds outside the Old Reich Chancellory at 12 noon to witness the assembly of the guard, a ceremony provided by the Wachtbattalion of the German Army's crack Grossdeutschland Regiment, which was now fighting in Russia. Just around the corner was the New Reich Chancellory, designed by Albert Speer and opened by Hitler in January 1939. Outside its gaudy colonnades and halls of polished marble, under the exterior's huge golden eagles grasping swastikas, soldiers in a different uniform stood guard. Instead of German Army feldgrau, these men, a detachment of the SS-Leibstandarte Adolf Hitler, wore black uniforms and helmets with white leather webbing. On their uniform collars they wore the distinctive siegrunes, resembling a double lightening bolt, of the SS. The Leibstandarte, a fully motorised division of volunteers, were now also in the thick of the fighting in Russia.[20]

It is rather unlikely that Harold Lechtweiss would have shown his Irish charges one large building just off Wilhelmstrasse. Number 10 Prinz Albrecht Strasse was infamous as the headquarters of the Nazi secret police, the Gestapo.

Codd and Stringer made no mention of seeing any of Berlin's Jews. They would have been easily identifiable; on 15 September 1941, German Jews were ordered to wear the infamous yellow star on their clothing for the first time. By October most of them had disappeared, having been deported to the ghettoes of eastern Europe as a preliminary to their awful eventual fate.

Elsewhere in Berlin, another Irishman was offering his services to Nazi Germany. Having worked for the Luftwaffe in Jersey, John Francis O'Reilly eventually learned German well enough to act as a translator between the Germans and the Irish workers still trapped on the island. Having made an agreement to recruit some of these men as war workers in Germany, O'Reilly and seventy-two other Irishmen set off

for the Hermann Goering Steel Works at Watenstedt in July
1941. The behaviour of the group on the train journey there
was less than exemplary. Chaos ensued when the drunken
group invaded other carriages and repeatedly pulled the communication cords. Their conduct did not improve at the factory where they aggravated their German hosts by their continued riotous behaviour and constant flouting of the blackout regulations. Eventually nearly all of this group returned
to Jersey, and the Germans made no attempt to bring them
back to Watenstedt, suggesting that they regarded them
as less than indispensable to the German war effort. After
two months at the Hermann Goering Works, a disgruntled
O'Reilly applied for a post with the Irish section of German
radio (Irland-Redaktion). He later recalled: 'When I reached
the German Propaganda Ministry, in the Potsdamerplatz,
Berlin, I had an interview with Herr Bock, an executive of
the Ministry. Then I was sent to the Rundfunkhaus for a
voice test. There I was asked to read an extract from a speech
by Mr Winston Churchill. This was recorded and later played
back to me and to those who were testing my voice. The test
was satisfactory.'

Dr Hans Hartmann, the head of Irland-Redaktion, signed
O'Reilly up immediately. As O'Reilly was to discover, he was
actually the only Irish national in the Irish section: 'When
introduced to my colleagues, I began to wonder if I had
joined an international brigade. There were two Frenchmen,
an Englishman who had been living in Paris, a Russian typ-
ist, and two German girl translators who had a perfect knowledge of English.' After a short time writing scripts, O'Reilly
began broadcasting under the name 'Pat O'Brien', but from
October began broadcasting under his own name.[21]

After two weeks of 'sightseeing', John Codd 'became difficult', according to Stringer, and objected to being continuously
being accompanied by Lechtweiss. Claiming to the Germans
to have been a member of the IRA in pre-war Britain, Codd
claimed that 'he had been able to walk about in London as

a free-lance and without escort, and could look after himself in Germany'. According to Stringer, 'Haller and Rheinhorst had Cod[d] interviewed by an Irish civilian named Moloney and it was proved that Cod[d] was not an IRA man.'

'Maloney' was another pseudonom used by Frank Ryan in late 1942, which suggests that Codd told Stringer some detail of the following events later in the war. Frank Ryan invited Codd and Stringer to a house, 'a bungalow with a large garden' in the wealthy Berlin suburb of Nicholassee. Codd began to speak to Ryan in Spanish, but Ryan 'told Codd to forget all that and carried on the conversation in English'. Codd was sparse in detail with regard to this interview, recalling only that Ryan told him that 'anything he might do to help the Germans would be all right so far as the Irish organisations in the USA are concerned'. Later, Codd claimed that he 'told Rheiners (making an unusual reference to Hoven's cover name) he did not feel too satisfied about Richards and to impress Rheiners said he had given Richards some IRA passwords and signs and that he did not respond. Rheiners assured him that Richards was OK, but gave no additional information.' This can hardly have helped Codd's credibility; Ryan was, of course, a famous IRA activist, although it is interesting to note that it was claimed that he had been virulently opposed to the IRA's bombing campaign that Codd had claimed to have been involved in. Stringer later claimed that the interview 'proved that Cod[d] was not an IRA man'. He was mistaken; although the interview might not have gone well for Codd, Ryan had in fact told Haller that he believed Codd to be an IRA member. Ryan kept in contact with Codd and Stringer, becoming a regular visitor to their Ludwigskirstrasse flat.

Codd and Stringer were issued with 'passports' under cover names which they now adopted as their own. Since Haller referred to these as 'alien's papers', these were presumably Fremdenpasses, German internal passports for foreigners. Stringer's new identity was now 'Willy Le Page', born in Guernsey on

24 July 1920 (Stringer's actual birthday); Codd became 'Juan Louis', a Spaniard born in New York in 1913 to Hawaiian parents.[22]

On 6 October 1941, the Abwehr war diary mentioned that: 'It is intended to send two trained Irishmen to London with sabotage materials and to provide them with a wireless set. Training of Irishmen in radio procedure started October 5th.' The mission was to be codenamed 'Operation Innkeeper'.[23]

The different accounts of Codd and Stringer vary slightly in detail here, but both are agreed that, three weeks after their release from Friesack, they began training in radio communications in their own flat. The radio instructor in their Ludwigkirchstrasse flat was a German civilian called Bubblitz, who was involved in the German television service. Codd formed the opinion that he might have been involved in some 'behind the lines role' in 1940, based on his knowledge of methods of concealing radio equipment and aerials. The pace of training was 'quite leisurely' lasting from 9 a.m. to noon, and 'sometimes' from 2 p.m. to 4 p.m., and seems largely to have consisted of transmitting and receiving in Morse code. During this time each Irishman claims they were paid 72 marks per week (the average German wartime wage was 200 marks per month), the money being delivered by Lechtweiss.

Codd and Stringer's accounts both become rather hazy here, but their radio training seems to have lasted until at least November when, according to Codd, Lechtweiss was replaced by a German civilian who was introduced to them as 'Stinzing'. Haller supplied the reason for this: 'Codd had already made difficulties in Berlin. He exceeded his monthly allowance (RM450), and when additional funds were not forthcoming, flew into a violent and sometimes dangerous temper. In Berlin he had shown a vast and indiscriminate capacity for drink and women.' He continued, 'Lechtweiss, who was supposed to look after him, could not control him. He was relieved by Pastor Risch from Mecklenberg, who also proved unequal to the job.' Many German pastors served in the Wehrmacht, often in a lay capacity. 'Risch had spent some years in Canada and spoke good English. He was registered as a V-Mann [i.e. 'man of trust'] with Abw II, but except that he looked after Codd and Stringer, his services were not used by Abw II.'

On 7 December 1941, Japan attacked the US naval base at Pearl Harbour, the US declared war on Japan and, in turn, Germany declared war on the US. Stringer's account made no mention of a conference which included himself, Codd, Bubblitz, Stinzing, Hoven, Haller and a new arrival, Herr Norman, who spoke good English with an accent. This was actually Abwehr agent Nissen, 'a professional artist who worked for the Deutsche Verlag in Berlin'. He was an amateur yachtsman and had just returned from a mission to South Africa. Operation Weissdorn had been under the command of Christian Nissen (no relation). On this occasion the able 'Heine Mueck' had been supplied with a fully seaworthy vessel (the *Kyloe*, an English-built ocean-going yacht), a crew of experienced German yachtsmen, and a competent agent, the South African saboteur Robby Leibrand. Nissen successfully brought the *Kyloe* the 8,000-mile journey and landed Leibrand 150 miles north of Cape Town. For several months afterward, Leibrand conducted a successful sabotage and propaganda campaign until finally being apprehended. Nissen brought the *Kyloe* safely back to Spanish Morocco, from where the crew returned to Europe.

The purpose of this meeting was to discuss the possibility of sending Codd and Stringer on a sabotage mission to the US. Other than the method of transport (U-boat) and possible landing sites, no details were discussed.

On completion of their radio training, Codd and Stringer were sent on a train journey through Potsdam, and on to the Quentzee lake in the Brandenburg region, where they were accommodated in the Quentzgut, a large isolated house by the lake. This in fact was the Abwehr explosives training

facility; a previous guest of this facility was Seán Russell, the
IRA leader who had died on a U-boat off the Irish coast in
August 1940. The Quentzsee's lake and dense forests provided an ideal training ground for the Abwehr's Brandenburg
commandos. Although locals were well used to the constant
noise of explosions and gunfire in the vicinity, by December 1941 the area was relatively quiet, the Brandenburgers
being heavily committed in Russia. Stringer only remembered the Quentzgut as being referred to as the 'Quentz', not
knowing whether this was a 'house or street, or district, or a
code-name'. The Quentzgut itself consisted of an old lake-
side estate with a large park and gardens of several acres, surrounded by a high fence, well guarded. The house itself, which
originally had been the property of a Jewish businessman,
was a two-storey stone building consisting of a cellar, a huge
living room and twelve bedrooms, which were used for ac-
commodating trainee saboteurs. The Abwehr had constructed a newer building with a garage on the ground floor and
a classroom and laboratory upstairs. There was an explosives
testing range on the grounds, which included several lengths
of railway track to practise on. Codd and Stringer were the
only two students there at the time, and their only instructor
was a man introduced to them as 'Dr Krug', remembered as
'Kruke' by Stringer and as 'Dr Cook' by Codd. This was in
fact Dr Gunther König of Abwehr II's technical laboratory.
Codd and Stringer's training concentrated on improvised explosives, incendiaries and detonators, which the pair could
construct from chemicals and materials readily available in
their area of operations. This training included the sabotage of railway lines, and one method for this that Dr König
taught them was to construct a bomb from charcoal, potas-
sium, iron oxide and other materials, which would be placed
in a metal container against a railway track, to be detonated
by a passing train. The pair were also taught to improvise incendiary devices to start fires in factories and aboard ships.
At the completion of their training, in late December 1941,

Stringer admitted that he was 'not as competent as Cod[d]. He was actually supposed to carry out the explosives and I to do the radio operating.'

Lechtweiss then re-appeared on the scene, taking the pair by train back to Berlin. They were now accommodated at a hotel near the railway station at Charlottenburg. Lechtweiss delivered their pay, seventy-two marks weekly to Stringer and 400 marks per month to Codd, the latter apparently having received a 'raise'. At the hotel, Stringer recalls, 'Rheinhorst [Hoven] and Norman [Nissen] gave me a suitcase fitted with a radio transmitting and receiving set.' Codd recounts a meeting that took place here, which involved Hoven, Nissen, Haller, Stinzing 'and another man', to discuss financing a possible sabotage operation in Britain or the US. This projected mission would involve Codd, Stringer and another six or eight individuals, and a figure of £35,000 was discussed to finance this team over an eight-year period. This sum would be made up of dollars, sterling and gold bullion, to be delivered by submarine.[24]

Later in 1942, the Abwehr would actually attempt such an operation, sending Germans rather than Irishmen. However, in late December 1941, sending a team of Irishmen on such a mission may have seemed a viable option to the Abwehr, to judge by their activities in Friesack at that time.

In November 1941, 'Gestapo Joe' (Jupp Hoven) had run another recruiting drive among the Irishmen at Friesack camp. 'In fact,' according to Haller, 'Cushing, in whom Hoven appeared to have some confidence, suggested the names of the other four.' In his own account, Cushing claims that he had been detailed to select these men by Colonel McGrath. James Brady, it will be recalled, had already been interviewed by Hoven after his arrival at the camp in May 1941, but had not apparently been of particular interest at the time. This time Brady was asked if 'he would like to work for the Germans'. Brady claims that he gave Hoven no definite answer, saying that he 'wanted to think it over'. Brady further claimed that he 'went to see Major McGrath [*sic*] and told him about the suggestion put to me by Rheinherst [i.e. Hoven] and Major McGrath advised me to accept any work that the Germans gave me and if possible to report to the British Authorities and to use his name to substantiate any information I might possess'. Brady was to make this claim to the British Army in September 1946; he may not have been aware that McGrath, although retired from the army and living in Dublin, could have been contacted to substantiate this claim. There is no record that he was called upon to do so at Brady's subsequent trial, but by then Brady was being called to account for his eventual involvement with the SS, not with the Abwehr. In fact, it was later to transpire that Brady was not the only Irishman to have made such an arrangement with Colonel McGrath. 'Col McGrath had given Cushing the address of a 'British agent' in Dublin, whom the latter was to contact on arrival in Éire.' McGrath gave Cushing a watch on which he crudely scratched the address '19 Eden Quay'. This was actually the address of a small garage in Dublin situated a short distance from the Theatre Royal of which McGrath had been manager before the war, and was almost certainly a bluff for the Germans' benefit, perhaps to increase Cushing's standing with them. Just after the war, McGrath himself made this startling comment to an Irish journalist who until very recently had been an officer in Irish military intelligence: 'Before he left the camp, Colonel McGrath saw to it that other Irishmen got out. This part of his story is rather mysterious. He says, 'I let some of the men go. They had important jobs to do. They did them, magnificently. I'm afraid I can't tell you anything about it.'[25]

Brady contacted Hoven, and when Hoven visited the camp a few days later, he invited Brady to leave the camp and live as a civilian in Germany. Hoven did not go into detail about what Brady would be doing, but did ask him if he 'knew anything about radio'. Brady agreed to the proposal, and in December 1941 Hoven returned to the camp and interviewed Brady again. The Roscommon man was told that arrangements had been made for him to leave Friesack camp and that he would be supplied with a passport and other papers under a different name. Afterwards, Brady discussed Hoven's offer with Cushing, although neither discussed their motives for accepting with each other. Cushing apparently wasted no time in betraying Colonel McGrath to the Germans: 'Cushing disclosed the Dublin address, given to him by Col McGrath, to Hoven. For some reason [Haller] no longer remembers, Hoven discounted this info as unimportant. No action had been taken against Col McGrath at the time.'

Just before Christmas 1941, James Brady and 'Sergeant' Cushing left Stalag XX A (301) in the company of three other Irish POWs. These were Corporal Andrew Walsh and Private Patrick O'Brien who, like Cushing, were Tipperary men, and Private William Murphy from Enniscorthy, Co. Wexford. Wexford men are said to be volatile people, and the red-haired Murphy certainly was.

Ostensibly being transferred to another camp, they were in fact being driven in a large car to Berlin. Having changed into civilian clothing which they found in the car (apparently while travelling through a blacked-out Berlin), they were taken to a comfortable communal flat at number 208 Hohernzollerndamm. Here they met Hoven and another German. The latter was either Gefreiter Dexheimer or Gefreiter Kucki of the Brandenburg regiment, both detailed to look after the Irishmen. The five Irishmen were supplied with money, and 'spent the night on celebrations, Rheinherst [*sic*] paying the bill'.

The next morning, doubtlessly suffering from hangovers, the Irishmen were told by Hoven that they 'were going to a school to learn about explosives, after which he would have a proposition to make to us. Subsequently the five were taken to the Quentzgut, where they were the only students. There were two instructors, 'German chemists, one of whom was named Kruck [i.e. Dr König]', who took the Irishmen through the same training that, unbeknownst to them, had been undertaken by Codd and Stringer very recently. It is obvious that the Germans did not wish any contact between their two groups of Friesack Irishmen.[26] According to Brady:

> The training consisted of instruction in the use of high explosives and incendiary compositions. We were taught about eight formulae … The mixtures were to be placed in bottles or tins. We were instructed how to place the explosives between two railway lines, so that it would be exploded by a train passing over the joint. We learnt how to mix the incendiary compositions in order to start fires in factories; also about the use of electrons and fuses. We were not told where our work would be carried out, but were informed how to use ordinary batteries, watches, etc., to make the explosions possible. Instruction was also given on how to buy the chemicals from chemists. We were all passed out as being competent after about fourteen days course, but were supposed to return to 'Quintz' later for a refresher course. Whilst we were at 'Quintz' we were confined to the house. We were paid about 80 marks per week from our arrival in Berlin.[27]

While in Germany, Brady carried papers which identified him as 'Charlos de Lacy', citizen of a South American country not specified in any of the Irishmen's accounts.

On the completion of their explosives training, the five Irishmen returned to their flat at 208 Hohernzollendamm where they began their training in radio, their instructor being the same 'Bubblitz' who had trained Codd and Stringer, although they were not made aware of this. Here, they learned 'about the working of wireless sets, and the receiving and transmission of messages'.

Although Jupp Hoven had high hopes for his latest group of Irish recruits and for Cushing in particular, whom he had designated the leader of the group, his high opinion was not shared by Kurt Haller. Haller regarded Cushing as 'a rank opportunist, without backbone or moral fibre, a loud mouthed braggart with little courage or intelligence, whose reliability was highly doubtful', and refused to consider him for any mission in the UK or Ireland. Murphy he described as a 'colourless individual' whose volatile temper, especially when drunk, was a constant source of complaint from his colleagues. O'Brien appears to have been a particularly strange case; 'Like Murphy, O'Brien was only intended to be a companion to one of the others. Mentally, he was subnormal and he seemed to live in a dreamworld of his own.'

Corporal Walsh and Fusilier Brady, however, were considered to show potential. Walsh he found to be 'a mature, determined and quiet person, who seemed to have genuine Irish nationalist feelings to which was added an adventurous streak. Mentally he was above average; his weakness was an overfondness for drink.' Haller added: 'His tech abilities were good, and he passed his WT training and sabotage course in Quentzee with flying colours. While he was training, Abw II proposals that he should go on a sabotage mission against the UK were accepted by him without apparent reserve. He asked little financial reward, and received, like the others, RM 12 to 25 per day.' Brady also apparently made a good impression. He appeared to be 'a strong Irish nationalist, and claimed to have contacts in IRA circles, although he was evasive about names and addresses'.[28]

By mid-January 1942, Germany was suffering serious setbacks in Russia. 'General Winter' had halted the German advance at the gates of Moscow, and now the Russians were on the offensive. The Germans were forced to withdraw, suffering heavy casualties, and eventually managed to establish a line east of Smolensk. The parent division of the SS Leibstandarte guards outside the Reich Chancellory, now wearing greatcoats against the bitter winter, had suffered particularly heavily. When the newly organised division had started its Russian campaign in July 1941, it had a strength of almost 10,000 men. By the end of November, nearly half that number had been killed or wounded.

Shortly after the arrival of the second group of Irishmen in Berlin, John Codd and Frank Stringer were informed by Dr Jupp Hoven that they were being sent away from Berlin, without any reason being given. Hoven and Nissen brought the pair to Cologne, then to 'Rösrath, a small village between Cologne and Dusseldorf, where Ii of Nest Cologne [an Abwehr unit] had a small WT station, in order to practise WT. The second group was then being recruited, and the two groups were being kept separate.' At Rösrath, the two Irishmen were accommodated (in a 'house' according to Stringer, a 'hut' according to Codd) near a 'truppenfuhrungsplatz' (army training ground). Codd and Stringer shared their accommodation with Nissen, another 'guide/interpreter called Reuter' (Pastor Risch) and a German soldier called Gefreiter Carl Krumbach, who instructed the Irishmen in radio transmission and receiving. Stringer was taught to operate the suitcase radio he had received in Berlin, and made daily contact with radio stations at Cologne and Breslau, operating 'on frequencies varying from 5,000 to 8,000 kilocycles'. He claimed to have been able to transmit Morse at seventy letters per minute, and to receive at forty/fifty letters per minute. They were paid weekly visits by a civilian called Schumacher, who travelled from Cologne with their wages, now 80 marks per week for Stringer, 100 marks weekly for Codd.

Codd apparently did no radio training while in Rösrath, telling Stringer only that 'he was training to disguise his features, as he was too well-known in England to go as he was'. He was continuing to test the patience of Kurt Haller, who later claimed that 'the enforced isolation in Quentzee and Rösrath drove Codd into fits of violence'. At about this time, Codd met a local girl whom he wished to marry. Permission from the Abwehr was not forthcoming. Deciding that Codd was having a bad influence on Stringer, it was decided to separate the pair. Codd was sent to live in Dusseldorf, while Stringer continued with his radio training in Rösrath. He spent April 1942, 'just waiting', now living in the Hotel

Vogtmann on Strasse der SA. Schumacher still continued to deliver his pay, now 600 marks per month, along with ration cards. Apart from occasional visits from Stringer, Hoven and Nissen, he lived alone. Hoven occasionally discussed possible missions to Britain, the US or Canada. Although the Germans had tentatively suggested possible missions for Codd in Malta or Gibraltar, 'Codd's irresponsible behaviour gave rise to doubts whether Abw II would be justified in sending him on a mission ... In spite of warnings about his behaviour,' complained Haller of Codd, 'he continued his drinking and riotous living in Cologne and Dusseldorf.' [29]

Codd's account does not mention a meeting that took place at the end of April 1942 at the Lindenhof Hotel in Dusseldorf where Stringer met Codd, Hoven, Nissen and a new face, 'Lieutenant Holborn'. This in fact was 'Lt Kappe of Abwehr II's Referat W/N [West/Nord], dealing with USA and Canada'. An exasperated Kurt Haller had transferred Codd and Stringer to his command, due to 'Codd's increasing irresponsibility', although the pair do not seem to have been immediately aware of this. Leutnant Walter Kappe, a short, eloquently spoken man, had been resident in the United States until 1937. He had been a founder member of the German–American Bund, an overtly pro-Nazi and anti-Semitic organisation of about 40,000 Germans living in the US; this body featured an 'Ordnungs Dienst', a group of paramilitary enforcers dressed in a grey and black uniform similar to Hitler's Brownshirts! Although the Bund had been eliminated as a political force by an FBI clampdown in early 1942, there were thousands of former members sympathetic to Nazi ideals still resident in the US. Since the previous December, when Hitler had authorised sabotage attacks against the US, Kappe had been working to identify and recruit any Germans who had lived in America, and in the same month that he was meeting with Codd and Stringer had gathered twelve of them in the Quentzgut to undergo a course of sabotage training markedly similar to that undergone by the two groups of Irishmen selected at Friesack. Suggested targets for this group of Germans included railway lines, aluminium plants, and the water and electricity supply for New York city, including the Niagara Falls hydroelectric plant. Kappe also suggested terrorist bombings of railway stations and Jewish-owned department stores. The codename for this intended mission was 'Operation Pastorius', named after the first German emigrant to America.[30]

It was intended that 'Operation Pastorius' would be only the first of a series of similar sabotage operations, hence Kappe's apparent interest in Codd and Stringer. At the Lindenhof Hotel, the possibilities of a mission for the two Irishmen were discussed. It was proposed that the pair would be flown by seaplane to the east coast of England, where they would slip ashore in a rubber dinghy which they would sink after use. They then went on to discuss the documents to be carried (British identity cards and Irish passports), the money they would bring (£8,000 sterling) and the Irishmen were told that they should book a hotel room and establish radio communications with an unspecified German station. This discussion had reached an advanced stage before 'Lieutenant Holborn' (Kappe) pointed out (correctly) that most of the British coastline was mined, making such a landing impossible. 'Rheinhorst' (Jupp Hoven) then suggested that Codd and Stringer be taken by submarine to the coast of Donegal, from where they would make their way to Antrim in Northern Ireland. Here, they 'would be met by two men' (not identified by Hoven) who would give further instructions, after which Codd and Stringer would proceed to England. Codd's mission would be to sabotage railway lines and other targets in England, to be specified by instructions from Germany. The conference then closed and it was decided that another meeting would be held later.

There would seem to be more to this meeting than met the eye. Kappe's department, after all, was concerned with operations in North America, not in Britain or Ireland. In

Kurt Haller's opinion, 'a discussion of an operation against the UK can only have been intended to serve as an introduction. Kappe at no time mentioned to [Haller] that he intended to send Codd and Stringer on a mission to the UK. The details of landing, equipment and methods of operation were also merely suggestions by Kappe to test the men's reaction, and cannot have been concrete proposals.' As for Hoven's suggestion that the pair be sent to Donegal to rendezvous with two men in Antrim, 'it could only have been thrown out on the spur of the moment; in fact there were no two men who Codd and Stringer could have met there.' Haller did admit, however, that 'Ryan and Clissmann were standing by to leave on their mission, and he may have had them in mind'.[31]

After the meeting in the Lindenhof Hotel, Codd remained in Dusseldorf while Nissen and Stringer returned to Rösrath and Hoven and Kappe returned to Berlin. Afterwards, Stringer was told by Nissen that Hoven 'had been transferred to other work and that Holborn (Kappe) would take his place'. Despairing of his efforts in Friesack, 'Jupp' Hoven had transferred from the Abwehr to a Fallschirmjager unit.

Stringer continued his radio training at Rösrath with Gefreiter Krumbach. As he continued to transmit radio messages to the station at Breslau, he was unaware that this station was also receiving similar radio messages from his old colleague, James Brady. Brady and Walsh, regarded by the Germans as worthy of promise, had been separated from the other Irish in Hohernzollerndamm in May 1942 and transferred to Stettin where they began more advanced radio training.

This reduced the population of the flat at 208 Hohernzollerndamm to O'Brien, Murphy and Cushing. Murphy 'acquired a German girl-friend to whom he trustfully confided full details of his training'. 'Like Codd,' according to Haller, 'Cushing was mainly interested in women and drink.' Also like Codd, Cushing too was transferred by Haller to Lieutenant Kappe's Referat West/Nord. Kappe evidently considered

him for a mission codenamed 'Operation Rothar', which involved blowing up a lock in the Panama Canal, where he had
once been stationed during his US Army service. However,
Cushing became involved with a former model called Ellen
Schultz, through which he 'was drawn into a circle of shady
characters and black-marketeers. These associations brought
him to the unfavourable notice of the internal security section
of Abw II (a section under Z Arch of Obst Schrader).' Cushing was placed under surveillance, which would have serious
repercussions for him and Walsh.

At Stettin, Brady and Walsh transmitted and received
several coded messages on frequencies (like Stringer's) ranging from 5,000 to 8,000 kilocycles, Brady was now able to
transmit and receive at a rate of eighty letters per minute.
Brady was now being paid '120 marks per week by Doctor
Haller who had replaced "Rheinherst"'. Haller was apparently seeking a mission for the pair, and discussed several
possibilities with Brady. The continuing buildup of American forces in Britain was causing the Germans some concern,
and Haller suggested that Brady could go by submarine or be
parachuted into England or Northern Ireland to learn about
the US force's numbers, training and equipment, details of
which he would transmit by radio to Germany. He also suggested that Brady could build up a network of agents in his
area.

Dr Haller apparently had another mission in mind for
Walsh. The Abwehr war diary records that on 16 May 1942,
Haller discussed with Dr Koerfer (of Economic Group Electricity Supply) the technical details of the power station in
Fort William in Scotland, with a view to landing agents in
northern Scotland to carry out a sabotage operation. According to Haller:

> The target selected for Walsh was chosen by the GAF
> Fuhrungsstab [Luftwaffe HQ]. He was to interrupt production
> in an aluminium works near Fort William in Scotland. Walsh
> was to attempt to destroy with special explosives the water-pipes

leading to the electricity plant supplying the works. Electric power was generated by turbines driven by water passing through pipes from a loch at a lower level and discharged into a river or loch lower down. This pipe-line had already in 1941 been the target of a special GAF sortie, but the aircraft had failed to attack the target because the mountains in the vicinity interfered with the bombing run. The GAF had excellent aerial cover of the works, complemented by most detailed descriptions which had appeared in a British tech magazine (name forgotten).[32]

Haller added:

In case Walsh should find it impossible to reach his target, he was given a secondary target, a smaller power plant in the vicinity, also connected with an aluminium works. Walsh was to be dropped by parachute in the North Midlands, at a spot chosen by himself. His WT set and explosives were to be dropped on a separate parachute, linked to his by a thin cord. Walsh was further given false papers in the name of Thomas Dunphy, secret ink and an address in Portugal supplied by KO Portugal via Abw 1.[33]

To prepare Walsh for his mission in Scotland, he was brought to the Eder dam in the Ruhr industrial area, where he was given detailed instruction in the demolition of the pipeline by Dr König, who had earlier instructed him in improvised explosives. The Eder dam was a mighty fortification; 1,300 feet long and 139 feet high, it held back over 200 million cubic metres of water. Walsh would have trained on the two power stations below the dam, one at each extremity. There were no anti-aircraft defences at the Eder dam; like the power station near Fort William, the terrain surrounding the area made an attack by aircraft all but impossible. The German dam was situated deep in hilly terrain, with surrounding ridges rising to over 1,000 feet.

Along with the other dams of the Ruhr industrial area, the Eder dam was a priority target for the British. From as early as 1937, the Ruhr dams had been targeted for attack, and several options were considered, including air-launched torpedoes and anti-submarine bombs, but it soon became obvious that a colossal amount of explosives would be required to breach a gravity dam. Independent research by aircraft designer Barnes Wallis drew the same conclusion, abandoning his original concept of a ten-ton bomb dropped from 40,000 feet by a six-engine bomber of his own design (never built) and instead proposed a missile which would bounce over the surface of a reservoir, detonating against the dam. In July 1941, not long after Walsh had been training on the Eder dam, a 500-pound sea-mine was detonated against the disused Nant-y-Gro dam near Rhayaden in Wales, successfully breaching the dam and proving the feasibility of Wallis' concept. This set in train a series of events that would culminate on the night of 17 May 1943 with the legendary 'Dambusters' raid on the Ruhr dams. On that night, 617 Squadron of the RAF, flying converted Avro Lancaster bombers, launched an assault utilising Wallis' secret weapon, the 'bouncing bomb' codenamed 'Upkeep'. Having successfully breached the Mohne dam at 12.49 a.m., Wing Commander Guy Gibson led five Lancasters to attack the Eder dam. In misty conditions and over treacherous terrain, each of the three aircraft still carrying 'Upkeep' bombs were obliged to make several passes before dropping their load. After the first two bombs were dropped, causing damage but not destruction, the massive Eder dam was breached an hour after the Mohne, in a skilfully executed attack by Pilot Officer Les Knight. Through a gap 230 feet wide, nearly 155 million cubic feet of water escaped, causing flooding in the Eder, Fulda and Weser valleys, and even in the city of Kassell.[34]

On 22 June 1942, the Abwehr war diary announced that two proposed missions, Seagull I and Seagull II, had been approved. 'Seagull I' involved the parachuting of an Irish agent codenamed 'Vickers' (Walsh) into Scotland, where he was to live in Glasgow and recruit two other men, with a view to sabotaging the electricity supply to the aluminium works at Fort William and Kinlock Leven.

'Seagull II' was to involve Brady (alias 'Agent Metzger') parachuting into Northern Ireland to 'contact the IRA' and carry out as yet unspecified sabotage attacks. In July 1942, Brady and Walsh returned to the Quentzgut to carry out refresher training in explosives, although 'Walsh did all the "swotting up"'.[35]

Back in Rösrath, Frank Stringer had got into the habit of listening in to foreign radio broadcasts. This does not seem to have been part of his normal duties, and in fact was a highly illegal act in Nazi Germany. One morning in July 1942, Stringer heard an electrifying broadcast on an American station stating that 'two German submarines had been captured off the south coast of the United States of America and that about twenty-four saboteurs had been found on board together with a quantity of sabotage equipment, including bombs in the shape of coal'. This was apparently an early and garbled report of the end of Operation Pastorius. At the end of May 1942, eight of the German saboteurs selected by Walter Kappe had set off for the east coast of the US aboard two U-boats. Divided into two groups of four men each, they carried a two-year supply of fuses and explosives and $160,000 between them. One group, transported by the *U-202*, landed on a beach in Long Island, New York on the night of 13 June. They were noticed by a single and unarmed coastguard man who overtly accepted a bribe from them before returning to his post and raising the alarm. Having buried their explosives on the beach, the party proceeded to New York city where one of their number contacted the FBI and betrayed the entire operation. The FBI had tracked down all eight Germans by 27 June, including the second party, who had been landed in Florida by the *U-584*. All were tried and sentenced to death; six died in the electric chair while two had their sentences commuted and were deported back to Germany in 1948.[36]

Stringer told his news to Gefreiter Krumbach, and he told Nissen who passed it on to Berlin. Schumacher, a local police official attached to Abwehr Nest Cologne, turned up, brought Stringer away to Bonn and booked him into a hotel there, where he was warned to remain, and under no account to travel to Rösrath or Dusseldorf. Once left alone, Stringer, with amazing naivety, immediately set off for Dusseldorf, where he found John Codd residing at the Hotel Lindenhof where the mission conference had been held in April. Stringer, having updated Codd and being booked into the hotel by him, contacted Schumacher to inform him of his move. The next day a furious Kappe turned up and informed Codd and Stringer that they were both now in 'cold storage'. This apparently provoked Codd to take a rash action that he would later regret.

Kappe brought Stringer back to Bonn, booked him into another hotel and again warned him not to travel to Dusseldorf or Röstrath. Again, Stringer wasted no time in disobeying this order, and having decided to pay a visit to Rösrath, noticed Gefreiter Krumbach training a group of agents that the Abwehr had not wanted the Irishman to meet. Returning to Cologne, Stringer was arrested by the police (at the Abwehr's behest), imprisoned and interrogated. After three weeks, Schumacher turned up at the prison and Stringer was released. He was brought to Cologne (which had been the target of the RAF's first thousand bombing raids the previous May), booked into a hotel and warned that 'Holborn' (Kappe) would be coming to see him later. Kappe turned up at 6 p.m. in a surprisingly conciliatory mood. 'He said it was not his fault that I was arrested, and that as things had not gone the way they were supposed to, there was no work for me.' According to Haller, 'Abw II were at a loss what to do with Stringer. He was too young and stupid to be sent on a mission on his own, and he would therefore have to be kept waiting until he could go with someone else.' Haller, however, had made arrangements. Kappe suggested that Stringer could work on a farm or he could return to prison. He was not offered the option of returning to a POW camp. Stringer accepted the offer, and the following morning he and Kappe set off on the train to Berlin. They caught a connecting train there, and that evening arrived at the Stettin Bahnhoff (railway station) where they were met by Dr Lotz, a friend of Haller's, and the owner of a farm at Klein Kiesow, near Griefswald in eastern Germany. Stringer was handed over to Lotz, and began work on his farm the following day at a weekly wage of twenty marks.

Stringer's erstwhile Abwehr employers appear to have kept an eye out for him. In August 1942, Kurt Haller and his wife paid a visit, asking Stringer how he was getting on and whether he 'liked the work'. In mid-September, Kappe showed up, bringing Stringer some clothes, books and a very interesting piece of information: 'He told me that Codd was in prison because he had written a threatening letter to him over not getting enough money and general conditions.' By Haller's account, Codd, with breathtaking arrogance, 'wrote a letter to Kappe, which in the eyes of Abw II bordered on impertinence and blackmail, threatening that unless he was given a certain sum of money and a number of special privileges by a certain date, he would no longer consider himself bound by his promise'.

Codd did not have to wait long for the Abwehr's answer to his ultimatum. On 25 August 1942, Codd was visited by a man in civilian clothes who politely introduced himself as 'Mr Thomas of the Dusseldorf Gestapo'. Codd was informed (quite truthfully) that he was to be moved to new accommodation, and he accompanied Mr Thomas to his car which was parked outside the hotel. There, he found himself sitting on the back seat between 'two rather burly gentlemen', after which he was driven to Dusseldorf prison and put into 'schutzhaft' (detention) where he was to remain for several months.[37]

After their refresher training in the Quentzgut in July 1942, Brady and Walsh travelled to Hamburg, Brady bringing a small portable radio, and stayed at the Berlinerhoff Hotel, occupying three rooms. They were assigned a 'minder', Johann Dexheimer, an Obergefreiter in the Brandenburg regiment. Brady continued to work on his radio procedure, and the pair were instructed by a chemist in the use of invisible inks. Brady recalled that he 'was issued with three codes – a book code, written by Jack London, a machine code, and a small emergency code, which I was to use if I lost the other two codes. These codes were not used in our practice transmissions.' In Hamburg, 'Walsh entered into a contract with Abw II (referred to in the contract as Neuhaus) which settled financial details: £8000 in English currency, part of which was for expenses and a yearly fee for several years (about RM 40,000 in all) after the successful completion of the mission; heavy expenses incurred during the mission would be generously refunded.' In August 1942 the pair returned to Stettin, where they would stay until 15 September, and were visited on a daily basis by Kurt Haller. (On one occasion he visited them shortly after visiting Stringer at Klein Kiesow.) On that date Brady and Walsh returned to Berlin for one night, before flying out to Norway the following morning. Despite strict instructions not to contact Cushing or any of the other Irishmen at Hohernzollendamm, Walsh gave Dexheimer the slip and arranged a covert rendezvous with Cushing. Unfortunately for both, Cushing was still being followed by a member of Abwehr's internal security section who 'had reported a clandestine meeting between Cushing and a man who corresponded in all particulars to Walsh. This meeting took place the evening before Walsh left for Norway. The two men behaved very furtively, and apparently exchanged notes.'

Haller met Brady and informed him that he would be flown from Norway to parachute into Northern Ireland. 'Brady was to be dropped in Northern Ireland and find employment in Harland & Wolff's shipyard in Belfast. There he was to recruit four or five sub-agents – if possible, IRA members – and undertake small-scale sabotage in the ship-yard. Brady was not given any IRA addresses, since there was as yet no proof of his reliability.'

It was a lunatic concept; the Harland & Wolff shipyard was famous throughout Ireland as a hotbed of extreme union-ism, where in the past any Catholic employees had frequently suffered injury or death at the hands of their Protestant 'co-workers'. Although the exigencies of wartime had obliged the shipyard to hire large numbers of Irishmen from south of the border, these were regarded with deep suspicion even at cabi-net level. Any attempt by Brady to set up a group of saboteurs in the shipyard would, if he were lucky, have merely resulted in denunciation to the authorities. Yet Brady did not point this out or complain to Haller.

Haller issued Brady with £8,000 sterling and $3,000, and three British identity cards in his own name, but not, Brady observed, any ration books which would have been essen-tial for anyone trying to live unnoticed in wartime Northern Ireland for any period of time. The Abwehr's ignorance of conditions in Northern Ireland was perhaps partly explained by the fact that, unlike Walsh, Brady was not required to place coded messages by newspaper advertisements, due to the non-availability of Northern Ireland newspapers to the Germans.[38]

The following day Walsh, Brady and Dexheimer flew to a Luftwaffe base near Trondheim in Norway. Trondheim-Vaernes was a base for Kampfgeschwader (Bomber Wing) 40, which had been operating the long-range Focke-Wulf 200 'Condor' since April 1940. The Condor was a convert-ed civil airliner, a prototype of which had flown direct from Berlin to New York in August 1938. With a small external bombload, the Condors initially proved effective against lightly defended shipping, but by 1942 the increasing avail-ability of small aircraft carriers to the British spelt the end of their usefulness as an anti-shipping aircraft. Its extremely long range, however, still made it useful for meteorological

and maritime reconnaissance missions, and the Condors often flew from Bordeaux in France several hundred miles out
into the Atlantic and into Trondheim on missions that typically lasted sixteen hours. At least five of KG 40's Condors
are known to have crashed in Ireland or off its coast throughout the war, the surviving crew members being interned by
the Irish authorities. By 1942, the Focke-Wulf 200 C-3 was
in production. With this new aircraft capable of flying over
4,000 miles, the Condor staffel (squadron) at Trondheim-
Vaernes was capable of flying reconnaissance missions over
Iceland and to the coast of Greenland.[39]

Brady and Walsh had not received any parachute training.
It was Abwehr policy not to provide this in the belief that
successive parachute jumps only increased the likelihood of
eventual injury, and in fact few, if any, of the German agents
parachuted into Ireland during the war had received anything
more than a quick briefing before the flight. In the opinion of
Oberleutnant Gollnow, a Luftwaffe officer who was involved
in final preparations for the mission in Trondheim, 'practice
jumps often frightened people more than the experience was
worth'. This was a questionable policy with regard to the German RZ series parachute, which required German paratroops
to undergo an intensive sixteen-day course which included six
jumps. Rather than suspending the user from the shoulders,
the RZ series parachute suspended him from the waist, in a
crouching position. From this position, a German parachutist would face the direction of landing as best he could before
landing in a very tricky forward roll; German paratroopers
wore rubber pads over their elbows and knees in an attempt
to protect them from all too frequent injuries. Training was
simplified by the fact that there was no reserve parachute. It
was therefore not necessary to teach Brady and Walsh such
details as recognising a parachute malfunction as there was
nothing they could have done in such an eventuality.[40]

James Brady's training as a spy therefore consisted of
extensive radio training, a two-week course in improvised

explosives, a quick briefing in the use of invisible ink and a forthcoming briefing on how to make a parachute jump. This did not compare favourably with his Allied equivalent. An agent of the British Special Operations Executive, for example, began his/her training with an initial two- to four-week course of physical conditioning and basic military training. This was followed by a harder course of three to five weeks' duration, held in Scotland, which included more physical training, 'silent killing', training with British and German weapons, fieldcraft, survival, map reading, Morse code, and advanced raiding. The latter included demolition of railways with plastic explosives, and routinely involved all-night exercises. Parachute training followed, at the British Army's Central Landing School in Ringway, Manchester. Each agent made four to five jumps, including one at night. The British parachute was superior to the RZ in several ways. Although it did not feature a reserve parachute, the jumper was suspended from lift webs rising from the shoulders, which gave him/her a small measure of steerability, and allowed a roll when landing, to absorb the force of impact. It also featured a quick-release mechanism, vital under certain circumstances. The next phase of training for an SOE agent consisted of security and clandestine techniques: spotting a 'tail', assuming an identity, resistance to interrogation (often featuring staff wearing SS uniform) and learning codes and ciphers. The training culminated in a four-day exercise, which involved the reconnaissance of a target, the contact of other agents, and sometimes the smuggling and planting of dummy explosives. The trainee agents were subject to constant surveillance, and were liable to be arrested and interrogated by civil or military police, or even approached by 'professional seducers!' Further training was available for specialists.[41]

James Brady at least would appear to have had the benefit of several months' radio training. However, in the opinion of one Sir John Masterson, almost all the German agents who landed in wartime Britain were unable to make radio contact with Germany without the aid of the British Security Service (MI5), due to poor training or faulty equipment. Masterson was the organiser of the 'double-cross system', which involved the apprehension of German agents as quickly and discreetly as possible, their 'turning' from the Nazi cause, and their broadcasting of disinformation to their unsuspecting chiefs. It is no exaggeration to say that the German intelligence effort in wartime Britain was controlled entirely by the British themselves.

It is possible that MI5 knew that Brady and Walsh were on their way. They knew of the existence of Friesack camp since late 1940, and thanks to the only Irishman at the camp to be actually deployed on a mission, they had up-to-date information on the German enterprise. In the summer of 1942, James O'Neill of Wexford had been dropped off on the border between Vichy in France and Franco's Spain with instructions to make his own way to Ireland, preferably via the Irish legation in Madrid. O'Neill was actually a civilian when sent to Friesack, having been captured aboard a British civil freighter. He had been trained in Hamburg as a radio operator, and also to build an improvised radio. Having crossed the Spanish border, however, O'Neill then crossed into Portugal and contacted the British authorities there. He was soon in London, being debriefed by British intelligence, after which he was permitted to return to Ireland. Like Lenihan, instead of providing information *to* the Abwehr, O'Neill ended up providing intelligence *about* them.[42]

Whether or not the British knew of the forthcoming Operation Seagull, the presence of Oberleutnant Gollnow at Trondheim-Vaernes made it almost a certainty that the plan was known to the GRU, Soviet military intelligence. Oberleutnant Herbert Gollnow, a desk officer for 'air-transported and parachute troops' in Abwehr II, began taking English lessons the previous year from the American-born Mildred Harnack, who was married to Dr David Harnack, a senior civil servant in the Reich Ministry of Economics, a man whose position allowed him access to the highest levels of the Nazi regime. The couple gained the young officer's confidence, and he was soon beguiled into boasting of secret Abwehr missions behind Russian lines.

In July 1942 the Gestapo succeeded in decoding an intercepted message from the GRU, which allowed them to identify Dr Harnack as a member of the Berlin branch of the 'Red Orchestra', the Russian spy network operating throughout German-occupied Europe. In the parlance of German espionage, an enemy radio operator was termed a 'pianist', hence a network of operators was an 'orchestra'. The Gestapo placed Harnack under surveillance along with two other named suspects, and by August 1942 over fifty of their accomplices had been identified. A series of arrests began at the end of August, and by the end of September over sixty members of the Red Orchestra were filling the cells of Gestapo headquarters at Prinz Albrecht Strasse. These, under 'interrogation' identified others, and Oberleutnant Gollnow was soon implicated as an unwitting Soviet agent. He was estimated to have betrayed at least twelve Abwehr sabotage operations, all participants of which were killed or captured by the Russians. That December Gollnow was placed on trial. Although the court accepted that he was not guilty of deliberate treason, he was sentenced to death for breaching military discipline and was executed by firing squad in February 1943. Dr Harnack was hanged and his wife beheaded, on Hitler's orders. Nearly fifty other members of the Red Orchestra were executed by August 1943.

It is by no means beyond the bounds of possibility that Gollnow had betrayed details of Brady and Walsh's forthcoming mission to the GRU via the Harnacks, who were arrested only two weeks before the Irishmen were due to fly out from Trondheim. Whether the GRU would have informed the British is another matter.[43]

In light of Colonel McGrath's postwar statement, there is every possibility that the pair may have intended to con-

tact the British authorities after their arrival. Even had this
not been the case, almost all Abwehr agents parachuted into
Britain during the war were captured immediately and discreetly inducted into the 'double-cross programme'. An un-
lucky few, whose capture became public knowledge, were executed. This might have been James Brady's fate had he been
insane enough to attempt to carry out his orders to carry out
sabotage at the Harland & Wolff dockyards. Fate, however,
was to intervene.

On 22 September 1942, the day before Brady was due to
fly out from Norway, Kurt Haller received a telephone call
from Berlin. Major Astor, director of Abwehr Section WN,
excitedly ordered Haller to place both Irishmen under arrest. Haller sadly obeyed the order, informing both Irishmen
separately. Brady was told that 'he would have to return to
Berlin', and was taken away by three members of the Geheime Feld Polizei, a military version of the Gestapo. When
Haller informed the other Irishman, he noticed that Walsh
seemed particularly nervous. Brady and Walsh were both
brought separately to Oslo where they were incarcerated in
the military prison there. Haller flew back to Berlin where he
learned of Walsh's illicit meeting with Cushing. Brady and
Walsh spent three weeks in Oslo military prison, before being taken by ship to Denmark, separately and under close
arrest. Brady glimpsed Walsh on the train from Denmark
to Berlin, and again as they were taken into Moabit military
prison at Lehtre Strasse, but was unable to speak to him on
either occasion.

After the pair's incarceration in Moabit, Haller arrived
there to interrogate Walsh, bringing Thomas Cushing with
him as a witness. Finding himself apparently confronted by
Cushing, Walsh reacted furiously. It is a standard tactic of interrogation to attempt to convince a subject that a colleague
has betrayed him. It would appear that the Germans were
successful in convincing Walsh:

Both men were interrogated together and accused each other of mutual double-crossing. Walsh told of Cushing's conversations with Col McGrath in Damm 1. Hoven at one time must have hinted something about a landing by U-boat, and Walsh now alleged that Cushing had proposed to seize the U-boat and bring it as a war trophy into a British port, and that these plans had been discussed with Col McGrath. Cushing, on the other hand, accused Walsh of never intending to carry out his Scottish mission. The meeting in Berlin had served the purpose of arranging mutual alibis in case of their being interrogated in England. The evidence of the two men was contradictory, but damning for both of them.

Haller left Moabit prison alone; Cushing remained there.

Brady spent three weeks in the military prison under constant interrogation from the Germans, 'who said they had evidence that Walsh and myself were going to double-cross them, and go to the British Authorities'. While Cushing and Walsh incriminated each other, and Murphy incriminated himself, Brady, however, remained silent under interrogation; 'I knew this could not be true because Major [*sic*] McGrath was the only person I had spoken to regarding double crossing the Germans.' Brady seemed to gain the impression that Cushing had betrayed them. Much later, Frank Stringer would be told by him that 'Walsh had told Cushing that when they got to Ireland they were going to give the game away. Cushing told the Germans.' John Codd would later hear a similar version. According to his account: 'Walsh informed Cushing that as soon as he reached England he would get in touch with the police and retain for himself the money given him by the German authorities with the result that Walsh, Cushing and all the members of the group were arrested and imprisoned in Berlin, with the exception of Codd who was arrested in Dusseldorf and imprisoned there.' In fact, by his own account, Codd had been arrested on 25 August 1942, a full month before the other Irishmen had been arrested, and for an entirely different matter. When appraised of Codd's claim after the war, Kurt Haller sourly noted: 'Codd was fully aware why he had been imprisoned.'

The other two Irishmen from the group, O'Brien and Murphy, were also placed in Moabit prison pending investigation. Murphy was already suspected of informing his German girlfriend of details of his training and proved to be a most troublesome prisoner, causing many problems for the guards and on one occasion injuring one of them. 'He asserted in prison that he considered himself a British soldier, and had always intended to double-cross the Germans. This was believed.'[44]

Back at Friesack camp, the Germans had continued to improve conditions. By early 1942 a new inmate, Tim Ronan from Cork, described the camp as 'quite a beautiful place with well laid out walks and gardens, a separate wash and showering hut, and our billets although severe, were more than adequate. We were allowed to move around the camp and associate freely with other prisoners, the only restriction being a head count twice daily. During the summer, a German soldier taught German to anyone who wanted to learn … in the winter, we had card games, reading and talk.' Tim Ronan, like James O'Neill was a merchant seaman aboard a British ship who had been captured in the south Atlantic earlier the previous year. 'Life was quite tolerable but very boring and everybody after a while became resentful of being confined and having their freedom curtailed, some more than others … Escape was discussed in increasingly emotional terms.' According to Colonel McGrath, 'a change came over the camp. The Irishmen began tearing down the propaganda posters and burning them. They cut the wires of the loudspeakers. They succeeded in digging a tunnel and twelve men escaped. The Germans, from looking upon them as potential allies, began to regard them as an intolerable nuisance.' This escape attempt actually took place in February 1943; after several months of digging by twelve Irish POWs, nine actually made an escape attempt but were captured having left tracks through the snow. Subsequently, the Germans transferred fifty of the most troublesome prisoners to the real Stalag XX in occupied Poland. Another small group of POWs had succeeded in sending coded messages 'back to the authorities in England' through the POW mail system, but were unable to report on much other than 'descriptions of life in the area and the morale of the German soldiers as we saw it.' Ronan claims that 'working independently, Lt Colonel McGrath from Dublin had been in communication with the Dutch resistance, how I don't know as we all made a point of minding our own business with regard to such matters'.[45]

In November 1942, Lieutenant-Colonel McGrath was arrested, having been caught attempting to secretly pass information about Friesack camp to the Irish legation in Rome. A search of his possessions disclosed a list of names of some of the Irishmen who had left the camp to be trained by the Abwehr. Haller claimed that McGrath was arrested on the orders of Oberst Lahousen, who commanded Abwehr II from 1939 to 1942. He also alleged that Lauhousen wanted McGrath court-martialled, but instead he was handed over to the Gestapo, who placed him in solitary confinement in the notorious Sachsenhausen concentration camp. Although Haller claimed that they were to provide 'conditions suitable for a British PW of officer status', McGrath's own account does not indicate this:

> I was transferred after this to the prison section of Sachsenhausen concentration camp, and there I was locked up in an ordinary prison cell, with not even the privileges of a convict. I was now under the SS, for whom I have not a good word to say. Life in these places was something beyond description, and, even though you may have read accounts in the newspapers, it is almost impossible to convey the misery and feelings of the prisoners who were confined.

In the words of the Sachsenhausen Memorial and Museum,

this prison within the camp was 'a place veiled in secrecy, a place of torment and murder'. In December 1942 McGrath, at the request of Abwehr II, was interrogated by the Gestapo with regard to Cushing's claims of having arranged with him to surrender to the British at the first opportunity. 'McGrath flatly denied knowledge of the alleged conversation but evidence from other PW showed that McGrath was trying to shield Cushing.'[46]

Abwehr II eventually decided that it would be undesirable to return the four Irishmen being held in Moabit prison to a conventional POW camp, and applied to the POW directorate to have them held in isolation. The Kriegsgefangenwasen OKW, however, would not undertake this, but 'pointed to the case of Col McGrath as a precedent for having the men transferred to a concentration camp'. In February 1943, Cushing, O'Brien, Walsh and Murphy were also transferred to Sachsenhausen concentration camp. They were, however, spared the worst privations of the camp and were billeted together in a special compound for important prisoners; it would appear that Cushing and Walsh had made their peace with each other. The Irishmen lived in their own room in a large hut and were afforded certain privileges – they wore British Army uniform, were supplied with Red Cross parcels and one was even allowed to retain an expensive watch. They were later joined by two Russians: Senior Lieutenant Jakov Dzhugashvili, son of the Soviet dictator Joseph Stalin, and Wasili Kokorin, nephew of Foreign Minister Molotov. A month after the commencement of the invasion of Russia, Dzhugashvili had been captured by the Germans while serving as an artillery officer on the front line. Joseph Stalin ordered the arrest of his son's wife Yulia, and later refused an offer to exchange him for Field Marshal von Paulus, allegedly remarking: 'I have no son.' Unlike the Russians, the four Irishmen were exempted from work details and adopted such practices of standing to attention in the presence of German officers; a series of related small incidents led to a growing animosity between the two groups.[47]

The sending of the Irish POWs to a concentration camp had postwar repercussions for those involved, but although the British speculated about with whom the fault lay, they did not conclusively allot responsibility to any individual. Lahousen, who by the end of the war held the rank of Major-General, vehemently protested Haller's accusation against him. He was an important witness for the prosecution for the Nuremburg war crimes trials, and was one of Admiral Canaris' co-conspirators in the plot against Hitler. According to the British assessment:

> Lahousen has strongly resented Haller's statement that he (Lahousen) was mainly responsible for the transfer of the 'unreliable' Irish PWs recruited as saboteurs to Sachsenhausen Concentration Camp, and has denied all knowledge of the incidents preceding this measure. Although he does not allegedly recollect it, Lahousen uneasily agreed that he might have ordered the men's 'isolation', but was thinking in terms of their separate internment in a PW camp. It seems to be a case where Lahousen originally gave a vague order and left it to his subordinates to carry it out as best they could. The decision to have the men transferred to a concentration camp was made somewhere between ZR, the PW Directorate, and possibly Abw III. Lahousen is guilty of neglect of duty in permitting his subordinates to deal with a matter which involved a principle of the first importance and taking no steps whatever to interest himself in the outcome. Haller is equally at fault in not informing his Chief of a decision which he claims to have regarded as a violation of principle. It is submitted that in truth both men were profoundly indifferent to the fate of a few men who they looked upon as double traitors, and although bearing no ill-will, accepted their disposal to a concentration camp as the simplest solution to a ticklish administrative problem.[48]

On 14 April 1943, the animosity between the group of Irishmen and the two Russians in Sachsenhausen finally boiled over. A heated argument led to Patrick O'Brien punching Molotov's nephew, and a Russian source claims that Stalin's son was also assaulted by an 'Englishman' named 'Cushings'. Already a broken man, the outraged Jakov refused to return to his room at curfew and demanded a meeting with the camp commandant. When this was refused, he lost all reason and ran towards the perimeter wire surrounding the compound. He was shot in the head by an SS guard as he grabbed an electrified fence. Cushing, peering through a hut window, 'saw Jakov running about as if he were insane. He just ran straight onto the wire. There was a huge flash and all the searchlights suddenly went on. I knew that was the end of him. Afterwards the Germans tried to make me take him off the wire and wrap his body in a blanket. It was the first time I felt sorry for the poor bastard.' When approached by journalists in 1980 he would 'remember it as if it were yesterday. It was one of the saddest events of my life.' The Germans, fearing retribution, gave no publicity to Jakov's death, and in fact when an Anglo-American investigation team discovered the details of the affair in July 1945, the British Foreign Office decided against informing Joseph Stalin because of the role played by British soldiers in the death of his son.[49]

After a year in Sachsenhausen, Lieutenant-Colonel McGrath was transferred to the even more notorious Dachau camp. Here, even important prisoners had their hair shaved, were forced to wear the striped camp uniform and were subject to regular physical assault by SS guards. 'It was the SS and Gestapo,' [McGrath] said, 'who thought up and put into execution all the punishments that had brought disgrace to the German nation. He, for one, who had been through these things, side by side with real Germans who were prisoners, would be very sorry to think that they should be classed with the SS and Gestapo, and he had often wondered how it was possible to breed and train such people so different from the average German fighting soldier.'[50]

3

THE SS

According to John O'Reilly, an interesting, if extremely brief, meeting took place in Berlin in the summer of 1942. O'Reilly and his flatmate, another Irishman called Liam Mullally, were in the Berlin Sportspalace when they encountered Frank Ryan, who was accompanied by Francis Stuart. Mullally immediately recognised Ryan and called 'Hello Frank, how are you?' To his amazement, Ryan stopped and answered, 'I haven't the pleasure of knowing you', before walking away.[1]

Francis Stuart had been making radio broadcasts for the Germans since March that year, although after a discussion with Ryan, he had decided not to use any anti-Russian material. Liam Mullally had been working for the Berlitz language school since November 1939, and would begin working for Irland-Redaktion, the Nazi radio service targeting Ireland, in September 1942, as O'Reilly's replacement. In June 1942, O'Reilly had volunteered his services to German intelligence; according to his often vague account he claimed to have approached a member of the SS for this. In September, O'Reilly was informed that he had passed background checks and was ordered to leave Irland-Redaktion to commence spy training. The Irish section's chief, Dr Hans Hartmann, was reluctant to lose one of his only two Irish broadcasters and having unsuccessfully attempted to dissuade him, agreed to O'Reilly's departure if he could provide a substitute. Mullally volunteered, and O'Reilly left for Bremen to commence training with German Naval Intelligence on 17 September 1942.[2]

As evidenced by the meeting with Mullally in the Berlin Sportspalace, Frank Ryan preferred to keep a low profile during his stay in Germany, avoiding the company of other Irish expatriates apart from Francis Stuart. In a magazine article in 1950, Stuart painted a saccharine picture of Ryan as a man 'with a deep love of country in the old romantic and noble sense, and an equally deep faith in the possibility of a reign of social justice and equity'. Stuart claimed that 'I got to know him well and ... we became close friends.' According to this account, he first met Ryan in Berlin in August 1940, just after Ryan's abortive mission to Ireland with Seán Russell, the story of which he chose to 'unburden' himself to Stuart. Of Ryan's decision to voluntarily return to German-occupied France aboard the *U-65* rather than return to Ireland, Stuart went into some detail:

> Frank had then to decide whether to continue the journey alone or to turn back. After some hesitation he asked the submarine commander to return with him to Germany. I think he later regretted this decision, but being in the dark as to the plan behind the voyage, he was reluctant to land in Ireland and meet his old comrades with nothing to tell them but the news of Russell's sudden death. Expecting, as they were, long awaited news from America, where Russell had been up to a month or two previously, and also from Germany, Frank was loath to return from his own exile (it had been, I think, four years or more since he had left home for Spain) on a German submarine with only a tale of disaster. I was aware, as he spoke, of the conflict of feelings he had experienced when, somewhere off the Irish coast, after Russell's burial at sea, he had decided to turn back.[3]

Stuart claimed not to have seen Ryan at all throughout 1941, and in the spring of 1942 found him 'living in a large, gloomy flat full of heavy furniture which he shared with a German friend'. Ryan's flatmate was Helmut Clissmann of the Brandenburg regiment. Another German friend was the sailor Christian Nissen, and Stuart claimed that he 'had the idea that the little, freckled Kapitan-zur See was the one hope left to Ryan of being able to return to Ireland'. As a guest of the Reich, Ryan enjoyed a diplomat's privileges. He himself admitted: 'So far as comforts go, I lack nothing. I have special privileges with regard to food and clothes.'

In 1989, however, Stuart would give a very different account of Frank Ryan in an interview with Dr David O'Donoghue, claiming that 'I never liked Ryan, we didn't really get on.' He further alleged that Ryan had told him that in the event of a German victory, he expected to receive a ministerial rank in the postwar Irish government. While in 1950 he claimed not to have met Ryan at all throughout the year of 1941, in 1989 he claimed that in that year he went with Ryan to a Kurfurstendamm night club where they met a friend of Ryan's, who was a senior member of the Nazi party.

The most likely explanation for this apparent change of heart is Dr O'Donoghue's own. The 1950 article was written for *The Bell*, a journal under the editorship of Irish republican Peadar O'Donnell, who had been a close associate of Ryan. At this time, Stuart was stranded in France without a valid Irish passport, and was evidently trying to ingratiate himself with Irish republicans, and particularly Seán MacBride, his former brother-in-law and current Irish foreign minister.[4]

In early November 1942, James Brady was released from prison and was checked into the Hotel Continentale in Berlin, where he was visited by Kurt Haller. When Haller suggested that Brady could broadcast propaganda on German radio, the Irishman initially refused, but eventually agreed having been warned that he could be returned to prison. 'Irland-Redaktion' was desperate for genuine Irish broadcasters. Brady reluctantly attempted a written and voice test, at which he was unsuccessful. John Codd later mentioned that Brady had 'worked with Mullally' for this. Later events would suggest that, like Ryan, Brady might have preferred to keep a low profile while in Germany. After his failed audition for German radio, Haller suggested that Brady might work on a farm instead.[5]

John Codd, still languishing in Dusseldorf prison, received occasional visits from Kurt Haller, who found that 'Codd was most contrite, apologised for the letter, swore he would turn over a new leaf, and assured the Germans – by now somewhat sceptical – of his desire to prove his loyalty to their cause.' On another occasion, Haller was accompanied by Frank Ryan, who he introduced as 'Mr Moloney', apparently forgetting that Codd already knew him as 'Frank Richards'. Ryan told Codd that 'he had friends in high places and that he would try to get him out of prison as quickly as he could'. Very significantly, in view of the horrible ordeal that he had suffered in the Spanish prison (although Codd knew nothing of this) he told Codd: 'You may think you are really bad in here, but this place is nothing compared with some of the places I have seen.'[6]

In January 1943, Frank Stringer, still working on the farm at Klein Kiesow, received a visit from Kurt Haller and was told that 'some Irish friends of mine would probably be coming to the farm'. When Haller had been transferred to the German Foreign Office the previous month, Abwehr II had insisted that he take Stringer with him! Stringer had therefore also been transferred to the German Foreign Office, although he was not aware of this. Shortly afterwards, Stringer was joined on the farm by five POWs; Corporal Cawley, Private Strogen, Private Johnstone, Private Lee and his old colleague, Fusilier James Brady. Stringer and Brady, who had not seen each other for fifteen months, wasted little time in catching up on news, in particular details of the similar training that they had received.

The other four POWs represented the Abwehr's last-ditch attempt to salvage anything from the Friesack camp. They had been selected by Jupp Hoven and released from Friesack in summer 1942, not because there was any specific mission for them, but because they might have lost interest in the German offer. They were brought to Berlin where they lived in conditions identical to Brady's group. 'So far,' according to Haller, 'the use of Irish PWs had proved a fiasco. Abw

II had become chary of running risks with Irish PWs; by Oct 42 it was certain that those men would not be operationally committed.' It speaks volumes that Haller found this third group to be 'much inferior to the previous groups', who had not provided the Abwehr with a single viable agent:

> Strogen, who acted as spokesman for the group, was far too young and inexperienced to lead a mission, and the other three were unsuitable even for taking part in a mission. None of them had learned a trade or profession, and they seemed to have drifted into the British Army by accident. Their political convictions, for what they were worth, were Irish nationalist, but not marked by any great enthusiasm. They were callow young boys, with no background or education ... Beyond a general statement that they would be required for work against Britain, no Abw mission was ever discussed with them, and when [Haller] saw them – which was rarely – he took them to lunch or to the Berlin Zoo, or some equally innocuous diversion.

As in Brady's case, it was at one stage suggested that this group might find employment with Irland-Redaktion, always keen to find genuine Irishmen for their service. Haller 'at one time tried to interest the Irish section of the German radio; Prof Mahr and Dr Hartmann, Clissmann (as additional observer), Kucki (their mentor) and [Haller] were present, but the men were not told the purpose of the interview; Hartmann declined to have anything to do with the men, as they were below the standard required.'

As with Stringer, when Haller was transferred to the German Foreign Office, 'Abw II insisted that he should take "his" PWs with him'. Veesenmayer reluctantly agreed to take responsibility for the group after Frank Ryan had met them and reported 'that they were perhaps not entirely useless'. The five Irishmen were sent to Dr Lotz's farm in Klein Kiesow, along with Haller's former secretary who was given a job as secretary on the estate 'to keep an eye on them'.

'All went well for a time. After some time, they refused to do any more farm-work, and one week-end took a train to

Berlin, strictly against orders. The estate bailiff notified the police, and they were arrested as they left the train in Berlin and held in Griefswald Prison. The estate bailiff refused to have the men back.'

James Brady recalled: 'In February 1943 Haller came to the farm and took Calley [*sic*], Strogen, Lee and Johnstone away as they had complained that the farm work was too hard. We were all fed up with farm work, but he only took those four away, as I think he had reason to believe that he could use Stringer and myself later.' Haller 'could think of no other solution but to have them returned to Damm 1, which was done about a week after their arrest'.[7]

Brady had a welcome surprise in early February 1943, when he received an unexpected parcel from Ireland containing clothes and chocolate. This welcome treat had been sent by the farmer in Roscommon who had found himself named as the mysterious James Brady's next of kin. In 1941 the same farmer had received a letter from the British Red Cross informing him that Brady was a POW at Stalag IIID. This was a German cover address; Stalag IIID was in fact a large camp for French POWs in Steglitz, south-west Berlin. Brady was actually at that time in Friesack camp. Despite not knowing Brady, he had posted the parcel to him in June 1942 (giving some indication of the speed of wartime mail) along with a letter requesting details of his identity and family.

Brady replied by 'Kriegsgefangenenpost' (POW mail) on a card dated '7.3.1943' from 'James Brady 7815, M Stammlager IIID, Duetshland [*sic*] (Allemange)[*sic*]'. The letter was written on one of the standard forms issued by the Germans to POWs for writing home, printed on glossy paper which was designed to prevent messages being written with invisible ink. The form had printed lines and was written in pencil. Brady's handwriting is neat and the letter largely grammatical, if occasionally mis-spelt.

I hope that you are well and in good health. I received your welcome letter last month, also the parcel yesterday for which

I was very thankful. They were both lost for some time. The weather is very good here at present. We had a very good winter. I hope it is the same with you. Please rite [*sic*] and tell me how things are going in Ireland. Also if you could manage to send me on some German Grammars, or you could write to the [R]ed [C]ross and they would send them. I will finish now hoping to see you when the war is over.

With best wishes to yourself and family.

Hoping to here [*sic*] from you soon.
I remain yours very sincerely
Signed. James Brady.

The request for German Grammar books suggests that Brady was making an attempt to learn to speak German. The Roscommon farmer subsequently made arrangements for Brady to receive these as well as food parcels.

A German censor would have examined Brady's letter, but evidently did not see anything that needed to be deleted. The letter would then have been passed to the international postal system through Sweden or more likely Switzerland. Long delays were frequent with POW mail.

On arrival in Dublin, the central sorting office in the General Post Office would have forwarded Brady's letter to the nearby postal censorship board, where all wartime mail from the European continent to Ireland was opened and read as a matter of course by a staff of 160, all of whom had had their backgrounds vetted by G2 (Irish military intelligence) and the gardaí. The censorship board was empowered to detain or return 'objectionable' letters, but some, among them Brady's letter, were considered worthy of G2's attention. G2 made a copy of the letter and forwarded the original to the designated address. Their suspicions were aroused when, on further investigation, they discovered that James Brady was not known to the man named as his next of kin. A G2 report on the matter noted that:

The position regarding Brady's identity is unsatisfactory. He is not known to his registered next of kin ... who says he completed the next-of-kin form following the receipt of a letter from Delaney Trimble I/C R.I. Fusiliers and Prisoner of War fund, Armagh in January 1943. Prior to that he had been informed by Records Office, Edinburgh that he had been registered as next-of-kin by Brady. So far as can be ascertained Brady is not known in the district where the next-of-kin resides, neither is he known to the next-of-kin who says that he regarded the completion of the form as an act of charity, so as to enable Brady to get Red Cross parcels.

[X] is a well-to-do and generous man and there is no need to believe that he has not been candid in the matter. He says he forwarded a parcel to Brady in June 1942 containing shirts, socks and chocolates and that he had a card from Brady dated 7.3.43. This card had been noticed, and it is written in rather formal terms.

It was part of G2's brief to monitor such men as Brady who conceivably could return to Ireland as German spies. They already maintained a substantial file on John Codd. A letter marked 'confidential and secret' to a senior officer at garda headquarters, dated 13 May 1943, noted:

From what we can ascertain, it appears that Brady was in some prison in France or Belgium when the Germans arrived and he was then sent to Germany as a Prisoner of War. It is suggested also that Brady was a 'ne'er to do well' if not worse and this may account for his imprisonment on the continent.

I would be glad if you would have further enquiries made regarding the identity of Brady.

A subsequent garda investigation by a Chief Superintendent established this: 'With reference to above I beg to report that confidential enquiries made in respect of the subject of this file have produced information to corroborate previous reports that [X] is neither relation or guardian of this James Brady and this James Brady is not known and did not ever reside in or near this area.'

One more thing is certain: the Irish General Registry Office has no record of anyone by the name of 'James Brady' being born anywhere in Co. Roscommon during the year 1920. Thus it would appear that the 'true' identity of 'Abwehr Agent Metzger' alias 'Charlos de Lacy' was a pseudonym in itself!

There are several reasons why a young man would join the British Army under a false name, but the most likely, given John Codd's claim that 'Brady's' family were unaware of his enlistment, would appear to be that 'Brady' had run away from home and did not wish to be tracked down. Given the fact that Brady's given date of birth made him a little older than eighteen years, the minimum age of enlistment without parental consent, it is possible that he was younger than this. It was not always the practice of British Army recruiting offices to demand a birth certificate, especially given the dire need for recruits as the war progressed. It would not have been a foolproof measure in any case; at least one elderly lady in Co. Kildare made a living from forging such items for this specific purpose.

Whoever James Brady was, he was certainly an Irishman.[8] None of the other Irishmen in Friesack ever suggested otherwise. Codd noted that he seemed very familiar with the Roscommon area; it was also apparent that Colonel McGrath, the senior British officer at Friesack and native of Roscommon, knew his family. Moreover, even if his named 'next of kin' did not know who he was, Brady evidently knew *him*, and this was in an age when personal telephones, and hence telephone directories, were rare in Ireland.

G2 also intercepted two POW cards posted by Frank Stringer to his mother. One was dated '4.4.1943' (when Stringer was still at Klein Kiesow farm) also addressed from 'Stalag IIID'.[9]

Just as Brady and Stringer were unaware that they had been transferred to the Auswartige Amt, they were also unaware that they were being held in reserve for Operation Taube (Osprey) II, a possible German military operation involving Ireland. In early 1942, a special Waffen-SS unit,

'SS Sonder Lehrgang Oranienberg', had been established and headquartered at the notorious SS Totenkopf Division's barracks at Berlin-Oranienberg, twenty kilometres north of Berlin. Commanded by the Dutch SS-Hauptsturmführer van Vessem, this unit comprised seventy NCOs and thirty privates, 'all fanatical SS men who had volunteered for dangerous missions'.[10]

After the entry of the United States into the war in December 1941, the Americans began a considerable build up of forces in Northern Ireland. It was speculated in high circles in Germany that this could be a precursor to an Allied invasion of the twenty-six counties. In fact, the American forces in Northern Ireland actually had a plan to 'invade' neutral Ireland; codenamed Operation Nist, this was apparently a contingency plan to be implemented in response to a German attack. It may have been almost mistakenly implemented on the night of 3 June 1942 but was fortunately cancelled before any American troops crossed the border:[11]

> Through Obergruppenführer Juttner [CO of Waffen-SS Operational HQ] ... the Waffen-SS put at the disposal of Amt VI a unit of about 100 picked men, commanded by Hptstuf van Vessem, a Dutchman. These men were to act primarily as instructors to Irish regular and irregular forces. The Ryan mission was to land a few days in advance of the main party, which was to be dropped later at points notified by the mission by WT. Arms would simultaneously be dropped by air, and later sent to Éire by blockade-runners from France (Christian Nissen had already been vaguely earmarked for this job). The SS men were to train Irish volunteers and units of the Irish Army in the use of modern weapons, and take charge of small dets of irregular forces. It was Ryan's first task to ensure that the Germans would be welcomed as allies and liberators. In the event of Éire being overrun by the British within a few days, it was hoped that the Irish, by temperament and tradition, would be suitable for conducting guerrilla warfare, provided they received the stiffening of German instructors.

The sending of small groups of instructors to train and

organise resistance forces in enemy-occupied territory is a classic special forces role, one that the Allies made much use of in all theatres during the Second World War. But were the SS commandos at Oranienberg suitable for this type of operation? In preparation for their prospective deployment to Ireland the SS unit was given training in sabotage techniques and captured British weapons. As a security measure, a rumour was circulated among them that they were preparing for a raid on the Suez Canal. A Focke-Wulf 200 was requested from the Luftwaffe to transport small parties of SS commandos to Ireland. This was the same type of aircraft that had been designated to fly James Brady to Nothern Ireland the previous September.

Unbeknownst to James Brady and Frank Stringer, 'after the unfortunate experience with Walsh, Irish PWs were viewed with distrust and it was intended that they should go to Éire with the Waffen-SS det, where, under close supervision, they would operate sub WT stations and act as local guides'. Their erstwhile acquaintance at Friesack, Oberleutnant Jupp Hoven, now serving with a Fallschirmjager unit, was also earmarked for the operation, as was Lieutenant Hocker of the Brandenburg Regiment. It is interesting that the Germans had considered seconding Brady and Stringer to the Waffen-SS special forces; later in the war both men would become members of this same unit, or more accurately, its successor.

Another Irishman was suggested as a radio operator for 'Operation Osprey II'. This mysterious figure, O'Duffy by name, had been a civilian labourer on the Channel Islands at the time of the German occupation. He had accompanied John O'Reilly as a volunteer to the Hermann Goering Works at Waterstadt, after which he had gone to Berlin and offered his services to the SS Security Services (SD) Having been screened by Clissmann, he was trained as a radio operator and was employed as such at the main radio station of the Auswartige Amt, being given the cover name of 'Winter'.

Significantly, 'he was considered reliable enough to work without supervision'.[12]

Although SS-Sonder Lehrgang Oranienberg was clearly intended to be a rival, the Abwehr's Brandenburg regiment were grudgingly willing to lend expertise, and in November 1942 Obergefreiter Bruno Reiger and Feldwebel Helmut Clissmann arrived at the Totenkopf barracks and spent three weeks there, ostensibly to give English lessons but actually to assess the SS unit's suitability for the Irish operation. Clissmann was uniquely qualified in this area. Apart from being a member of the Brandenburgers, his pre-war residence in Ireland (to say nothing of his Irish wife) gave him an intimate insight into the Irish character. It was not the first time that Reiger had accompanied Clissmann on an Irish-related matter; in September 1940 the pair had been involved in the abortive attempt to land a small party on the coast of Sligo.

Although Clissmann would form a favourable impression of the men as soldiers ('old campaigners with rows of ribbons'), and did not doubt their ability to fight well as a conventional military unit, he was less certain of their ability to conduct irregular warfare effectively. He also found them 'arrogant and contemptuous of all foreigners', and was doubtful as to their ability to cooperate with Irish guerrillas without causing friction.[13]

Partly as a result of Clissmann's report, but mostly due to the decreasing likelihood of any Allied invasion of Ireland, the SS commandos were released for other duties. In early 1943, the unit was involved in Operation Franz in Persia (present day Iran), an effort which bore striking similarities in concept to Operation Osprey. In August 1941, Persia was invaded and occupied in a joint Anglo-Russian operation, the pro-German Emperor Reza Shah abdicating in favour of his son, Mohammed Reza Pahlavi. The Persian Gulf oilfields were secured for the Allied cause, and Persia became a vital supply route for Russia, over five million tonnes of supplies passing through the country throughout the war. Operation

Franz was conceived in a bid to send Waffen-SS instructors to organise resistance to the Allied occupation among the Kashgai and other mountain tribes. A Junkers 290, a Luftwaffe four-engined transport similar to the Folke-Wolf 200, took off from an airfield in the Crimea and, operating at extreme range, parachuted two officers and three NCOs of the SS Sonder Lehrgang into an area south-east of Teheran where they succeeded in contacting local insurgents. Logistical difficulties prevented the Germans from sending further men and material, and the five German instructors remained with the Persian hill tribes until the end of the war.

> By the end of 1942 no-one, least of all Veesenmayer, believed that Operation Taube II would still materialise. He officially notified Ribbentrop that about twelve men were nevertheless still standing by. This was an overstatement. Available were: Ryan, Clissmann, Rieger, possibly Brady, O'Duffy and Stringer. Veesenmayer added to these Oblt Hoven, Lt Hocker and Christian Nissen, who could be made available.[14]

On 20 February 1943, John Codd was released from Dusseldorf prison. He was met outside by the ever-polite 'Mr Thomas of the Dusseldorf Gestapo' (who had arrested him the previous August) and driven to a hotel near the Dusseldorfer Bahnhof, where he met Kurt Haller. Since they were unable to travel to Berlin that day, Haller and Codd spent the night in the hotel and went to Berlin the next morning. On arrival, 'to satisfy formalities', Haller delivered Codd to the 'Heimgefengenis' (home prison) at Moabit, where he would spend the next two weeks. During that time Haller visited, bringing Red Cross parcels, which Codd, nominally still a POW, was apparently entitled to receive.

Codd also received another visitor while still in Moabit prison; a man who introduced himself as 'Captain Drescher' and who invited Codd to work for 'his people'. Codd assented. Drescher was actually a Hauptsturmführer, the SS rank equivalent of captain, and 'his people' were in

fact the Sicherheitsdienst (SD), the intelligence service of
the SS. More precisely, Codd was being invited to work for
the RSHA Amt VI. In September 1939, the SS established
the Reich Security Main Office (Reichssicherheitshaupamt),
thereby achieving Himmler's aim of integrating offices of the
Nazi party with those of the German government. The new
organisation was arranged into six departments; among these
Office (Amt) III was responsible for domestic intelligence,
Office IV was the dreaded Gestapo, while Office VI (foreign
intelligence) was clearly a rival intelligence organisation to
the Abwehr and would supersede it in early 1944.

Major Astor of Abwehr II had finally assented to Codd's
release, but made it clear that neither his own nor any other
department of Abwehr was interested in employing Codd.
Although Veesenmayer of the Auswartige Amt had agreed
to take responsibility for several of Kurt Haller's Irishmen,
he also refused to have anything to do with the troublesome
Laoisman. He did, however, talk to SS-Brigadeführer Walter
Schellenberg, the commander of RSHA Amt VI, who agreed
to recruit him.

Codd later offered some biographical details on SS-
Hauptsturmführer Drescher; he spoke English and Norwegian and was given to 'drunken habits'. It is noteworthy that
Codd appeared to be sanctimonious when discussing other
people's drinking habits; other contemporaries did not speak
highly of his own. Drescher, according to Codd, was also involved in black market dealing in stolen Red Cross parcels.
His office was in 'Berlin-Wilmersdorf, Delbruckstrasse 3',
which was the headquarters of RSHA VI-F, the technical
department of SS foreign intelligence.[15]

By March 1943, it was obvious that the war was not going
well for Germany. A staggering 300,000 men had been lost in
the disaster at Stalingrad, and the Germans were in retreat in
North Africa. In that month, SS-Obergruppenführer Hans
Juttner, who had authorised the formation of SS Sonder

Lehrgang Oranienburg the previous year, conducted an interview with an SS-Obersturmführer by the name of Otto Skorzeny. Juttner, who had held high rank in the tiny and very select officer corps of the pre-Hitler Reichswehr (German Army), was evidently satisfied with Skorzeny's military record, and at the interview's conclusion offered him command of the Waffen-SS special duties unit, and also a sabotage school in occupied Holland. Skorzeny immediately accepted.

Physically, the Austrian-born Skorzeny was an impressive specimen. At 6'4" and weighing over two hundred pounds, he easily exceeded the exacting physical requirements for a Waffen-SS officer. He would later be nicknamed 'Scarface' by the Americans, due to a particularly prominent duelling scar that ran down the left side of his face. Several senior SS officers bore such scars, although less obviously. SS-Brigadeführer Walter Schellenberg, chief of SS foreign intelligence, also carried one, and even the prissy SS-Reichsführer Heinrich Himmler sported a tiny mark.

Apart from his imposing appearance, Skorzeny may have seemed an unlikely candidate for Juttner's offer. At thirty-five he was a relatively elderly subaltern (he was promoted to SS-Hauptsturmführer on acceptance of his new post) who was medically classified 'GvH', fit only for garrison duty. Such a choice might outwardly indicate a low priority for the development of special operations in the Waffen-SS. By this stage of the war, the Wehrmacht was moving away from such concepts, eventually converting the elite Brandenburg Regiment into a conventional line infantry division.

Juttner, however, had made a good choice in Skorzeny. A civil engineer by profession, Skorzeny had originally volunteered for the Luftwaffe on the outbreak of war but had been deemed too old for aircrew training. He transferred to the Waffen-SS, and as an artillery officer with the Leibstandarte took part in the invasion of Russia, winning the Iron Cross second and first class. Wounded and stricken by a serious case of dysentery followed by biliary colic, he was evacuated on

medical grounds and returned to Vienna. After convalescent
leave he was eventually appointed to the SS Totenkopf Division as an engineering officer. This was, however, while the
division was refitting in France, therefore Skorzeny was not
involved in that division's more notorious exploits. During
this time he gained a thorough knowledge of the operation
of German and Allied tanks. Skorzeny's health collapsed late
in 1942, and he was returned to 'garrison duties'. Like the
founder of the British SAS, David Stirling, Skorzeny used
his enforced free time to formulate certain ideas on uncon-
ventional warfare, which brought him to the attention of SS-
Obergruppenführer Juttner.[16]

According to Skorzeny's original account in 1945, SS
Sonder Lehrgang Oranienburg, as its name implies, was
based in that town, in the SS Totenkopf Division's barracks.
Skorzeny was more evasive about this detail in later years,
possibly not only due to fears of any perceived association
with that notorious formation, but of confusion with the
even more notorious 'special' unit that was founded there in
1940. In that year Oskar Dirlewanger, SS-Obersturmführer
and convicted paedophile, took command of a special unit
comprised largely of convicts. When this unit, now designated SS-Sonderbattalion Dirlewanger, was posted to occupied Poland, it quickly established a reputation for brutality
that surpassed even that of other SS units there, not least
due to Dirlewanger's favourite diversion of injecting naked
young Jewish girls with strychnine and observing their death
agonies. Despite being under suspicion of 'racial defilement'
(for suspected sexual relations with a Jewish woman in Lu-
blin) Dirlewanger was promoted to SS-Sturmbannführer in
late 1941. This was an indication of his privileged position
in the eyes of the Nazi hierarchy. When in early 1942, SS-
Obergruppenführer Friedrich Kruger threatened that unless
Dirlewanger's 'bunch of criminals' were removed from his
jurisdiction he would lock them up personally, SS-Gruppenführer Hans Juttner had them placed under the direct

command of SS-Reichsführer Himmler's staff, and they were transferred to anti-partisan operations to the east of Minsk. There they 'distinguished' themselves by such tactics as forcing villagers into their barns, which would be then set alight, and marching women and children across minefields to clear them.

It should be noted that Dirlewanger's SS Sonderbattalion had absolutely no connection with Skorzeny's SS Sonder Lehrgang. Although in June 1944 a special order invited members of Dirlewanger's unit to volunteer to participate in an operation with 'SS Jager Battailon 502' (as Skorzeny's unit was then designated), this seemed to originate from Himmler rather than Skorzeny, and there is no evidence that any such personnel volunteered or were accepted.[17]

Skorzeny reviewed the training programme of his new unit and, like Helmut Clissmann before him, was unhappy with certain aspects of it. In keeping with their 'stormtrooper' ethos, Waffen-SS units tended to favour aggressive assaults utilising heavy firepower. Such an approach had its drawbacks, as the German General Kurt Student could testify; in 1940 he had been mistakenly shot by over-aggressive Waffen-SS troops in Rotterdam. Skorzeny had made a study of British commando operations, in particular the daring attempt to assassinate Rommel, the commander of the Afrika Korps. Skorzeny had concluded that the raid had failed primarily because of faulty intelligence (Rommel was not at the base when the raid occurred) but also because the vital element of surprise was lost due to unnecessary gunfire, which resulted in the loss of most of the British force. In Russia, Skorzeny witnessed for himself how a single shot by a nervous sentry could result in an entire German position firing wildly at nothing, and began to instil a strict weapons discipline in his unit, the results of which became evident in its two most spectacular operations.

Early in the summer of 1943, Skorzeny's unit moved to a purpose-built facility in nearby Friedenthal and was re-designated 'SS Sonder Lehrgang zbv Friedenthal'. The 'zbv' in the unit's title indicated 'special duties', just as in the official title of the Wehrmacht's Brandenburgers (Bau-Lehr Battalion zbv Nr 800). The Luftwaffe would form their own special operations unit later that year, namely 'Staffel Gartenfeld zbv', named after its commander, Major Gartenfeld, who had flown Hermann Görtz to Ireland in 1940. In February 1944, this squadron was expanded to form Kampfgeschwader 200, which became infamous for its utilisation of captured Allied aircraft for covert missions.

By now, Skorzeny's new command consisted of one full company led by SS-Hauptsturmführer van Vessem, as well as part of another company and a transport element. There were 300 men in all, all members of the Waffen-SS. Even at this early stage some members of this force were non-Germans. Apart from van Vessem, nearly fifty members of the unit were Dutch or Flemish, with a few 'Volksdeutsche' (ethnic Germans) from Hungary. Skorzeny wished to expand his command to battalion status and obtained authorisation to activate 'SS Jager Battailon 502' in June 1943, Sonder Lehrgang zbv Friedenthal being absorbed into the new unit. There were, however, difficulties in attracting suitable personnel. The Waffen-SS envisaged a '500' series of battalions for dangerous missions, one of which was the SS-Fallschirmjager Battalion 500. These units were to recruit personnel from SS penal institutions; under the draconian disciplinary code of the Waffen-SS, soldiers could be imprisoned for such offences as sleeping on sentry duty or 'defeatist comment'. Skorzeny received a draft of personnel from an SS penal camp in Chlum in occupied Czechoslovakia, but ninety per cent of them were deemed unsuitable and were returned. Obergruppenführer Juttner then allowed Skorzeny to recruit volunteers from the Wehrmacht, and apart from one hundred SS personnel, fifty Luftwaffe and one hundred and fifty Heer (army) personnel were also admitted, allowing the formation of a headquarters company and two line companies. Thirty men were sent to the Havel institute for radio training. 'The others underwent strenuous infantry training and engineer and motor courses were added later.'[18]

In early March 1943, John Codd was released from Moabit prison and brought to a flat on the Hermannplatz, which he shared with a Fleming called Mr Bach. He was issued with a new Fremdenpass, which gave his name as Jacob Collins, born in Metz, France. Kurt Haller credited Frank Ryan for Codd's eventual release from prison. When Codd told Haller that he would like to express his thanks to 'Mr Moloney', he was told that his benefactor was very ill in Dresden. Frank Ryan had suffered a stroke on 15 January 1943, leaving him bedridden with a paralysed arm in the Charite hospital. 'It was,' noted Frank Stuart, 'a bad time to be ill with all the hospitals full of wounded, with the air raids that were increasing in violence, the lack of food.' Although Ryan recovered from his stroke that summer, ulcers kept him hospitalised until October.

A week after his release from prison, Codd spent two weeks being instructed in cryptography by Frau Dr Hiempel. His training was supervised by SS-Hauptsturmführer Schultz, who Codd presumed to be in charge of SD radio, cipher and demolition training. Codd was then directed to a public house in Hubertsalle near the Halensee lake. This turned out to be a disguised training centre where Codd received ten days' training in manufactured explosives, as opposed to the improvised explosives training he had undergone at the Abwehr training facility at the Quentzgut. He was also trained to handle various pistols and submachine guns, including the British Sten gun, which he fired on the range at the SS barracks at Berlin-Zehlendorff.

On 15 April 1943, Codd's fiancée, Irma Schoenhorff, arrived in Berlin. This was the girl who Codd had met in Cologne in March 1942 and had wished to marry. Permission from the Abwehr had not been forthcoming. The day after Fraulein Schoenhorff's arrival, Codd left his flat on the

Hermannplatz to share a flat with her at Katherine Strasse 16 at Halensee. His erstwhile flatmate, Bach (who would later apparently work for the SD in Italy and Norway) gave Codd the address of a public house called the 'Weldeck' at Halensee, which turned out to be another concealed training centre, where Codd was trained in telegraphy. Also in training here were a group of twelve Arabs from Algeria and Tunisia. Since Codd spoke French and German, he was able to act as interpreter between them and their German instructors.[19]

At about this time Codd had an 'interview' with SS-Hauptsturmführer Drescher and SS-Untersturmführer Schubb about his German fiancée. While Codd's original application to marry a German girl had been refused by the Abwehr on grounds of security, the SS could regard such an application with suspicion on ideological grounds. Although the SS was prepared to employ foreigners as agents (as the presence of the Arabs at Halensee testified), marriage between Germans and foreigners could be very much frowned upon in the Third Reich. However, Codd was granted permission to marry Schoenhorff. A very detailed wartime German military survey of Ireland declared that: 'Racially, the population is a mixture of Western and Nordic components', which would seem to indicate that Codd was acceptable by the warped standards of Nazi racial ideology. This survey was believed to be partly the work of Professor Ludwig Mulhausen, the holder of the chair of Celtic studies at Berlin university since 1937. A brilliant Celtologist, Mulhausen had been a regular visitor to Irish-speaking areas of Ireland since the late 1920s. By now an officer in the SS, he made several wartime propaganda broadcasts to Ireland in flawless Gaelic.[20]

A few marriages took place between German men and Irish women, for example between Helmut Clissmann and Elizabeth Mulcahy. From a practical point of view, the SS on this occasion had shown more imagination than the Abwehr. As Codd himself later noted, it made sense for the SS to employ a foreign spy with a wife in Germany, to ensure his loyalty while abroad on a mission.

In May 1943, Codd was introduced to SS-Hauptsturm-führer Giese, later described by Skorzeny as 'Born 1914, 1.82m, strong build, black hair, square face, pale'. Giese was based in 32–35 Berkaerstrasse in central Berlin, the head-quarters of RSHA VI (SS foreign intelligence). This was a very large brick and concrete building of classic 1930s circum-linear layout. Until 1941 it had been a retirement home for elderly Jews; in that year the occupants had been evicted and sent on the trains to their eventual deaths in eastern Europe. Giese's office was in room 228 on the third floor. The only other occupant was a secretary that read Irish daily newspa-pers and marked items of interest. Giese informed Codd that he had a plan to send him to Northern Ireland on a mission; before this, he would attend the SS radio school at Lehnitz to improve his radio skills.

In about June 1943, Giese would make a phone call to John O'Reilly, with an offer of employment by SS intelli-gence. O'Reilly had completed an extensive course of train-ing at Bremen, and it had originally been proposed that he be returned to Ireland by U-boat. This scheme had been halted by Edmund Veesenmayer, who was anxious not to jeopardise the possibility of a similar mission involving Frank Ryan. He was currently living in Berlin, although not involved in Irland-Redaktion.[21]

At about the same time that the RSHA was taking an interest in recruiting Irish agents, the SS were holding another group of Irishmen under hellish conditions. Apart from the four Irishmen being held in Sachsenhausen and Dacau, a number of others, who had been serving with the British Merchant Navy when captured by the Germans, were interned in the Milag Nord prison camp. In March 1943, thirty-two Irishmen were transferred to the SS-Arbeitserziehungslager at Farge, near Bremen. As they arrived, they were beaten with hosepipes by the SS guards, who lined them up and warned them that no-one knew of their location and that the SS could treat them as they pleased. Along with 10,000 concentration camp prisoners, POWs and forced labourers (4,000 of whom died), the Irishmen worked on the construction of a massive bunker for the construction of U-boats. They were forced to labour there for twelve hours a day for six days a week (Sundays being spent labouring on a farm), continuously beaten and threatened by the SS. Each man survived on a daily ration of a bowl of soup and three slices of black bread. Five of the Irishmen had died by the time the Irish legation in Berlin became aware of their plight. Representations were made to the German government and the Irishmen returned to Milag Nord. After the war, three of them gave evidence in the war crimes trial of thirteen of the Bremen-Farge camp guards.[22]

At the end of April 1943, Brady and Stringer, still working on the farm at Klein Kiesow, received a visit from a man who introduced himself as 'Franz Richter'. This was, in fact, none other than Brandenburger Obergefreiter Bruno Rieger, who had accompanied Clissmann in his abortive voyage to the Irish west coast in 1940, and had participated in Clissmann's evaluation of the SS commandos at Oranienberg the previous November. He produced a small radio set and tested the pair in receiving and transmitting Morse code. Commenting that after a little practice they 'would do', he left, and a few days later Brady and Stringer were ordered to travel to Berlin. They travelled by train, alone and unescorted, and at the railway station in Berlin were met by Rieger, who brought them to the Hotel Nationale near Savignyplatz. After a few days they were brought to a large house at 21 Florastrasse at Lehnitz, just south of Oranienberg.

Although Haller considered the pair's reliability to be 'doubtful', he suggested to Veesenmayer that 'they should be kept as possible reserve WT operators for Operation Taube II'. Bruno Rieger, still on standby in Berlin for this operation, had been detailed to take Brady and Stringer in hand and to supervise their training. 'Veesenmayer arranged for their

training through the Haven Institut of the SD near Oranienberg.' This was despite the fact that, by Haller's own account,
Operation Taube II had been abandoned the previous year.

Lehnitz, ostensibly a 'school of languages', was actually an
SS radio training school in a village north of Berlin. It appeared to be part of the huge SS complex which had grown
up around Oranienburg. This complex included a 'colony' for
SS families and the notorious Sachsenhausen concentration
camp. Another Irishman who later trained at Lehnitz described it as 'a wooded area more than a town'. The school
itself was described as a three-storey building. On the ground
floor there was an office in which a secretary worked (named
by Stringer as Ruth Boem, later replaced by Fraulein Rotke),
a radio instruction room, a kitchen and a lounge. The first
floor consisted mainly of a large room with a long bench running down the centre. The pupils would sit here and practise
sending and receiving Morse code. The top floor consisted of
rooms for advanced students to practise long-distance transmission to other radio stations in Germany.

When Brady and Stringer began training at the school, the
school commandant was called Siegal, although he also used
the name Walthers. The instructors at the school did not wear
uniform and were addressed by their students as 'Herr'. They
included Walther Odenthal (Siegal's deputy), Meyer (also
known as Schiele) and two Dutchmen, Becker and Polman.
It seems that, like the Abwehr, the staff at Lehnitz attempted
to use pseudonyms for security reasons, though apparently
without success. In June 1943, Siegal was replaced as commander by a man called Schultz; he in turn was replaced by
the Dutchman, Polman. Other students at the school varied
in number between twenty and thirty. They included French,
Danes, Norwegians, Bulgarians, an Arab and a Turk. The in-
clusion of the latter pair, nominally 'untermensch' as far as
strict Nazi ideology was concerned, showed that the SS was
prepared to suspend racial considerations as far as recruiting
agents was concerned.

Brady and Stringer remained at the school until the end of July 1943, mostly training to transmit and receive Morse. They were also taught the transmission of telegrams and the use of a simple code. This involved the use of a cardboard cipher wheel consisting of two discs, a smaller one printed with numbers superimposed onto a larger disc printed with letters.

Bruno Rieger remained at Lehnitz, keeping constant watch on Brady and Stringer. He also delivered their pay, seventy marks weekly. At the end of July 1943, Rieger brought the pair away, on a long journey to southern Russia.[23]

By his own account John Codd began training at Lehnitz on 22 June 1943. Apart from this date, the information he gives about the staff and students strongly suggests that Codd was actually attending the SS radio school at the same time as Brady and Stringer. Apart from Rieger's constant presence, it is obvious that the Germans had made every effort that the Irishmen should not meet each other.

Schultz was in command when Codd began training, having taken over from Siegal that month. Codd named the Dutch instructor as 'Bakker', adding the unsavoury detail that he had boasted to Codd of having persecuted Jews in Holland. Bakker is said to have had several children, both legitimate and otherwise. He instructed in WT and ciphers. SS-Scharführer Odenthal, according to Codd, was aged thirty-six and had served in Poland. He was friendly with Schultz, and took over his job for a while. Another instructor arrived in July 1943; Husenette (alias Housemann), born in Alsace-Lorraine. He had been a ship's radio operator before the war, and 'was far better than any of the others'. There was also Schnell, an interpreter who spoke good English, Spanish and French.

Codd's account also shed more light on the replacement of the school's original secretary, a 'French-German' according to him. Bakker had reported her for having an unusual number of ration cards, and she was arrested and taken away on suspicion of 'being in contact with the British'. She was never heard of again. An instructor called Kruger was also taken away, due to his strong association with the secretary.

There were six to twenty pupils at the school at any one time, according to Codd. Apart from the French, Norwegians, Danes and the Turk that Brady and Stringer had encountered, Codd later met the Arabs he had earlier encountered at the 'Weldeck'. He also encountered Belgians, Swedes, Russians, Poles and Italians. Codd continued training at Lehnitz 'with breaks' until May 1944.[24]

On 4 July 1943, Hitler launched a massive offensive on the Russian front, codenamed 'Operation Zitadelle'. Some 900,000 men, 2,700 tanks and 2,000 aircraft were launched in a massive assault to cut off the Russian salient at Kursk. One of the objectives of the assault was the capture of large numbers of Russian prisoners to be used as forced labour for the German war effort. The Russians were expecting the assault and had assembled a force of 1.3 million men, 3,300 tanks and 2,600 aircraft. In the biggest tank battle in history, the Russians, commanded by Marshal Zhukov, bled away the German strength in a series of defensive battles. After eight days of savage fighting with few gains and heavy losses, Hitler called off the offensive, worried by the Allied invasion of Sicily and a massive Russian buildup in the Donetz region. It was the decisive turning point of the war. From then on, the Red Army would continue an inexorable advance to Berlin.

Throughout August 1943, the Russians slowly pushed back Field Marshal von Manstein's 'Army Group South' along a line that ran from the Kursk salient to the Sea of Asov in the south. The port of Berdiansk, near Melitopol on the Sea of Asov, was therefore not conceivably the safest place in the Third Reich, but that was where Rieger and his two Irish charges found themselves at the start of that month, on 'a WT training trip'.

Throughout the month, Brady and Stringer, their call signs being changed daily, kept constant radio contact with

stations at Wannsee (Berlin) and Kharkov, until the latter fell
to the Russians on 22 August 1943, an event that can hardly
have improved the trio's morale. In the heat of the Crimean
summer, animosity developed between Brady and Rieger.
In September, Rieger decided that the two Irishmen 'would
never make radio operators' and the three returned to Berlin.
By the end of the month the Russians were advancing on
Melitopol.

On their arrival in Berlin, Brady and Stringer were again
accommodated at the Hotel Nationale. To Haller, 'Rieger
reported adversely on their ability as WT operators, their
reliability and character.' He 'thought very poorly of them
generally'. Kurt Haller visited the pair in their hotel where he
informed them that 'he had received complaints from Richter [Rieger] that we wouldn't take interest in our work'. Brady
admitted: 'I did very little as I couldn't get on with Ritter
[sic].'

Telling the pair that 'he had no more work' for them, Haller
spelt out the alternatives. In Stringer's version of events, these
were: 'go to work on a farm, or in a factory or join the German army. We both volunteered for the army. Neither of us
wanted to go back to Stalag. I don't know why, I just didn't
ask, and Haller would not have let us go back anyway, because
he knew we knew too much.'

Haller, however, would deny this version strenuously. He
claims that he had offered 'the choice of returning to a PW
camp, work as labourers on a farm or in a factory, or enlistment with the Waffen-SS. He made it clear that they could
only enlist in an infantry unit of the Waffen-SS and not in
the German Army. Without hesitation, both men chose to be
sent to the Waffen-SS. [Haller] states that there would have
been no difficulty about returning both Brady and Stringer to
a PW camp. The Strogen group had already been returned to
Damm 1 and a breach of security was inevitable.'

This discrepancy is understandable. Stringer was facing
possible charges for treason when he made his claims, and

would have been anxious to impress that his enlistment in the Waffen-SS was not entirely voluntary. Haller was desperately trying to evade any responsibility for sending five Irish POWs to Sachsenhausen concentration camp. Haller's version, however, is lent some credence by the fact that Strogen's group, the four Irishmen who were taken away from Klein Kiesow, were indeed returned to the Friesack camp. Brady's account does not mention any hint of duress: 'Haller said he had no more work for us to do, so we decided to join the German Army, as I knew it was easy to get into.'

Both the German Army and Waffen-SS enlisted foreign volunteers in the early years of the war, but in March 1943 it was agreed to rationalise the supply of manpower by enlisting all non-German personnel in the latter organisation. By September 1943, a quarter of the Waffen-SS was non-German, effectively making it, in part at least, Germany's foreign legion. It was, therefore, to the Waffen-SS recruiting office on Berlin's Scheerstrasse that Bruno Rieger brought the two Irishmen. When they enlisted (with Veesenmayer's assistance), they did so under the false names and nationalities originally provided to them by the Abwehr. Bruno Rieger took his leave of Charlos de Lacy from South America and Willy le Page from Guernsey (Brady and Stringer respectively) and the pair proceeded to Sennheim in Alsace-Lorraine the next day, unescorted and wearing civilian clothing.[25]

By the beginning of September 1943, Sicily had been lost to the Allies and Benito Mussolini, fascist dictator of Italy, had been deposed. On 3 September the Allies invaded mainland Italy and the Italian government surrendered, agreeing to hand over Mussolini to the Allied powers as a condition of the armistice. Mussolini was moved from location to location, until in early November he was brought under heavy guard to a requisitioned hotel on the peak of the 6,000-foot Gran Sasso mountain in the Appenines. The mountain could be accessed only by cable car and all surrounding roads were blocked; this ruled out any possibility of a surprise assault by land, and the mountain's altitude made a parachute assault impossible.

At about 2 p.m. on 12 September, a large glider swooped out of nowhere and crashed within 15 metres of the back of the hotel. Eight German soldiers and the pilot quickly emerged and sprinted to the building, led by a big man with a scarred face. Although they wore the uniforms and insignia of the Fallschirmjager, these men were actually members of SS Jager Battailon 502. SS-Hauptsturmführer Otto Skorzeny, leading the assault, had given strict instructions to his troops to hold their fire in order to preserve the element of surprise. The new Italian government had not yet declared war on Germany, although some skirmishes had taken place. The stunned Italian defenders were further confused when an Italian general clambered from the wrecked glider and began shouting 'non abagliare!' Seconds later, a second glider landed in front of the hotel, from which emerged another eight members of SS Jager Battailon 502. The first group had already reached Mussolini, scrambling up a terrace and a lightning conductor, while the second secured the ground floor of the hotel. It was five minutes since the landing of the first glider. Within minutes, six more DFS-230 gliders (the same type that had been used in the assault of the Eban-Emaal fortress in May 1940) landed on the mountain top – these carried Fallschirmjagers who surrounded the hotel. One glider missed the landing zone and was wrecked on the steep mountain slopes. In the hotel, Skorzeny demanded and received the surrender of the Italian garrison and informed Mussolini that he was free. Word soon came through that other Fallschirmjagers had seized the cable car station in the valley. Due to large numbers of Italian forces in the area it was not advisable to attempt to bring Mussolini away by road. The original plan to bring Mussolini to safety required Skorzeny to bring him down to the valley in the cable car and transfer him to a nearby airfield which would be temporarily seized for the purpose, but Skorzeny's radio operator in the valley was unable to contact the Heinkel 111s designated to land there; in any case there was now a full Italian division in the vicinity. An alternative plan called for a light aircraft to land in the valley below the Gran Sasso, but this aircraft damaged its undercarriage on landing. As an absolute last resort, a tiny Feiseler Storch aircraft flown by General Student's personal pilot was ready to attempt a landing on the mountain top. Skorzeny's troops, assisted by Italian prisoners, moved as many boulders as possible from an improvised airstrip and Hauptmann Gerlach successfully landed his aircraft within 100 feet. He had a shock in store – not only was he expected to fly out Mussolini, but Skorzeny as well! All three were aware of the extreme hazards involved; Mussolini was a qualified pilot and Skorzeny had some flying experience. Gerlach performed another miracle by taking off from the Gran Sasso, the aircraft plunging into the chasm at the end of the improvised airstrip. Recovering from the dive, Gerlach flew the heavily overloaded Storch to Rome and landed safely despite a damaged undercarriage. Skorzeny and Mussolini transferred to a Heinkel 111 and the pair were in Vienna that evening where Skorzeny was immediately awarded the Knight's Cross and promoted to SS-Sturmbannführer on Hitler's personal order.

The raid on the Gran Sasso was subsequently hailed as an assault of exceptional daring, all the more remarkable for having been carried out without loss of life. This was purely accidental: when Skorzeny took off, four more DFS-230 gliders were missing and unaccounted for, along with the occupants of the glider that still lay wrecked on the mountain slope. It is worth noting that without the exceptional skill of Hauptmann Gerlach, to say nothing of the glider pilots, the rescue of Mussolini would have ended in a pile of twisted wreckage on the slopes of the Gran Sasso. Skorzeny originally admitted to 'vehement reproaches' from General Student and Hermann Goering for his decision to accompany Mussolini in the Storch. Ironically, the assault was planned with poor quality aerial photographs which did not indicate just how steep and rocky the intended landing zone really was; better information in this regard would almost certainly have led to the raid being cancelled. Goebbels' propaganda ministry exploited this rare victory to the full, leading to Skorzeny quickly becoming famous. For his part Skorzeny was happy to grab his share of the glory. When in early October 1943 the Nazi newspaper, *Illestrierter Beobachter*, mistakenly credited the Major in command of the party of Fallschirmjagers as Mussolini's liberator, Skorzeny took part in a widely broadcast radio programme to set the record straight.[26]

After the German occupation of western Europe in 1940, SS-Reichsführer Heinrich Himmler declared: 'We must attract all the Nordic blood in the world to us, and so deprive our enemies of it, so that never again will Nordic or Germanic blood fight against us', and began preparations to recruit suitably 'Nordic' non-Germans into the Waffen-SS. At the end of 1940, an SS-Ausbildungslager (training camp) was established at Sennheim (Cernay) in Alsace-Lorraine, exclusively for foreign recruits to the Waffen-SS. The disputed border region of Alsace-Lorraine, ceded to Germany after its victory in the Franco-Prussian war of 1870 and returned to France by the Treaty of Versailles, was seized again by Germany in 1940, despite Hitler's pre-war assurances that Germany had no designs on the territory.

In 1941, Himmler authorised recruiting to the Waffen-SS units 'Freiwilligen Legion Nederlands', 'Freiwilligen Legion Flandern', 'Freikorps Danmark' and 'Freiwilligen Legion Norwegen', composed of Dutch, Belgian Flemings, Danish and Norwegians respectively. Himmler was not willing to extend SS status to other, less 'Aryan', Europeans, and so French, Spanish and Belgian Walloons served in the Wehrmacht, where the Legion des Volontaire Francais, the Blue Division and the 373 Infanterie Bataillon carved solid combat reputations.[27]

Motivations for these foreign volunteers for the Waffen-SS were many and varied. The Waffen-SS offered German citizenship after a two-year contract of service as an inducement. Many of the volunteers had genuine Nazi sympathies, while others were enthusiastic to participate in a 'crusade against Bolshevism'. Others were professional soldiers with no army to serve since the German occupation of their country.

Many of these newly recruited SS Freiwilligen were in for a rude shock when they arrived in Germany. Apart from the fact that few spoke German, which led to natural misunderstandings, the harsh discipline and the tough training regime of the Waffen-SS came as a shock even to former soldiers. Many of the Waffen-SS training staff genuinely regarded any non-German as 'racially inferior' and treated the foreign recruits in a particularly brutal fashion. It should be noted that, at this early stage, foreign volunteers were regarded as 'attached to' rather than full members of the Waffen-SS; for example, even when some foreign recruits were eventually commissioned, they were likely to be officially designated as 'Waffen-Untersturmführer der SS', or 'Legion-Untersturmführer der SS' rather than 'SS-Untersturmführer'. After several foreign recruits resigned, Himmler himself eventually intervened, and some reforms were made.

Very few of the original volunteers lived to complete their two-year term of service, and these rarely extended their contracts. The Wehrmacht and the Waffen-SS suffered appalling losses on the Russian front. By the war's end, out of the 920,000 men to serve with the Waffen-SS (57 per cent of whom were non-German), 180,000 were killed, 400,000 wounded and 70,000 missing. Four full Waffen-SS divisions took part in the invasion of Russia: the 'Leibstandarte', 'Das Reich', 'Totenkopf' and 'Wiking'. The latter was comprised of the 'Germania' regiment, along with the 'Nordland' and 'Westland' regiments of western European volunteers; the division thus included Germans, Norwegians, Dutch, Belgian Flemings and Danes. Before the end of 1941, the four

Waffen-SS divisions fighting on the Russian front suffered over 36,000 casualties between them. Further heavy losses were sustained throughout the winter of 1941–2 (the 'Der Führer' regiment was reduced from two thousand to thirty-five men), but the Waffen-SS established such a combat reputation that in late 1942 these four Waffen-SS divisions were withdrawn to occupied France, not just to have their losses replaced but to be expanded to SS Panzer Grenadier Divisions, each with an establishment of 20,000 men and including a regiment of panzers. Three divisions together formed the first SS Panzer Corps, which took part in the desperate fighting around Kharkov in early 1943, further enhancing the combat reputation of the Waffen-SS at the cost of 11,500 casualties. Hitler was at first outraged when corps commander SS-Obergruppenführer Paul Hausser ignored his direct orders by abandoning the key city to the Russians, but was elated when the SS Panzer Corps retook the city in March. Hitler now began to manifest enormous faith in the abilities of the Waffen-SS, which would prove to be a double-edged sword; although more Waffen-SS corps were raised and the force given preference with regard to new equipment, Hitler's expectations were met at the cost of appalling casualties.[28]

Throughout 1943, not only had heavy casualties to be replaced, but new personnel had to be provided for the ongoing expansion of the Waffen-SS. More Waffen-SS divisions were established that year so that, by the end of 1943, of the thirty German panzer divisions, seven were Waffen-SS formations. This manpower crisis was not helped by a dwindling number of volunteers for service. In February 1943 a series of reports from the thirteen main recruiting centres pointed to an increasing lack of enthusiasm for Waffen-SS service, and noted the growing level of influence of parents and clergy in this. Desperate measures had to be resorted to. By May 1943, the elite Leibstandarte division had recouped its losses by effectively conscripting 2,500 Luftwaffe ground personnel. One of the new divisions, the Hitlerjugend, was comprised of seventeen-year-old volunteers. Of the first 27,000 personnel provided to establish the Hohenstaufen and Frundsberg SS Panzer Grenadier Divisions, 14,000 were conscripts. A particularly interesting feature of the latter two divisions was the chivalry that they displayed to captured British paratroopers (although not to civilians) following the ferocious fighting at Arnhem in 1944, proof that Waffen-SS formations could act correctly under the right leadership.[29]

In order to rationalise the manpower supply, the Wehrmacht agreed to transfer its 'foreign' units to the Waffen-SS, Himmler effectively abandoning all previous racial standards to the extent of authorising the formation of Ukrainian and Russian units. This development delighted such men as Leon Degrelle, the leader of the Rexist right wing association of Belgian Walloons. When the Germans originally began recruiting volunteers from the conquered countries of western Europe, only the Flemings of Belgium had been considered 'Aryan' enough for Waffen-SS membership. The Walloons, and Degrelle, joined the German Army's 373 Infanterie Battailon. By May 1942, Degrelle was a lieutenant with the Iron Cross second and first class. In June 1943, these Walloons were absorbed into the SS Sturmbrigade Wallonien, which was attached to the SS Wiking Division. Degrelle was pleased with his unit's new status, claiming: 'First there was the German, then the Germanic, and now there was the European Waffen-SS. 125,000 would then volunteer to save Western Culture and Civilisation.' Degrelle was so proud of his service with the Waffen-SS that in the 1960s, while in postwar exile in Spain, he wore his SS uniform to his daughter's wedding! Yet it is indicative of the true status of the foreign volunteers in the Waffen-SS that, despite the fact that Degrelle rose to the equivalent rank of Colonel and received the Gold Combat Clasp (awarded for seventy-five days' combat) and the Oak leaves to his Knight's Cross (indicating a subsequent award of this prestigious medal) from Adolf Hitler himself, the Belgian was never listed in the SS

Dienstalterliste, the official roll of SS officers. Likewise, non-Germans were far less numerous in the Allgemeine-SS, the unarmed branch of the SS concerned with racial, security and legal matters.[30]

In September 1943, a division comprised of Bosnian Muslims assembled in occupied France to commence training. The German SS instructors, however, could not bring themselves to regard these recruits as 'Aryan' by any stretch of the imagination, and treated them so harshly that they mutinied, killing several of the training staff. The division was not disbanded until 1944, by which time it had been named the 'Handschar' division by Himmler; although enthusiastic when committing atrocities against Serb civilians, the formation performed poorly in combat. Indeed, most of the Waffen-SS formations raised in eastern Europe (with the exception of those raised in the Baltic States) had mediocre battlefield records.[31]

New recruits to Sennheim SS-Ausbildungslager were typically 'welcomed' at the small railway station by NCO instructors, who usually left them in no doubts as to the strict discipline to which they were now subject. Recruits were then marched towards the camp. The main entrance was between two three-storey houses, before which two flags were flying; one was the swastika banner of Nazi Germany, the other was a black flag which carried the silver siegrunes of the SS. The house on the right was a security post, in which were based an NCO and three men of No. 9 Company. This was the Wachcompanie, the permanent unit responsible for camp security and honour guards, at this time commanded by SS-Hauptsturmführer 'Papa' Krone. The house on the left was the resident of the camp commandant, SS-Oberführer Ernst Fick. Born in 1898, Fick served in the German Army during the First World War. He joined the Nazi party in 1928 and was an early member of the SS, receiving the SS number 2853. He became a fervent exponent of Nazi ideology, and served as an instructor in this pseudo-science at the Waffen-SS officer schools at Bad Tolz and Braunschweig. From May to August 1941, he served with the artillery regiment of the SS-Wiking Division, which was comprised partly of non-German volunteers. While one source claims that he spent most of this period (during which this division was heavily involved in the invasion of Russia) as the commander of an artillery battalion, another claims that he was in fact the division's 'ideological observer', a non-combatant role. Either way, Fick evidently incurred the contempt of the artillery regiment's commander, SS-Standartenführer Gille, who contemptuously informed him that he would not have 'a brown shirt' in his command, a particularly insulting remark for an SS officer. Gille, who later rose to high rank in the Waffen-SS, was known to be an officer who cared little for Nazi 'ideology'. Whatever the truth of the matter, Fick's frontline career was not a lengthy one and he was named commandant of SS-Ausbildungslager Sennheim in June 1942. In January 1944, he was named 'inspector of ideological instruction' for the whole Waffen-SS.[32]

Sennheim camp was located in picturesque surroundings, at the foot of the 1,000-metre Hartmannkeilerkopf mountain. Before the war it was the St-Andre psychiatric institute, and comprised a number of permanent buildings spread over a large area, ideal for a military camp. This area was the site of fierce fighting during the First World War, and there were large French and German military cemeteries in the vicinity. After its acquisition by the Waffen-SS as a training facility for foreign volunteers, several changes were made in the camp, notably to the institute's Catholic chapel. Although the pews remained, the altar and all religious statues were removed, and the chapel was converted for use as an assembly hall, where training and propaganda films were screened on occasion. Sometimes ceremonies were convened here; on such occasions, the former altar was draped in the flags of the SS and Nazi Germany, and on either side, instead of the religious statues that formerly stood there, two armed and uniformed Waffen-SS soldiers stood instead.

Recruits arriving late in the day were usually registered at the administration block before being provided with their accommodation. Although the original recruits were usually housed in the camp buildings, by 1943 the large numbers of foreign recruits were usually billeted in large prefabricated wooden huts imported from occupied Yugoslavia. Brady and Stringer's hut mates represented several nationalities; by 1943 Sennheim was training hundreds of recruits from France, Belgium, Denmark, Switzerland and Sweden. New recruits were provided with bunk beds with blue and white sheets and brown blankets. Each recruit also had a chair, and large tables were also provided. Two recruits shared a large locker between them, which it was forbidden to lock. This was a standard Waffen-SS practice, intended to instil trust and camaraderie among its members. The crime of 'kamaradendiebstahl' (theft from a comrade) was considered a particularly heinous offence and was ruthlessly punished; this crime accounted for half of all prosecutions carried out by the SS internal judicial system in late 1943. One recruit at Sennheim at this time who stole a cigarette lighter from a colleague received a beating from his entire company, after which he was banished to the camp's cell block. During the short time the thief spent there, he was forced to eat from a rusty plate on all fours like an animal. He then disappeared from the camp. His most likely fate was a penal institution for SS members, the most notorious of which was Danzig-Marzgau in occupied Poland.

Brady and Stringer received their new uniforms soon after arrival. These were of the same 'feldgrau' colour as that worn by the German Army. The trousers were straight legged and high waisted, and supported by a belt; the tunic was belted at the waist and featured four large pockets. Both trousers and tunic were made of a mixture of wool and rayon, but due to wartime shortages the proportion of wool in Waffen-SS uniforms manufactured in 1943 was much smaller, reducing warmth and durability. Waffen-SS uniforms were in fact manufactured in concentration camps, clothing seized from victims being reprocessed and dyed for this purpose.

Boots were a very practical thick-soled ankle boot (called shnurschuhe) based on mountain boots, usually worn with canvas gaiters. Their introduction in 1942 was in fact resented by older troops, who preferred the jackboots (marchstiefel) that they replaced, despite the fact that these high boots, like the British Army puttees that Brady and Stringer wore in 1939, were often the cause of varicose veins in later life. Headgear was a feldmutze, a sidecap similar to that worn by most armies, known to the Waffen-SS as a schiffchen (little ship) due to its resemblance to an upturned boat. The uniform was completed by a koppel, a 42mm wide black waist belt, with a square metal buckle. At a glance, the uniform did not differ greatly from that worn by most armies. But Brady and Stringer's new uniforms carried some very distinctive insignia. The Nazi symbol of an eagle clutching a swastika was worn on the left arm, as opposed to being worn on the chest by the Wehrmacht. A different version of the eagle and swastika motif was embossed on the belt buckle, along with the motto of the SS: 'Meine Ehre Heisst Treue' (My Honour is Loyalty). Both the buckle and the motto were said to be the personal design of Adolf Hitler. On the front of the 'schieffchen' was another cloth eagle and swastika, over a cloth version of the SS death's head motif, the only symbol worn by all branches of the SS organisation.

On their right collar Brady and Stringer wore the symbol most commonly associated with the SS, the siegrunen. Resembling a double-lightening bolt, this was actually the Germanic runic symbol of victory. Until 1943, this collar badge was jealously reserved for the German units of the Waffen-SS, most foreign units wearing a variety of other collar badges, but after the Waffen-SS's virtual abandonment of racial standards in 1943, almost all foreign volunteers at Sennheim wore the siegrune on their collar.

Brady and Stringer were issued rifles far earlier than
was the case in the British Army. The standard rifle of the
Waffen-SS in 1943 was the accurate and reliable Mauser
KAR 98, a bolt-action 7.92mm rifle that compared favourably with the British Army's Lee-Enfield. These rifles were
most likely constructed by skilled workers in a concentration
camp, a death sentence mandatory for any prisoner attempting an act of sabotage. Combat equipment was also issued
at an early stage. In keeping with the 'stormtrooper' ethos of
the Waffen-SS, a minimum of equipment was carried in battle. The classic German stahlhelm (steel helmet), also painted
with the SS runes, was always worn during combat training.

The waistbelt was worn with leather ammunition pouches
and adjustable leather 'Y' straps which passed from the back
of the belt over the shoulders. Also worn on the belt were
mess kit (an aluminium plate and small pot), water bottle,
bayonet, entrenching tool and a canvas 'bread bag' which
could carry rations or grenades. Some flexibility was allowed
in deciding which items would be carried, but the gas mask
in its steel or aluminium cylindrical case was mandatory. This
case was often used to keep cigarettes dry. Also issued, but not
worn in combat, was the M39 pack, a square canvas backpack
which contained such items as rifle cleaning kit, wash kit,
rations and spare clothing. Worn on a cord around the neck,
Waffen-SS members carried a zinc identity disc on which
was engraved their SS number, unit and blood group.[33]

Brady and Stringer, beginning recruit training for the second
time in their lives, would soon notice many differences
between the regime at SS-Ausbildungslager Sennheim and
the British Army's training depot at Borden Camp. Brady
and Stringer were not in fact the only British soldiers serving
in the ranks of the Waffen-SS. The SS Leibstandarte division
was deployed in Italy after the fall of Mussolini, and in
the course of its duties there captured two escaped Allied
POWs; an Englishmen, Corporal James Conen, and a South

African, Corporal William Celliers. Both were persuaded
to stay with the Leibstandarte and were attached to the
division's anti-aircraft detachment as drivers. Both fought in
Russia throughout the hellish winter of 1943–4, winning the
Iron Cross second class. In March 1944 the Leibstandarte
(reduced to forty-one officers and 2,000 men) was withdrawn
to France to face the forthcoming invasion by the western
Allies. Since it was usually Waffen-SS policy not to deploy
its western volunteers on the western front (there were some
exceptions), the pair were withdrawn and invited to join the
'British Free Corps'. This was undoubtedly the most farcical
attempt by the Waffen-SS to recruit foreign volunteers, in this
case from the thousands of British POWs in German camps.
At no time did the 'corps' even achieve platoon strength,
and never saw combat. Conen and Celliers refused to join,
and apparently returned to a POW camp. Neither man was
punished after the war.[34]

For the typical recruit at Sennheim in 1943, the very first
lesson in military training involved crawling across open
ground on bellies and elbows. As opposed to Borden Camp
in 1939, 'square-bashing' assumed a much lower priority to
physical training and learning combat skills. In 1942, the
deficiencies in British Army combat training was addressed
with the introduction of battle schools, where trainees were
put through intensive simulated battlefield conditions which
involved the use of live ammunition and pyrotechnics.

Instruction was invariably in German, with a German-
speaking recruit translating for his compatriots whenever
possible. The training staff at Sennheim were almost invariably German, with the odd Dutchman. Although the French
in particular were surprised to find themselves being taught
by such junior ranks as SS-Sturmann and SS-Rottenführer,
the trainees at Sennheim were required to salute all instructors, regardless of rank, with the straight-armed Nazi salute.
The young Waffen-SS instructors were invariably combat
veterans, most of them invalided out of frontline duties. Not

a few were amputees; both the commanding officer and senior NCO of the 6th Company had each lost a leg in the service of the Reich.

The man-management techniques used by each NCO would depend on which Waffen-SS division he had served with; while former members of the Leibstandarte tended to use methods suited to training combat soldiers, recruits would quail at the sight of a former member of the 'Totenkopf', who was more likely to use 'management skills' influenced by his pre-war employment as a concentration camp guard.[35]

The daily routine at Sennheim began at 7 a.m. when the steel-helmeted 'Unterführer vom Dienst' (duty NCO) for each barracks stood outside the huts and signalled 'reveille' with a blast of a whistle. He then threw open the doors of each hut and any recruit not already in the act of getting dressed could expect trouble. Bare-chested, the recruits trooped to the washrooms: although these were well equipped with sinks and mirrors, only cold water was provided. One recruit from each hut ran to the dining hall and returned with 'breakfast'. This was usually a container of *ersatzcaffee,* a bitter tasting 'coffee substitute' usually made from crushed acorns. Any recruit who did not keep a piece of bread from the previous evening could expect to go hungry until midday.

At 8 a.m. the morning PT session would begin, which usually consisted of a fast run of five to seven kilometres outside the camp. On their return the recruits changed into their uniforms without delay (or a shower) to begin the day's training programme. This began with a classroom lesson in the German language or 'ideological instruction'. Otherwise, the recruits spent the morning running or crawling on tactical training and fieldcraft, or on the firing ranges training with the Mauser K98 rifle or the MG34 machine gun. This latter weapon introduced the concept of a belt-fed machine that could be used both at section level and as a heavier support weapon with minor conversion. In service in large numbers, it was eventually supplemented, but never replaced, by the improved MG42. Long hours were also spent learning to throw the distinctively shaped stick grenade with precision.

Between 11.30 a.m. and noon the recruits assembled for the main meal of the day. The NCOs first checked each man's hands to ensure they were clean and the fingernails properly trimmed. Any infringements to these requirements resulted in the whole company being punished together. The dining hall at Sennheim was well equipped with the most up-to-date equipment, including an automatic potato peeling machine which no doubt would have been a most welcome innovation in the British Army of the time. The fare, however, was, to say the least, spartan. The midday meal was usually a small bowl of meat and potatoes of sometimes dubious quality or a pint of soup. At a separate table, the NCOs, and sometimes an officer or two, partook of the same meal. If the recruits were spending the day on exercises in the mountains near the camp, pea soup was served to them on the ground.

After the half-hour designated for dinner, training continued. This was likely to involve a route march outside the camp in full kit, the distance of which increased daily until, by the final phases of training, the recruits were marching sixty kilometres. Alternatively, the foreign recruits spent the afternoon involved in sports. Athletics assumed a high priority in Waffen-SS training; all recruits at Sennheim were issued with a full set of sports gear on enlistment, the singlet bearing the SS runes. At Sennheim, the emphasis was placed on track and field sports rather than the ball sports which were more popular with the British Army. Ten-kilometre runs were commonplace, as were two-kilometre runs with ten men carrying a heavy log. An outdoor swimming pool was situated in the camp, and during the colder time of year an indoor pool in nearby Mulhouse was available.

At 6 p.m. the evening meal was eaten in the billets. This consisted of bread and water, the former consisting of 700 grammes of black bread. It was advisable to keep a piece of this for breakfast the following morning. 'Substitute sausage' and 'substitute honey' were sometimes available, examples of the synthetic alternatives to the actual foodstuff produced in wartime Germany. A daily ration of two cigarettes per man was also issued.

Night exercises were frequent, but at their termination the recruits returned to sleep in their billets rather than bivouac on the ground. Otherwise the four remaining hours of the day were used for cleaning and maintaining uniforms and equipment. There was a compulsory shower for each man in the evening, hot water only provided once a week. Although no luxuries such as radio were provided, propaganda films were sometimes screened in the camp's old chapel in the evening. The SS were acutely aware of the value of such a medium for indoctrinating trainees; the exceptionally anti-Semitic motion picture *Jud Suss* was often shown to SS units before attacks on Jews in occupied Europe. In fact, one of the films shown in Sennheim was *Mein Leben fur Irland*, one of a small number of Nazi propaganda films depicting Irish rebels of remarkably Teutonic appearance and disposition.

At night, sentries patrolled the camp perimeter, accompanied by German Shepherd guard dogs. At 10 p.m. a bugler signalled 'lights out' at which the duty NCO of each barracks gave a whistle blast. At this signal, each recruit immediately got into bed. [36]

At first glance, the training regime at Sennheim would not appear to be altogether different from that used by the elite units of most other armies. However, Brady and Stringer would have noticed many differences between Borden Camp in 1939 and Sennheim SS-Ausbildungslager in 1943. The draconian disciplinary code of the Waffen-SS cut a stark contrast with that of the British Army. This was amply illustrated when two of the French volunteers, when outside the camp on local leave, stole two geese to supplement their meagre rations. They were cooked on the stove in their hut and were greatly enjoyed by the hut's residents. The practice of 'scrounging' creature comforts, particularly for the benefit of comrades, was a time-honoured tradition of the British Army. It was not always condoned by the British military authorities, but it was doubtful that they would have meted out the kind of punishment that was handed down to the main transgressors. Having been convicted by a locally-convened court of inquiry, the two thieves were banished to Danzig-Marzgau, the notorious penal institute reserved for members of the SS. After a period of incarceration, the offenders were 'offered' the opportunity to redeem themselves by service in what were effectively suicide squads, popularly known to the Germans as *himmelfahrtskommando* (ascension commands). The 'luckier' of these personnel were admitted for service with SS-Fallschirmjager Battailon 500, a paratroop unit which would be wiped out almost to a man in May 1944. The less fortunate were likely to find themselves serving under the command of Oskar Dirlewanger. By late 1943, it was estimated that of the 500 men of Dirlewanger's SS Sonderkommando, 15 per cent were SS penal troops while another 30 per cent were Ukrainian or Russians.

Minor infringements of discipline were dealt with on the spot by press-ups or chin-ups. While any recruit in the British Army foolhardy enough to insult an officer was undoubtedly severely punished, recruits in Sennheim were warned that such an offence merited summary execution on the spot. Given the punishments awarded for such other offences as theft, the threat was naturally taken seriously by the trainees. While a prison block of a dozen cells with steel doors existed in the camp, they were, unsurprisingly, rarely occupied.[37]

Another major difference between Sennheim in 1943 and Borden Camp in 1939 that Brady and Stringer would have noticed was the different relationship between officers and men. It was difficult to obtain a commission in the Waffen-SS. One result of this was the Waffen-SS maintaining the classic 'one officer to twenty men' ratio that was the hallmark of many of history's most successful fighting forces, from the legions of Rome to the Israeli Defence Forces. In 1934, the Waffen-SS founded its own officer training academies (SS-Junkerschule) at Bad Tolz and Brunswick which by 1943 admitted some foreign officer candidates. These were founded by SS-Oberstgruppenführer Paul Hausser, who was a general in the very select officer corps of the pre-war Reichswehr. A Waffen-SS officer candidate had to serve a minimum of eighteen months in the ranks before being eligible for Junkerschule. This meant that most wartime candidates were extremely experienced combat veterans even before officer training. The Waffen-SS officer corps set less store by social status and educational background than the German Army, with the result that men from working-class backgrounds could aspire to higher rank than was possible in the army. Joseph 'Sepp' Dietrich, the semi-literate and illegitimate son of a butcher, rose in rank to SS-Oberstgruppenführer by the end of the war, the equivalent of a Wehrmacht Colonel-General. Kurt Meyer, the illegitimate son of a sergeant-major, rose to become an SS-Brigadeführer (Major-General) at the age of thirty-four, commanding the 12th SS Panzer division in Normandy in June 1944.

One of Hausser's innovations that distinguished the Waffen-SS from most other armies was his intent to foster a closer relationship between officers and their men. Even when training recruits, it was not unknown for officers to actively participate to the extent of crawling through muddy fields with their men. The prefix 'Herr', compulsory in the Wehrmacht, was not used when addressing a Waffen-SS officer, the officer being addressed by his rank only. In turn, officers commonly referred to their men as 'the comrades'. Waffen-SS officers were expected to lead from the front. By 1942, almost all of the first fifty-four SS officer cadets to graduate from Bad Tolz SS-Junkerschule in 1934 had been killed in action. By 1944, the average frontline Waffen-SS officer had a life expectancy of two months.[38]

By contrast, in the British Army of 1939 there was little contact between officers and men. Such a distinction was seen as essential to maintenance of discipline. Young officers graduated from the elite Sandhurst officer academy, and in 1939, 85 per cent of the cadets there would have come from a privileged public school background. Brady and Stringer would not have witnessed the fact that, elitist though this system was in peacetime, it still produced genuine leaders of men in wartime. After the outbreak of war, most new British officers were trained by Officer Cadet Training Units, service in the ranks being a mandatory condition of entry.

Also unheard of in the British Army was the weekly session of 'political instruction' in Nazi beliefs. This was a classroom lesson utilising slides and other 'educational' materials and was usually conducted by the elderly SS-Untersturmführer Binder, although SS-Oberführer Fick might give a lesson on occasion. This involved the tenets of 'national socialism', and the Nazi views of communism, capitalism and Zionism. Recruits were also taught racial theory, such as facial characteristics of the 'Aryan' race and its subdivisions into such ethnic groups as 'nordic' and 'westphalian'. While Nazi propagandists in occupied Europe might have paid lip service to such concepts as a united European federation, Waffen-SS recruits in Sennheim were taught only of a Greater German Empire.[39]

Three weeks after their arrival at Sennheim, Brady and Stringer were tattooed under their left armpit with their blood group, an 'A' in both cases with no quantifier. Although this served a practical purpose on the battlefield, enabling medial staff to quickly establish the blood group of a wounded soldier, it was also said to brand the wearer as a member of the SS. In the Waffen-SS, the tattoo was sometimes referred to as the 'schussel zu Walhalla' (key to Valhalla) in a reference to the likely fate of its wearer.

At Sennheim, the tattooing of the blood group was invariably preceded by another ceremony: the swearing of the SS

oath of allegiance. This was typically with a hand placed on a
junior officer's sword rather than on a bible. All wearing steel
helmets, the young SS officer held his sword in front of him
while four recruits each placed their left hand on the blade,
their right hand upraised. All four then recited the oath. The
standard oath taken by foreign volunteers to the Waffen-SS
was as follows, although this was subject to some variations,
especially in the case of some foreign contingents:

> *Ich schwöre Dir, Adolf Hitler, als germanischer Führer Treue und*
> *Tapferkeit. Ich gelobe Dir und den von Dir bestimmten Vorgesetzen*
> *Gehorsam bis den Tod, so wahr mir Gott helfe.*
> (I swear to you, Adolf Hitler, as Leader of Germany, loyalty,
> and bravery. I vow to you, and to those you have named to
> command me, obedience unto death, so help me God.)[40]

The Waffen-SS set great store by this oath, so much so that
foreign recruits with inadequate German could swear it in
their native language. Brady and Stringer's narratives, which
suggest that at this time they spoke passable German, omit
their taking of the oath although they could not deny the
blood group tattoo. While there are few obvious untruths
in the account that they gave to the British Army after the
war, there are a few glaring omissions of details that both
obviously felt might incriminate them further.

What brought two young Irishmen to swear an oath of allegiance to Adolf Hitler? At Brady's postwar trial, his defence
counsel would make the point that 'he was a man who at
that stage had been behind the German lines for more than a
couple of years and subjected during the whole of that period
to German influence.' Brady and Stringer had indeed been
'guests of the Reich' in various capacities; the Nazi media
would not after all have given great coverage to the atrocities
committed by the SS.[41]

There were certain aspects of the regime at SS-Ausbil-
dunger Sennheim that would not have been without appeal
to the two young Irishmen. Rather than 'SS-Schutze', the

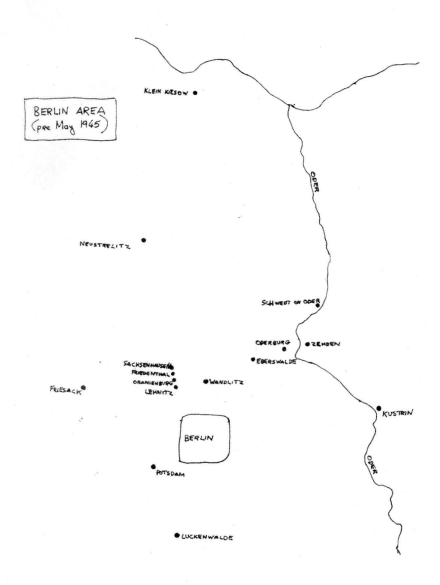

Sketch map of the Berlin area.

The prison compound within Sachsenhausen concentration camp, where Lt-Col John McGrath was incarcerated in 1942.

The interior of the Sachsenhausen concentration camp.

Berdjansk in Russia, where Brady and Stringer spent August 1943 on a radio training mission. Detail taken from a contemporary Wehrmacht map.

Skorzeny and Hitler, taken shortly after the rescue of Italian dictator Mussolini from his mountain-top prison.

John O'Reilly's passport photo, issued at the Irish legation in Berlin.
Image courtesy of the Irish Military Archives.

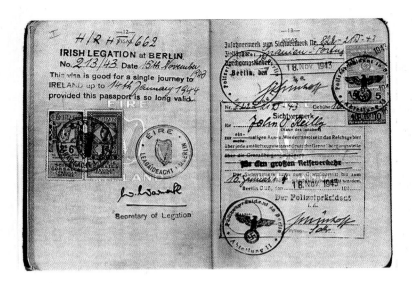

John O'Reilly's passport, displaying an entry visa for Ireland and an exit visa from Germany. Since an Irish passport holder did not require a visa to return to his own country, this was a very obvious forgery. Image courtesy of the Irish Military Archives.

September 1943. Members of SS-Jager Battailon 502 at their base in Friedenthal, shortly before the rescue of Mussolini (Bundesarchiv Bild101 III- Alber-183-19).

October 1943. Officers and NCOs of SS-Jager Battailon 502 who had been involved in the rescue of Mussolini. On the right is SS-Obersturmführer Ulrich Menzel, who recruited Brady and Stringer to the battalion in March 1944 (note the cane – Menzel had broken his ankle when his glider crash landed on the mountain). Second from the right is SS-Untersturmführer Otto Schwerdt who later organised terrorist attacks in occupied Denmark. Fifth from the right is SS-Hauptscharführer Manns; later commissioned, he was Brady's company commander at Budapest and Stringer's at the Zehden bridgehead, where he was killed in March 1945 (Bundesarchiv Bild 183-JO7989).

21 July 1944. Skorzeny walking through the inner courtyard of the German army headquarters in the Bendlerstrasse, where Colonel von Stauffenberg and his colleagues had been put to death the previous night. The Waffen-SS troops in the background are almost certainly members of SS-Jager Battailon 502 (Bundesarchiv Bild 146-1972-109-18A).

Budapest, 16 October 1943, following the successful conclusion of Operation Panzer-faust. Facing the camera are SS-Sturmbannführer Skorzeny, SS-Hauptsturmführer Adrian von Foelkersam and SS-Obersturmführer Walter Girg, all holders of the Knight's Cross and officers of the newly constituted Jagdverband Mitte battalion. Girg had been Brady's unit commander in Romania for Operation Landfried the previous August (Bundesarchiv Bild 101 I - 680- 8283A - 30A).

February 1945, during the fierce fighting at Grabow near Schwedt-on-Oder. Sko-rzeny (by now an SS-Obersturmbannführer) consults with the interestingly-named SS-Hauptsturmführer Karl Fucker, battalion commander of Jagdverband Mitte since October 1944 (Bundesarchiv Bild 183- R81453).

Grabow, February 1945. SS-Hauptsturmführer Fucker again, on the right with his arm outstretched.

1960. Skorzeny (on the right) working on his Kildare farm with a local man. Photo courtesy of Michael Sheehan.

standard Waffen-SS rank equivalent to a private soldier, the foreign recruits at Sennheim were given the title of 'SS-Freiwillige' (Volunteer.) Such a title had deep Irish nationalist connotations. In 1913, the Irish Volunteer armed militia movement was founded by Irish constitutional nationalists to counter a similar body set up by Ulster unionists, and was infiltrated by Irish republicans and used to fight the Easter Rising in 1916. The Volunteers provided the backbone of the Irish Republican Army (IRA) that fought the Irish War of Independence in 1919–21, and of the Free State Army established in 1922. In all these bodies the rank equivalent of private soldier was 'Volunteer'. Such was the appeal of the term 'Volunteer' that in 1934 the Fianna Fáil government established the part-time Volunteer Force to entice Irish republicans to the ranks of the Irish defence forces.

After the war, Frank Stringer claimed that: 'In 1943, I and other Irishmen [*sic*] were asked if we would join the German Army [*sic*]. At this time the war with Russia was being fought and being a Catholic I hate the Russians so I joined the German Army in order to fight them.' There was a certain amount of truth in this; hatred of communism was endemic in Catholic Ireland. When James Gralton, a member of the tiny Communist Party of Ireland, built a social hall in Stringer's native Leitrim in 1921, local Catholic priests denounced him as an 'anti-Christ' and warned that any local horses hauling materials to the site would die within the year. Having been arrested twice by government forces and accused by Redemptorist missionaries of forming a communist cell, Gralton emigrated to the United States. On his return in 1930 he re-opened the hall and was again denounced by local Catholic clergy as a 'communist anti-Christ and Russian agent'. Even the local IRA became involved, attacking the hall with gunfire and explosives and eventually destroying it. In 1933 Gralton was deported by the state without trial.[42]

There were several examples of the evils of communism to be seen at Sennheim, not least a unit of Estonian youths.

These had been orphaned during the brutal Soviet occupation of their country from 1940 to 1941, a regime so harsh
that the Estonians had welcomed the invading Germans as
liberators. The young Estonians were subject to a regime similar to that of the German teenagers in the 'HitlerJugend' SS
Division; for example, instead of alcohol and cigarettes, the
youngsters received an increased sweet ration. There was also
a contingent of Ukranians, chaplains to the newly formed
Ukrainian SS Division. As evidenced by the use of the former
Catholic chapel in Sennheim, the attitude of the Waffen-SS
to religion could be ambiguous. Although the standard sold-
buch (paybook) issued to each Waffen-SS soldier included a
space to specify their preferred religion, the most preferable
specification was 'Gottglaubekeit', a belief in God without
membership of an established church. Although Himmler,
a fervent Catholic in his youth, used so many Jesuit-inspired
principles in the foundation of the SS that Hitler referred
to him as 'my Ignatius Loyola' (the Jesuits' founder), he was
virulently anti-Church and avowedly wished to eventually
establish the SS as 'a Pagan order'.

Despite official discouragement, however, it is estimated
that half of even the original Waffen-SS members were regular churchgoers, apparently further proof of the old adage that
'there are no atheists in foxholes'. Himmler steadfastly refused
to allow chaplains in the Waffen-SS, until a precedent was
set by the establishment of the 'Handschar' divison of Bosnian Muslims, which included a complement of Imams. In
mid-1943 permission was given to seek Waffen-SS recruits
in occupied Ukraine, 70,000 volunteers coming forward. Although the Nazi occupation of this region was harsh, it did
not remotely compare to the brutality of the Soviet regime,
which deliberately engineered a famine in 1932–3 as a result
of which at least three *million* Ukrainians died. It was decided
to raise a 'Galician' division (the 14th Waffen-Grenadier Division der SS) with a strength of 14,000. Since the new volunteers were predominately Catholic, Himmler found himself

obliged to authorise chaplains for the new division. About twenty of the Ukrainian chaplains reported to Sennheim for their military training in August 1943. They were billeted in a separate barracks, two to a room, and received a full issue of combat equipment, including steel helmet and gas mask, but no weapon. They participated in physical training, including the morning runs with the other foreign recruits. Their course of military training required them to navigate with map and compass, and to identify both German and Soviet military equipment, apparently impressing their German instructors by their already acquired knowledge of the latter. SS-Oberführer Fick, however, was not altogether keen on the Ukrainian priests; shortly after their arrival he assembled the group and issued a denunciation of Pope Pius XIII for his alleged role in the overthrow of Mussolini. Apart from a few who were too elderly to complete their course of training, the chaplains joined the 'Galician Division' in November 1943. In mid-June 1944 the new division was nearly annihilated near Brody, less than 3,000 personnel surviving. At least two of the chaplains were killed in action while another finished up in a Soviet prison camp.[43]

Basic training at Sennheim lasted for seven weeks. After this the foreign volunteers were allowed a few privileges. Limited access was allowed to the camp library, situated near the cell block, for personnel who wished to improve their German. Normally the library was reserved for the use of officer and NCO instructors preparing lessons. On Saturdays, 'comradeship evenings' were sometimes organised, in which NCOs and men would share small amounts of alcohol and cigarettes.

Sunday passes were sometimes issued which allowed the volunteers to visit the local towns of Thann and Mulhausen (Mulhouse); in early 1941, local citizens were welcoming and such luxuries as pastries were freely available, but such delights were increasingly rare by late 1943. Those hoping to leave the camp on pass had to submit to a rigorous uniform inspection beforehand, and often walked five miles to avail of a glass or two of wine in a relaxed atmosphere at a local inn that might have been noticed on a route march during the week. Those hoping for female companionship had to walk even further. One young volunteer at the camp ruefully noted that it was near impossible for a private soldier to catch a female eye, in view of the competition posed by heavily decorated NCOs! Despite these constraints, however, Frank Stringer was able to acquire a girlfriend in nearby Mulhausen (Mulhouse) who John Codd would later claim was an Irishwoman. By now Brady and Stringer were being paid ten marks a week, supplemented by occasional 'pocket money' from Kurt Haller. Haller continued to keep in touch with the two Irishmen until he was posted to Hungary in early 1944, as aide to SS-Brigadeführer Edmund Veesenmayer who was appointed German ambassador there.[44]

In October 1943, a dark green BMW limousine appeared at the gates of Sennheim, bearing a very distinctive number plate: 'SS 1'. Reichsführer-SS Heinrich Himmler was paying a visit.

Himmler's visit to Sennheim came shortly after his infamous speech to several senior SS officers at Posen in occupied Poland, on 4 October 1943. This three-hour speech was recorded on magnetic tape, and a transcript was presented as evidence at the postwar Nuremberg trials. During the course of Himmler's long monologue, he made several damning statements regarding Nazi racial policy:

> One basic principle must be the absolute rule for the SS man: we must be honest, decent, loyal, and comradely to members of our own blood and to nobody else. What happens to a Russian, to a Czech, does not interest me in the slightest. What the nations can offer in good blood of our type, we will take, if necessary by kidnapping their children and raising them with us. Whether nations live in prosperity or starve to death interests me only in so far as we need them as slaves for our culture; otherwise, it is of no interest to me. Whether 10,000 Russian females fall down from exhaustion while digging an anti-tank ditch interest me

only in so far as the anti-tank ditch for Germany is finished.

We shall never be rough and heartless when it is not necessary, that is clear. We Germans, who are the only people in the world who have a decent attitude towards animals, will also assume a decent attitude towards these human animals.

But it is a crime against our own blood to worry about them and give them ideals, thus causing our sons and grandsons to have a more difficult time with them. When someone comes to me and says, 'I cannot dig the anti-tank ditch with women and children, it is inhuman, for it will kill them', then I would have to say, 'you are a murderer of your own blood because if the anti-tank ditch is not dug, German soldiers will die, and they are the sons of German mothers. They are our own blood'

Later, Himmler added:

I also want to refer here very frankly to a very difficult matter. We can now very openly talk about this among ourselves, and yet we will never discuss this publicly. Just as we did not hesitate on June 30, 1934, to perform our duty as ordered and put comrades who had failed up against the wall and execute them, we also never spoke about it, nor will we ever speak about it. Let us thank God that we had within us enough self-evident fortitude never to discuss it among us, and we never talked about it. Every one of us was horrified, and yet every one clearly understood that we would do it next time, when the order is given and when it becomes necessary.

I am now referring to the evacuation of the Jews, to the extermination of the Jewish people. This is something that is easily said: 'The Jewish people will be exterminated,' says every Party member, 'this is very obvious, it is in our program – elimination of the Jews, extermination, will do'. And then they turn up, the brave 80 million Germans, and each one has his decent Jew. It is of course obvious that the others are pigs, but this particular one is a splendid Jew. But of all those who talk this way, none had observed it, none had endured it. Most of you here know what it means when 100 corpses lie next to each other, when 500 lie there or when 1,000 are lined up. To have endured this and at the same time to have remained a decent person – with exceptions due to human weaknesses – had made us tough. This is an honour roll in our history which has never been and never will be put in writing, because we know how difficult it would

be for us if we had Jews as secret saboteurs, agitators and rabble
rousers in every city, what with the bombings, with the burden
and with the hardships of the war. If the Jews were still part of
the German nation, we would most likely arrive now at the state
we were at in 1916/17.[45]

Himmler did not repeat such sentiments at Sennheim; such
comments were only for the highest ranking members of the
SS, not for its footsoldiers. Himmler's visit was a short one;
after a review of the troops and watching an athletics contest,
he left.

In November, snow began to fall across the Black Forest
and Alsace-Lorraine. Training, particularly route marches,
continued regardless. In the final phases of training, the recruits could expect to be roused from their beds at all hours
of the night, given two minutes to dress in uniform and
combat equipment and spend hours running and crawling
through the snow on night exercises. The volunteers at Sennheim could expect much worse conditions in Russia, where
most of them were destined to serve, without the benefit of a
warm billet to return to.

Brady and Stringer spent several wartime Christmases
together, but surely few were as strange as 'Christmas' in
Sennheim in the winter of 1943. Rather than celebrating
the Christian feast of Christmas, the Waffen-SS personnel
in Sennheim were expected to observe the pagan festival of
'Julfest' on 21 December, the winter solstice. Mess halls were
decorated with flags and foliage, and recruits received small
gifts such as books with a dedication by the camp commandant. An unusually fine dinner was served, with dessert. There
was a genuine attempt to create a festive occasion in line with
the Waffen-SS proverb 'dienst ist dienst, schnaps ist schaps'
(duty is duty, schnaps is schnaps.) Although schnaps were not
in abundance, there was a good supply of red wine. Many of
the young soldiers in Sennheim celebrating 'Julfest' in 1943
would not live to celebrate another.[46]

Back in Berlin, shortly after Brady and Stringer's departure for Sennheim, SS-Hauptsturmführer Giese invited John Codd to a meeting at Adolf Hitler Platz, where he was introduced to John O'Reilly. Codd initially formed a good impression of his compatriot, later informing Giese that he would be happy to work with O'Reilly when the German mentioned the possibility of both men landing by submarine in Ireland before Christmas. The feeling was not mutual; O'Reilly was suspicious of Codd's claims to have been a member of the IRA who had infiltrated the British Army and informed the SD that he was not willing to work with him.[47]

Considering an alternative companion for O'Reilly on his forthcoming mission, another Irishman seemed to present an ideal candidate. From Kerry, where he joined the IRA, John Kenny had moved to London in 1937 and worked in a radio station near London, claiming to have picked up a knowledge of radio technology. He left for Jersey in a hurry in 1940, three weeks before the German invasion. Having offered to join the Wehrmacht, he worked for the German occupiers first as a waiter and later as a driver for a German officer, this duty taking him around occupied Europe.

Shortly after his unsuccessful introduction to John Codd, John O'Reilly, accompanied by a 'Gestapo officer', according to Kenny, arrived in Jersey and made enquiries about Kenny at the 'local Gestapo office'. There was not actually a Gestapo detachment on the island, although there was a unit of the Geheime Feldpolizei, its military counterpart. O'Reilly approached Kenny and made an offer of work in Germany. 'O'Reilly told him that the work was connected with the German SS … and that he would be home in Ireland before Christmas.' Kenny assented and accompanied O'Reilly back to Berlin; he was brought to the headquarters of RSHA VI at Berkaerstrasse, where he first met SS-Hauptsturmführer Giese. Kenny subsequently referred to him as 'Oberleutnant Geeser', which says nothing for his powers of observation, given the fact that he had worked for the German armed forces for over three years. Although the SS had their own rank structure, SS officers wore the same epaulettes as their army counterparts, and Giese's rank equivalent was Hauptmann (captain). Kenny claimed the officer who he had recently acted as driver for was also an 'Oberleutnant', a dubiously junior rank for an officer who was allegedly responsible for the defensive works of northern France. Having been issued with ration coupons by Giese (who also paid him at the rate of 450 marks per month), Kenny was booked into the Hotel Roxy where he stayed for three weeks. Although he received occasional visits from O'Reilly, who informed Kenny that he would soon be undertaking radio training, he found the hotel's other occupiers, Waffen-SS on home leave, 'unfriendly' and moved to a flat in Leibnitzstrasse. Shortly afterwards, he began training at the SS radio school in Lehnitz. He worked in a class which, although comprising only a dozen people, boasted such diverse nationalities as Norwegian, French, Belgian and Turkish. His training concentrated on 'the technical side of radio work, repairs to radio sets, aerial erection etc'. He was not taught how to transmit or receive messages, this apparently being O'Reilly's responsibility.

Kenny met another Irishman at Lehnitz, a man named 'John Collins', whom 'Kenny understood … was being trained as an agent in the same way as himself and O'Reilly'. This was of course the name that John Codd was using while he attended Lehnitz himself. Codd evidently talked quite freely about himself to Kenny, who later recalled: 'This man, Collins, was married to a German girl from Mannheim and has a child who would now be from 12 to 18 months old. Collins was living in a flat in Berlin … Kenny understood that Collins was born in Leix but had left Ireland when he was very young. He was much travelled and had spent some time in China and in America[48] … Kenny gathered that Collins had served in the British army and had been captured at Dunkirk'. By now, Codd spoke French and German 'fairly fluently'.

Codd, however, could never resist exaggerating his own importance: 'Prior to the war he was a middle-weight boxer and told Kenny that arrangements had been made which later fell through for him to fight for the middle-weight championship of the world in America.' He also untruthfully claimed to have managed a restaurant in London before the war.

Of limited intelligence and education, Kenny was soon struggling with his radio training. 'All of the class with the exception of himself were well advanced and the teachers seemed to pay little attention to him … He could not clearly follow and memorise what he was being taught.' Although he complained to O'Reilly, a regular visitor to Lehnitz where he was doing 'transmission test work', he found him 'unsatisfactory to speak to'. Later, O'Reilly stated that 'almost from the outset Kenny was a disappointment. He couldn't grasp what was being taught and made very little effort to learn. He drank frequently, overspent his pay, and grumbled at his cigarette and ration allowances. He associated with the tougher type of student in the school. When O'Reilly tried to reason with him he said he was discouraged and fed up and spoke of returning to the Channel Islands. As a result of all this and because he knew he would be useless to him, O'Reilly states he strongly urged the Germans not to send Kenny. When they persisted, he made up his mind to drop him as quickly and quietly as possible when they arrived. He therefore avoided Kenny as much as he could in Berlin and told him as little as possible.'

In subsequent years O'Reilly tended to be vague as regards the specifics of his forthcoming mission for the SD. He would usually claim that his brief was to land in Ireland, but to then travel to England and to infiltrate and report upon the British political structure. He would admit only to a limited military espionage role, having been briefed on captured Allied aircraft at a secret Luftwaffe base, a claim that is rather suspect given the German concern at the Allied buildup of forces for the forthcoming invasion of France.

He was similarly evasive when talking about his service with the SS. 'O'Reilly spoke guardedly of the growing
ascendancy of the Himmler organisation. The gist of his
remarks broke no new ground, and was to the effect that the
SS were determined that there should be no surrender and
collapse like that of the last war. In order to deal with any
panic, treachery or underhand dealings which might arise
from the increasing difficulties of the military situation they
were extending their tentacles and tightening their grip on
the Higher Command. As they knew an allied victory would
mean their extermination they would fight to the last ditch
and were determined to forestall any move leading to pre-
mature surrender. These remarks, O'Reilly said, were based
partly on information and partly on observation and surmise.'
Later 'O'Reilly mentioned that before he came to Ireland he
had seen the dossier of all the Irish people in Germany in the
Gestapo Headquarters but he did not elaborate.'[49]

Brady and Stringer's departure from Berlin to join the
Waffen-SS in August might not have seemed like the safest
of their possible options, given the casualties being suffered
by that organisation. Sennheim, however, was to prove a far
safer location than Berlin during the month of November
1943. Following a preliminary raid four nights earlier, on
the night of 22 November the RAF's Bomber Command
launched their biggest raid yet against Berlin. Sending a
force of 764 aircraft, nearly all of them four-engined heavy
bombers, against the capital of their enemy, RAF Air Chief
Marshal 'Bomber' Harris exhorted the bomber crews to 'burn
his black heart out'. When the British bombers arrived over
Berlin, the city was under complete cloud cover. The bombers
were obliged to blindly unload their deadly payloads into the
overcast and turn for home with no idea of the effect of their
attack. This was area bombing at its crudest.

The raid of the night of 22 November was the single most
devastating raid on Berlin throughout the war. The bombs
carved a 1,000-acre swath of destruction across the city from

the Tiergarten in the centre to Spandau in the west. The following morning, more than 150,000 Berliners found themselves homeless. Among them, formerly living at Wurzberger Strasse, Wilmersdorff, were John Codd and his wife. Heavy RAF raids on Berlin would follow throughout the winter, forcing the German authorities to evacuate a million Berliners from their city and relocate them. As an employee of the SS, Codd was at an advantage. He was rehoused in a bungalow at 23 Diana Strasse in Lehnitz, close to where he was then training at the SS radio school.[50]

During this time John Kenny, still living in a flat in Leibnitzstrasse, was unable to attend his classes at Lehnitz, not even the Deutsches Reichsbahn (German Railways) being capable of running services to Oranienberg under these conditions. For the first time, he was told that he would be returning to Ireland in mid-December. Kenny returned to Lehnitz, but finished within a week, telling an instructor that 'he was only wasting time. The teacher agreed that he had made very little progress and expressed regret.'

After O'Reilly's first arrival in Berlin in 1941, he had gone to the Irish legation in November and applied for an Irish passport, which was issued to him in April 1942. Early in October 1943, he had handed the passport over to the SD at their request, and this was returned to him at the start of December, now containing an exit permit from the Berlin police, and entry visas for Spain, Portugal and Ireland. It is evident that, if questioned in Ireland, O'Reilly was to claim that he had returned on the regular British Overseas Air Corporation (BOAC) civil air flight from neutral Portugal to Foynes, on the Shannon estuary in the west of Ireland. One of the aircraft on this route, a civilian version of the massive Shorts Sunderland flying boat, had crashed on Mount Brandon in Kerry the previous July with the loss of ten lives.

On Monday 13 December, following an instruction from O'Reilly, Kenny reported to Berkaerstrasse where he turned in his surplus clothing, keeping for himself clothes with no

German markings or labels. The SD staff there told him that he would be given cash with which to buy new clothes on arrival. That evening, Kenny and O'Reilly left Berlin on a train to Paris accompanied by two SS officers. One of these was apparently SS-Sturmbannführer Dr Schuddenkopf, the SD chief of operations in Britain. At one point, when the two Irishmen were left alone, Kenny began to question O'Reilly more closely on details of their forthcoming mission. O'Reilly, always evasive, told Kenny that he might have to go to England to collect information on troop movements and shipping, suggesting Kenny 'could make his way to Liverpool and there contact soldiers or sailors coming home on leave'. He also suggested that Kenny could contact any shipping workers 'who would be willing to help him place bombs on board ships.' When O'Reilly suggested that the Germans could parachute explosives into Ireland or Britain, even Kenny 'did not think such a scheme was feasible.'

Although of limited education, Kenny was a pragmatic individual and next questioned O'Reilly on exactly what the pair were expected to do after they had landed in Ireland. O'Reilly suggested that they proceed to his parents' house in Kilkee, Co. Clare, and he would introduce Kenny as a truck driver who had given him a lift; he claimed that 'he would have no trouble convincing the local gardaí of his regular arrival home'. After a short stay, they would take a train to Dublin. O'Reilly also said he would find out from his brother the situation regarding identity papers and ration books in Ireland, since neither man had been in the country since the outbreak of war and were ignorant of wartime conditions there. They were not helped in this regard by the rivalry between the SD and the Abwehr: 'O'Reilly said he found it impossible to get information from the SS people on present conditions in Ireland on such matters as ration books, identity papers etc. When asked why they did not seek this information from the people who could have given it to them, O'Reilly said that they would not look for it for reasons of jealousy. The SS would not ask Haller for the information nor did he think that Haller would give the SS the information even if asked for.' It might be noted that the Abwehr could hardly have been described as particularly professional in their dealings with Ireland.

On arrival at Paris, the two Irishmen and their SS escort caught the train to Rennes, arriving there at 4 a.m. on Wednesday 15 December. They were accommodated at a house locally, and that night O'Reilly was driven to Rennes airfield, accompanied by the two SS officers. The Luftwaffe unit charged with transporting the two Irishmen back to Ireland was Afklaerungsgruppe (Fern) 123 [Long range Reconnaissance Group 123]. Headquartered in a fine chateau near Versailles, this unit carried out regular reconnaissance missions over Britain, operating Junkers JU-88s and occasionally a Heinkel He-111.

The Luftwaffe decided that it was not practical to drop the two Irishmen together due to the likelihood that they would be separated in the darkness. For their drop zone, they selected an area near O'Reilly's parents' house in Kilkee, Co. Clare. BOAC operated regular flights from the nearby flying boat station at Foynes, and it was hoped that the Luftwaffe's flight might be mistaken for one of BOAC's flying boats.

O'Reilly's parachute training was limited to a quick briefing from the pilot just before he boarded the aircraft. According to O'Reilly's subsequent account:

I met the crew and then got up into the belly of the plane, one member of the crew coming with me to explain about the bomb door etc. I looked at my watch just before we started and it was 11.10 p.m. I could not see out of the plane but through two round holes in the roof, I could see that it was a moonlit night. I had been told that I would get over my destination at about 2 a.m. and until about 1 a.m. it was light enough to see my watch. Then somewhere at about 2 a.m. I noticed the plane rapidly losing height and one engine seemed to be missing and I began to get worried in case a forced landing was necessary. I had no idea where we were. The plane again levelled out and about a minute later, the bomb doors opened slightly. This was a signal to be prepared to jump. The doors closed back again and I got up and braced myself against the sides of the plane and a minute later the bomb doors opened to their fullest extent. I saw my suitcase go through and I sprang immediately afterwards, with my back in the direction the plane was travelling. I wanted to keep my eye on the suitcase. I landed safely and I was down before the case.

Later, Kenny was told that O'Reilly signalled his safe landing to the bomber crew by flashing a torch. The suitcase, which had its own parachute, contained two radio sets. O'Reilly was unable to dig a hole to bury his parachute in the soft field where he had landed, but he was able to hide it in a water hole. He then found his way to the nearest roadway and, struggling under the weight of the heavy suitcase, began to look for the road to Kilkee. The German pilot had actually dropped O'Reilly a short distance from his own house, but O'Reilly was unaware of this in the darkness. At about 3.30 a.m. a farmer on his way to the local fair came across O'Reilly. He had no problem believing the stranger's explanation that he had lost his way having stepped off the train at a nearby railway station; the West Clare Railway was legendary for its slowness, inspiring a famous Percy French ballad. Later, the farmer would recall: 'I noticed that he had difficulty in carrying the case and I took it from him. When I was carrying it I noticed that it was very heavy for such a small case. It was about two feet long and about one foot deep. It was over half a hundredweight and the weight appeared to be very unevenly balanced. I remarked this to him and he said one end of it was packed with books.'

O'Reilly accompanied the farmer to Kilkee, and eventually made his way to his parents' house, no doubt in a state of exhaustion. At about the same time back in Rennes, John Kenny awoke, had breakfast and went for a walk. He spent a leisurely day, going to the local cinema and returning to his accommodation at 9 p.m. Shortly afterwards, he was driven

to the airfield by his SS escort, who gave him £100 sterling. At the airfield, Kenny met the crew of the aircraft that
would transport him to Ireland, who had successfully brought
O'Reilly home the night before. O'Reilly subsequently claimed
that the aircraft had been a Junkers JU-88, but Kenny disputed
this, claiming that the aircraft was 'a new type of reconnaissance bomber of which the Germans were very proud'. This
may have been an attempt by the Germans to reassure Kenny,
who was after all preparing to make his first parachute jump.
Kenny was shown his intended drop zone on a map, kitted up
with his parachute, and climbed aboard the aircraft, one of the
crew sitting beside him. Kenny noticed that the bomber was
carrying a bombload; German military resources by then were
already becoming stretched and Auf (F) 123 evidently thought
it best to be prepared in case of a target of opportunity.

Taking off at 11 p.m., the German aircraft was over the
west coast of Ireland at 2 a.m. The area, however, was ob-
scured by fog, and the pilot decided to abandon Kenny's drop,
turning the aircraft south and flying along the coast, and then
out to sea. Like O'Reilly, Kenny's parachute training had
consisted of a quick briefing before take-off. He was soon
about to make a 'practice' parachute jump, although under
rather nerve-wracking circumstances. On the journey back to
France, the German aircraft carrying Kenny suddenly began
to take violent evasive action and the defensive gunners began
firing; the crewman sitting beside Kenny shouted that they
were under attack from two British fighters. 'Skimming the
water', the Germans flew over the French coast, and climbed
to gain altitude above the Luftwaffe airfield at Morlaix. Ordered to bail out, Kenny dropped through the bomb doors
into the slipstream, quickly followed by the bomber's crew.
The pilot remained aboard, and after Kenny and the crewmen
had landed safely, carried out a successful landing despite a
damaged undercarriage. After this the fortunate group had
breakfast together, and retired to sleep in the Luftwaffe mess.
In the afternoon they flew back to Rennes aboard the same

aircraft. That night (17 December) Kenny spent in Rennes, and the following night was preparing for a second attempt to return to Ireland. After landing, Kenny was supposed to locate O'Reilly as a prelude to commencing their mission. O'Reilly was by then already under arrest. His earlier claim to Kenny that he would have no difficulty in convincing the local Garda Síochána of the legitimacy of his return home was not proving to be well founded.

Far from passing unnoticed, O'Reilly's aircraft over west Clare in the early hours of the morning was not on the BOAC's regular flight path, and flew low enough to awaken several local people. According to the local gardaí: 'At about 2 a.m. on the morning of 16 December 1943, a plane of the heavy type was heard over Kilkee and from the sounds it appeared to hover at times in the vicinity of the town. Necessary messages were forwarded to the Military Message Centre at Limerick.' The following morning the mysterious aircraft was the cause of much excited speculation. By that evening, the Garda Sergeant in Kilkee had heard of 'a strange man' seen wandering near the town at four in the morning. 'Enquiries were immediately set on foot and Sergeant Carroll, suspecting that a family named O'Reilly whose son was recently broadcasting from Germany might know something of this man or have information regarding him, called at O'Reilly's.' To the Sergeant's surprise, he was told that the O'Reilly son had returned from Germany very recently; he suggested strongly to the family that it would be in John O'Reilly's best interests to present himself at the garda barracks for interview. O'Reilly did so, but waited until 11.30 p.m. on the night of the seventeenth. He had quite a tale to tell.

No doubt aware that any claim by him to have returned to Ireland on the BOAC service from Lisbon would be quickly disproved by a brief examination of passenger lists, O'Reilly admitted 'without hesitation that he jumped out of a plane and came down that morning at Moveen'. Instead, he offered a bizarre alternative to the flimsy cover story suggested by the

SD. He had, he claimed, originally travelled to Lisbon but had been warned there by a German friend that BOAC had refused travel to certain people, or were likely to divert the aircraft to Britain. O'Reilly then returned to France where he contacted a friend in the Luftwaffe, who apparently agreed to drop him off in Kilkee during a regular mission!

O'Reilly's cover story did not survive even a brief perusal of his passport. The SD had included a carefully forged entry visa for Ireland; an Irish passport holder, however, did not require a visa to visit his own country. O'Reilly himself was not aware of this, and went into some detail when describing his imaginary visit to the Irish legation in Berlin to obtain the visa. He was no more convincing when attempting to account for the heavy suitcase he had been struggling with on the road to Kilkee. O'Reilly claimed that his friend in the Luftwaffe 'was anxious that I should have a suitcase with me as my arrival without one would be difficult to explain, and the suitcase would give credence to my having travelled by ordinary means'. He added that, 'regarding the weight in my bag, I decided I would have to get rid of that, and on last night I was able to dispose of it by throwing it over the cliffs at George's Head'. The radios were subsequently recovered by the gardaí, along with £143 of the £300 given to O'Reilly by the SD.

O'Reilly began his lengthy statement just before midnight on the night of 17 December, and finished it in the early hours of the eighteenth. Later that morning O'Reilly was formally taken into custody.

That night, back in Rennes, Kenny was driven to the nearby airfield, where he was kitted out with his parachute. Later examined by the Irish Air Corps, this was of the RZ series which suspended the user from the waist, from two hemp ropes 'doubled and whipped, and eye-spliced at either end'. This made it extremely difficult to collapse the parachute in a high wind, as Kenny would shortly find out. Although the harness was fitted with quick-release shackles on the legstraps, cheststrap and waistbelt, these were nowhere nearly as effective as the chest-mounted quick-release box on Allied parachutes and later versions of the RZ. Even a properly trained parachutist would have had difficulty operating the shackles when being dragged along the ground at night in a high wind, and Kenny's 'training' amounted to no more than a quick brief, although he had carried out one parachute jump under adverse circumstances. The same aircraft and crew as before were waiting for him and took off at 11.30 p.m. The duty garda in Kilkee heard them flying low overhead at 2.32 a.m., and shortly afterwards Kenny was dropped through the bomb doors. Dropping a parachutist 'blind', without any ground crew to advise on conditions, can be a hazardous business, and the weather on the west coast of Ireland can be particularly unpredictable. Judging by his broken wristwatch, Kenny hit the ground (hard) before 2.50 a.m., suffering back injuries that would plague him for years to come. Although it was a bright, moonlit night, there was a high wind blowing, and the unfortunate Kenny was dragged by his parachute for 1,000 yards over fields and stone walls, leaving drag marks that were still visible the next morning. His nightmare ride mercifully ended when the camouflaged silk canopy was caught by bushes, but not before Kenny was rendered unconscious by a nasty gash to the head.

He was awakened not long afterwards by pouring rain and, soaked and bleeding, he attempted to find shelter. At about 4 a.m. a local farmer heard Kenny's moans of pain at his back door, quickly brought him inside and placed him on a mattress by the fireside. A neighbour was sent to summon the gardaí in Kilkee, and Garda Sergeant Carroll found himself dealing with a second parachutist in almost as many nights. Sergeant Carroll first alerted the local doctor and then organised a vehicle, a very rare item in a time of strict petrol rationing, before arriving at the farmhouse himself. He interviewed Kenny as best as circumstances allowed, and while gently searching him for weapons took possession of a rain-soaked wad of banknotes that Kenny had been given by the Germans. Shortly afterwards the doctor arrived, and having received treatment Kenny was transported to Kilrush hospital. The local Garda Superintendent soon arrived, and shortly afterwards armed troops from the base at Foynes placed a guard at the hospital.

As soon as his condition allowed, Kenny was interviewed by Irish military intelligence. To begin with, he was stubborn and reluctant to divulge information, but by mid-January G2 noted that 'Kenny's attitude has changed for the better since the last interview and he now states that he is anxious to give all assistance in clearing up any questions involved with his landing here.' He subsequently told whatever he knew of his recruitment and training by the SS, which G2 forwarded to the Allied intelligence services as a matter of course. This was in stark contrast to John O'Reilly, who G2 found not to be 'prepared to give the particulars and the identities of the people with whom he was in contact in Germany, or the location of the various SS schools and offices … He had told the truth of his mission in broad outline and he could not be more specific without betraying his trust.' On one occasion, O'Reilly appeared to let slip genuine Nazi sympathies when speaking of an acquaintance in Berlin: 'He always felt that there was something dirty about her in the same way as one gets a feeling about some Jews or Poles.' Shortly after his capture, he was challenged by G2 to demonstrate the code system provided him by the SD, which he regarded as impenetrable. Years later, O'Reilly is said to have boasted of taking the secret of his code to his grave. In fact G2, utilising the services of Dr Richard Hayes, an amateur but very capable cryptologist, cracked the code in January 1944.[51]

O'Reilly and Kenny were effectively interned, being placed in the military prison at Arbour Hill in Dublin. There were quite a few internees in Ireland by this time. At the Curragh, one camp held over 500 members of the IRA, while another held over 200 members of the Kriegsmarine and Luftwaffe. With the exception of ten airmen in a small camp at

Gormanston, Co. Meath, there were no internees belonging
to the Allied forces remaining in Ireland. After a secret agreement with the Allies, all but this token number had been released, and even this group was freed in July 1944, albeit only
after some diplomatic pressure.

In Athlone military barracks, a special compound housed
all the spies that had been sent to Ireland by the Abwehr,
including Hermann Görtz. In an attempt to contact his
masters, Görtz had bribed one of his guards to deliver coded
messages to contacts on the outside, for radio transmission to
Germany. Eventually, the guard delivered to Görtz the first
of several messages from the Abwehr, one of which was a request for a full account of Goertz's activities in Ireland. Görtz
dutifully complied, and was later informed that he had been
promoted to Major and awarded the clasp to his Iron Cross.
After the war he learned that, all along, his messages had
been delivered to G2 and decoded by Dr Hayes, who also
encoded the replies from the 'Abwehr'. Görtz later bitterly
commented of Colonel Dan Bryan, the wartime chief of G2:
'I always regarded him as an enemy of Germany and I am
convinced that he believed he was serving his country best
by being pro-British.' Bryan's 'pro-Britishness' was somewhat
belied by the black and brown medal ribbon worn on his uniform, which identified him as a participant in Ireland's War
of Independence. He nevertheless freely cooperated, on the
orders of the Irish government, with the Allied intelligence
services throughout the war and with MI5 in particular.[52]

In July 1944, O'Reilly escaped from Arbour Hill prison
and returned to his parents' house in Kilkee. His father, however, contacted the authorities and collected a £500 reward
which he kept for his son on his eventual release. O'Reilly's
father was the RIC constable who had arrested Roger Casement in Kerry in 1916.

Kenny, the more cooperative of the pair, continued to be
plagued by the injuries suffered in his parachute landing, and
by late 1944 G2 officers were expressing some concern for his

health, which appeared to be declining in Arbour Hill prison. One observed that: 'He has rendered all the assistance he could to this branch, and he was quite definitely of little importance to this mission.' Kenny's release was considered on the grounds that: 'It is not felt that Kenny's release will create any security problem or that he will undertake any subversive activities in the near future.' However, such a course of action was reluctantly rejected since it was feared that Kenny 'may be contacted by cross-channel or American press correspondents', which would result in 'undesirable publicity'. Kenny and O'Reilly remained in captivity until the end of the war.[53]

4

JAGDVERBAND MITTE

In January 1944, a massive Russian winter offensive broke the German siege of Leningrad and began driving the German forces back towards Finland and the Baltic states. Many of the foreign volunteers at Sennheim were dispatched to frontline Waffen-SS divisions; five of the NCO instructors were declared fit for combat duties again and were dispatched to an anti-tank unit in Estonia.

In March 1944, the camp at Sennheim was visited by an SS-Hauptsturmführer of particularly athletic appearance and a holder of the Iron Cross in second and first classes, who proceeded to interview the foreign volunteers. Since SS Jager Battailon 502 wore no distinctive insignia, there was nothing to indicate that Hauptsturmführer Ulrich Menzel was a member of that unit and was actually seeking replacements. The previous month, No. 1 and 2 Companies of the battalion had gone to Truppenfuhrungspaltz Kurmark (Kurmark troop training area) for four weeks' intensive training, after which they saw combat on the eastern front for over a month. 'Unsuitable officers and men were eliminated to the extent of 10–15 per cent.'

Menzel had taken part in the rescue of Mussolini the previous September as an SS-Untersturmführer; he was in the second glider that crash-landed on the Gran Sasso. Promotion followed rapidly, and in March 1944 he succeeded van Vessem as battalion second in command and commanding officer of No. 1 Company.[1] Menzel selected thirty men, including Brady and Stringer, who were informed only that they had been picked 'for a special job'. It was an unorthodox means of selecting personnel for a special forces unit, but it had much to recommend itself in the often Byzantine world of the Third Reich. When in late 1944 Skorzeny sought English-speaking personnel for a secret mission in the Ardennes, he was stunned when the Wehrmacht circulated a routine order advertising this fact. Likewise, when Oberst von der Heydte was ordered to form an airborne unit to carry out an operation at the same time, commanders of Fallschirmjager units on the western front were ordered to each supply one hundred of their best men. Predictably, the officers concerned availed themselves of a heaven-sent opportunity to rid themselves of their worst troublemakers, and von der Heydte later lamented that he had never 'been in command of a unit with less fighting spirit'.[2] After all, apart from their obvious language skills, the men at Sennheim had volunteered for Waffen-SS service and were the beneficiaries of several months' intense military training, an increasingly rare state of affairs in early 1944.

The men selected by Menzel were taken away, with the exception of Frank Stringer, who was taken ill with scarlet fever. It is tempting to suspect that he was reluctant to be separated from his girlfriend in Mulhouse, but any suspected act of malingering would have been ruthlessly punished in the Waffen-SS and would likely have resulted in Brady being sent to Danzig-Marzgau. In any case, a scarlet fever patient would have been kept in quarantine.

James Brady's group eventually found themselves at the headquarters of SS Jager Battailon 502 at Friedenthal. Situated just north of the town of Oranienburg, the camp was not far from Lehnitz, the SS radio school where Brady and Stringer had trained a year before. A short distance to the east was the Sachsenhausen concentration camp where his former colleagues from Friesack camp were still incarcerated.[3]

Friedenthal (the 'valley of peace'), a vast park surrounded by heath and woodland, was originally a hunting lodge for the Hohenzollerns where the Kaiser once entertained guests. It consisted of two large pavilions, around which a barracks camp of prefabricated huts was erected in early 1943. Sitting astride a road between Oranienberg and Sachsenhausen, the camp was surrounded by a four-metre high wall, fitted with an alarm system and patrolled at night by sentries with trained dogs. The part of the camp to the north consisted of a riding circuit, an athletic field and the hutted accommodation for the Jager Battailon's three companies. A third company was established in February 1944, from mainly Flemish and Dutch personnel with Hauptsturmführer Hoyer as its commanding officer.

To the south, just over the road, were the quarters of the camp guards and administrative personnel, including some civilian secretaries. Behind these was the main camp, bordered to the south by a canal, central to which were a pair of three-storey permanent buildings which contained the officers' quarters and offices. There were also such buildings as a communications centre, garages and several ammunition dumps. In a special compound to the south-west of the camp, to which access was only granted with special permission, was a branch of RSHA VI-F, which dealt with special weapons and sabotage equipment. This contained offices, weapons and ammunition storage, a machine shop, a parachute storeroom and a chemical laboratory. Among the more exotic weapons available to Skorzeny were silenced submachine guns from Britain which had actually been intended for the Dutch resistance movement.[4]

At this time, a small detachment of SS Jager Battailon 502 were conducting what amounted to terrorist activities in occupied Denmark, an episode in the unit's history that Skorzeny was most reticent about in his postwar accounts. In April 1940 Germany occupied Denmark but announced that it would not interfere with the Danish government's independence. In that year only ten acts of resistance took place against the German occupiers. By 1943 this figure rose to nearly 1,000, including the spectacular escape of 7,000 Jews to Sweden in October, and in August the Germans dissolved the Danish government. In December 1943 Hitler ordered that acts of terror should be carried out against the Danish population to retaliate for acts of resistance. Himmler directed Skorzeny's unit ('thugs experienced in the use of explosives' in the estimation of the Americans) to carry out this task, and von Foelkersam selected a group of six men. These included Untersturmführer Otto Schwerdt, Oberscharführer Fritz Himmel and Unterscharführer Hans Holzer, all of whom had accompanied Skorzeny in his rescue of Mussolini from the Gran Sasso. These men travelled to Copenhagen and were issued with false papers, Schwerdt's identifying him as 'Peter Schafer', which led to the group being known to the Danish as the "Peter Group'. They were soon in 'action'. On 30 December, they attempted to assassinate Danish journalist Christian Damm, who survived despite being shot twice at close range by Schwerdt. Three days later they kidnapped and shot dead Pastor Kaj Munk, a figure in the Danish resistance. The group was known to have carried out ten assassinations in all, over thirty attacks on public gatherings and nearly twenty attacks on Danish factories; Himmel was killed during one such attack. The group was recalled to Friedenthal in September 1944, and the job of 'counter-terror' operations was handed over to the Gestapo.[5]

Back at Friedenthal, James Brady began a three-month course of training even more intensive than he had undergone at Sennheim. This included 'small arms, map reading, grenades and anti-tank warfare'. The last of these assumed particular importance for German troops, since German tank production was being vastly outstripped by the massive industrial capacity of the Soviet Union and the United States. The German infantryman, however, had increasingly effective anti-tank weapons for the task, which usually utilised the hollow charge warheads pioneered at the Eban-Emaal fortress in 1940. These included the Panzerfaust, a single shot recoilless weapon which was effective at close range and was produced in vast numbers. Another such weapon was the Panzerschreck, essentially a heavier version of the American 'bazooka'.[6]

In May 1944, John Codd, still living with his wife in a bungalow in Lehnitz, received an unexpected visitor. Frank Stringer had travelled to Friedenthal after his recovery where he took the opportunity to check up on a familiar-sounding Irishman named 'Collins', of whom he had learned from his girlfriend in Mulhouse. Stringer, accompanied by Brady, were to pay many weekend visits to Codd's bungalow. Codd got to know Brady well and considered him to be 'well-educated, well-mannered and considerate'. It is doubtful that Sergeant le Lievre of the Guernsey police would have agreed with this assessment; at this time le Lievre was still serving as a policeman, under the control of the German occupation forces. While Codd considered Brady to be well-educated, it should be noted that while he was an intelligent individual his own education was limited; in any case, given Brady's age when he joined the British Army, it is doubtful that he could have proceeded beyond secondary school. In an apparent attempt to support his assertion, Codd claimed that Brady 'appeared to have little or no experience of manual labour as he was very awkward when using gardening tools. Brady (and Stringer) used to help Mrs Codd to till and plant the garden on occasion.' It is, however, singularly difficult to believe that Brady had no experience of manual labour having spent six months in the British Army, fifteen months' hard labour in Guernsey prison, several months on an Arbeitskommando in Germany, four months as a farm worker in Klein Kiesow and eight months in the Waffen-SS! Codd, however, claimed that Brady had mentioned a father who was 'well to do but fond of the bottle' and a brother who had studied at a German university. This is particularly intriguing since third level education in 1930s Ireland was strictly the preserve of the most privileged classes, far less the ability to send a son to study at a foreign establishment. Others noted that Brady seemed brighter than the simple farm boy he claimed to be; the Military Police detectives who interrogated him in 1946 found him to be 'fairly intelligent' and were 'surprised by what he could say'. Most intriguingly, both Codd and his wife were 'satisfied that Brady was not his correct name, but they could not offer any alternative'. There was an immediate benefit for Brady and Stringer when they contacted John Codd: although the trio were in the service of the SS they were still nominally POWs and entitled to Red Cross parcels which Codd drew weekly for the three of them from Stalag IIID at Steglitz in south-west Berlin![7]

After his eventual arrival at Friedenthal, Stringer reported to SS-Hauptsturmführer Menzel. 'He did not say why I had been ordered to come, but he did ask me whether I wanted to be a motor-driver or go horse-riding.' Scarlet fever tends to be a debilitating disease and Menzel obviously did not consider Stringer yet capable of undergoing combat training. The proffered choice of a driving course or 'horse-riding' might sound bizarre, but throughout the war the Germans remained heavily dependent on horse transport and the Waffen-SS even maintained horse cavalry units on the eastern front. In fact there were small stables and a 'blacksmith shop' in Friedenthal, although this was probably a leftover since the camp's origin as a riding school. In the event, Stringer commenced a driving course.[8]

In April 1944, Hauptsturmführer Menzel was replaced in his dual role as battalion second in command and commander of No. 1 Company by Hauptsturmführer Adrian von Foelkersam, one of the legends of the German elite forces. Then aged twenty-six, von Foelkersam was born in Riga to a Baltic German family; his uncle was an Admiral in the Tsar's navy during the Russo-Japanese war in 1905. Having studied in universities in Berlin and Vienna he spoke fluent English and French and particularly flawless Russian. He joined the Brandenburgers on their inception and won the Knight's Cross in 1942 for a successful mission in the Causcasus in August of that year. Leading a Brandenburger unit of sixty

Volksdeutsche who spoke fluent Russian, and who also were wearing the uniforms of the NKVD (Stalin's dreaded security police), von Foelkersam presented himself at the important oil centre of Maykop and was provided with quarters for his unit. Having waited until the 13th Panzer Division was within twenty kilometers, von Foelkersam's unit destroyed the communications centres for the local military and for the north Caucasus region, which made it possible for them to convince the local Red Army commanders to withdraw their units. Maykop was successfully captured with minimal resistance. Disillusioned by the German high command's increasingly wasteful use of the Brandenburg commandos as conventional infantry, von Foelkersam and ten other officers of the regiment applied to transfer to Skorzeny's Waffen-SS unit in 1943. Abwehr Chief Admiral Canaris prevacariated, but the transfer was effected by Skorzeny regardless.[9]

On 25 May 1944, John Codd was introduced to a tall skinny American named 'Koller' and was told to teach him German. This was actually the alias of William Colepaugh, aged twenty-six and born in Connecticut to an American father and German mother. His pronounced pro-German sympathies eventually led him to sign on to a Swedish cargo vessel in January 1944 and jump ship in Portugal where he contacted the German consul to whom he announced that he wished to join the German Army. Accompanied by a Gestapo agent, Colepaugh was sent by train to occupied France and later to Berlin where he was accommodated in the Hotel Excelsior. He spent the next three months being vetted by RSHA VI before he was eventually interviewed by Skorzeny himself, who informed the American that he would be permitted to serve with the SD. According to Codd, 'it was he who had arranged the Koller-Codd combination'. On 27 May 1944, Codd and Colepaugh left Berlin for The Hague, in the company of a German friend of Giese.[10]

When Skorzeny took command of SS Sonder Lehrgang

Oranienburg in June 1943, he also took command of A-Schule West (Agent School West), established by RSHA VI at a country estate called Park Zorgvliet near The Hague in occupied Holland. The main house was built in the seventeenth century, and was since upgraded by businessmen who added a swimming pool, small outhouses and a surrounding wall. According to Skorzeny:

> Subjects covered were sabotage methods, demolitions, W/T operation, and firing of weapons. The training schedules were determined by VI-S/3 in Berlin. Two to four weeks before the beginning of each course the schools received instructions as to the number and nationality of the prospective students, and the purpose and length of the course. The training was designed to be as varied and interesting as possible. Students were given the opportunity to swim, attend movies, engage in sports, and read books in their own language. Their teachers were constantly with them. Upon completion of each course individual progress reports were issued, determining the student's further employment.

The staff, provided by RSHA VI-F, included:

> SS-Sturmbannführer Knolle Director of Training
> SS-Hauptsturmführer Winter Deputy CO
> SS-Hauptsturmführer Faulhaber Sabotage Instructor
> SS-Hauptsturmführer Besekow Foreign Sabotage Methods
> SS-Hauptsturmführer Westphal Explosives

Between November 1943 and June 1944, the following groups of agents were trained in classes lasting four to six weeks at the school:

> Appr. 25 Arabs from the Italian-Arabian Legion. Few were ever used as VI-S and Jaeger Btl 502 did not take any.
> 60–75 Italians (three classes). Unsatisfactory with the exception of one class.
> 20 Serbian militia. Good material, eager to learn and act.
> Appr. 15 Frenchmen.
> Appr. 10 Belgians.[11]

The spy school in The Hague was surrounded by a barricade which separated it from the rest of the city. Most trainee agents there were confined to the premises, although Codd was allowed to return home at weekends. There were a hundred trainees there at the time Codd attended, which included several Arabs from Algeria, Morocco and Iraq, presumably members of the Italian–Arab Legion. Designed to be 'varied and interesting', the daily programme ran from 8 a.m. to noon, and from 2 p.m. to 5 p.m., a rather leisurely regime compared to the training undergone by Brady and Stringer in the Waffen-SS.

The training at the Hague included the use of plastic explosives, radio operation and maintenance, and weapons training with German and British firearms. Also covered were electronics, espionage and counter-espionage techniques, swimming, sports, horse riding, motor cycling and driving. Codd claimed that the commanding officer of the school was 'SS-Sturmbannführer Dr Peters'. This may have been SS-Sturmbannführer Dr Pechau, who was deputy commander until May 1944 and who was succeeded by an officer named by Skorzeny as SS-Hauptsturmführer Winter, but who Codd and later Frank Stringer named entirely independently as 'Winterfeld'. This SS officer was an Austrian with a sense of humour, who sometimes was known to do a 'comic turn' during lectures. He instructed mostly in sandtable exercises, espionage and counter-espionage. One of the radio instructors was SS-Oberscharführer Pollman, who taught Brady and Stringer at the SD radio school at Lehnitz. Although Codd had not, apparently, met him there, he discovered that they had a mutual acquaintance in Bakker, the other Dutch instructor at Lehnitz. Codd described Pollman as a proficient radio instructor who spoke English, German and French. Other instructors named by Codd included sports officer SS-Untersturmführer Bemmer and SS-Untersturmführer Jansen, who instructed in radio but not very proficiently. There was also SS-Scharführer Heggemann, another Dutchman who instructed in the technical and theoretical side of radio and electricity. Codd described him as 'proficient, although a good deal of his stuff was above the students' heads.' Other members of staff included a quartermaster, Brinkman, and two junior NCOs who instructed in driving and motor sabotage.[12]

According to Codd's account of this spy school, 'related rather disjointedly', he made the acquaintance of three other German trainees named 'Polzany', 'Maxy' and 'Johnny'. All spoke Spanish and excellent, if accented, English. 'Polzany' was actually the alias of Erich Gimpel, a thirty-four-year-old electrical engineer from whom Codd learned that he had been arrested in Latin America, sent to the US and repatriated to Germany. This was true: in 1935, Gimpel had accepted a post with Telefunken, a German radio corporation, in Peru. He was interned in January 1942 and repatriated through the US by special agreement via a Swedish vessel to neutral Sweden from where he returned to Germany. The Auswartige Amt used him as a courier to Spain on occasion, and he also helped to vet repatriated Germans. In the summer of 1944, he accepted a proposal from RSHA VI that he spy for Germany. Codd claimed that the original projected mission for Gimpel, 'Maxy' and 'Johnny' was for them to attack the Panama Canal. 'Maxy', however, was removed from the group after an argument with Gimpel.

Gimpel subsequently decided that Colepaugh might make a good partner and greatly impressed the younger man with tales of his alleged espionage activities. According to Codd, 'at this time the officers in the school were drinking heavily … things were not looking good and they seemed to realise that Germany was on her last legs. Codd says that 'this was general all over Germany'. Having returned to the school after the weekend, Codd found Gimpel, Colepaugh and the officers showing evident signs of a recent 'binge'.

Codd and Colepaugh attended the Hague school for ten weeks, after which Codd returned to Berlin, where SS-Hauptsturmführer Giese informed him that Colepaugh did not want to work with him. Colepaugh subsequently referred to Codd as a 'fake Irishman' who did his translating for him. 'Codd was dropped in favour of Gimpel, who went to the USA with Koller.' The Hague school was disbanded shortly afterwards; SS-Sturmbannführer Knolle was relieved of command and transferred to Heinrichsburg near the Fruska Gora mountains outside Ruma in occupied Yugoslavia, where another A-Schule had been set up in a former tourist hotel. This was a rather less tranquil area than A-Schule West; German forces in the area were under constant attack by Tito's partisans, which it was thought would give the students combat experience. In fact both the A-Schule in Heinrichsburg and the local partisans shared the same doctor, who divided his time between them! The school cadre was comprised of a company of Serbian Muslims and a platoon from SS Jager Battailon 502. Between July and September 1944, the school trained '40 Italians (two classes), 25 Serbs, 120 Russians and 20 Hungarians'. The school was abandoned in September 1944 with the approach of the Russian army: the Russians and the Muslims were sent to the front and Knolle was recalled to Berlin. The school's remaining staff were relocated to Austria.

In the meantime, SS-Hauptsturmführer Winter took the staff of A-Schule West to the barracks at Neustrelitz in eastern Germany where it re-opened as a 'Kampf Schule' in July/ August 1944, classes commencing in September. 'The Kampf Schulen were conducted on a much more military basis than the A-Schulen. In addition to the necessary fundamentals of sabotage, the students were taught to shift [sic] for themselves when left behind the enemy lines singly or in small groups. This implied intensive terrain intelligence training and toughening courses. W/T instruction was given sporadically.'[13]

As subsequent events proved, Codd was lucky not to have accompanied Colepaugh to America. Gimpel completed his training at A-Schule West: his final test was to gather information on the German garrison in The Hague and transmit it to Germany. Colepaugh and Gimpel then returned to Berlin and underwent further training in photography, invisible ink and producing microdots. They were soon briefed on their mission; RSHA VI was giving them a sensible task in low-level intelligence gathering. They would be expected to live in the United States for a two-year period, gathering technical information on such matters as aircraft and shipping that was freely available in American books and journals. Vital information would be transmitted by a radio that Gimpel would construct in situ, more bulky data by means of microdots mailed to cover addresses in neutral countries. The pair were issued with pistols, secret ink and forged personal documents. They were also provided with a staggering $60,000 in cash (Colepaugh having convinced the SD that this was the minimum that the pair would need to survive two years in America) and ninety-nine diamonds in case of emergency. In late September 1944 the pair boarded the *U-1230*, an ocean-going Type IXC U-boat, and set off on a difficult two-month voyage across the Atlantic.

On 29 November, the pair were successfully landed on the coast of Maine and began walking inland. They eventually managed to take a taxi to Bangor, where they made their way by train to New York, arriving there on 1 December. Colepaugh opened a bank account and the pair, with some difficulty, found an apartment – most apartment houses were of steel construction and unsuitable for covert radio broadcasts. While the pair soon purchased a second-hand radio receiver and some instruments necessary to convert it to a transmitter, they did not go to any great lengths to gather information. John Codd later claimed that if he had been sent to America, 'there were good prospects of the mission being carried out. He would certainly not have gone on a drinking bout as these did when they got to the USA.' While this was an exaggeration of the pair's conduct, they certainly lived the high life in New York, spending an average of $100 a day on restaurants, stage shows and tailored suits. Despite this comfortable existence, funded by the Germans, Colepaugh soon displayed divided loyalties and deserted Gimpel on 21 December. He spent the Christmas period with an old school friend, and through him alerted the FBI and provided them with a description of Gimpel, who was arrested on 31 December. Both were tried by a military court and received the death sentence, which was later commuted by President Truman. Gimpel was released from prison in 1955 while Colepaugh was eventually freed in 1960.[14]

After the Codd–Colepaugh mission to the US fell through, other projects for John Codd were suggested by Hauptsturmführer Giese but nothing came of them. 'Giese then suggested that Codd could join an 'English Fascist Unit' which had been formed from a number of British soldiers who had joined the German side to fight against the Russians. Codd was told that it was a new unit which had been formed about August or September 1944. Codd knows nothing about this unit except that they wore German uniform.' This was in fact the British Free Corps, the handful of British POWs who were persuaded to join the Waffen-SS. Codd prudently refused, alleging that 'he had no wish as an Irishman to fight alongside Englishmen', a claim that had not prevented him from joining the British Army. Giese suggested that Codd go to work in a factory, and he 'also brought pressure on Codd to join the German army, but Codd stood firm'. Giese was relieved of command in January 1945, when the RSHA was ordered to evacuate Berlin. Skorzeny may have had Giese in mind when he lamented of certain RSHA VI officers: 'Personnel were selected without regard for suitability. None of the men in leading positions had ever been abroad or spoke any foreign languages. Most of them were too young for the responsibilities they were supposed to assume.'[15]

By the middle of May 1944, Irish military intelligence was evidently wondering where James Brady had got to. In a report dated 15/5/44 a G2 officer noted:

PTE [sic] James Brady, Irish Fusiliers, POW no. 7815
The identity of this man has not been fully established. He

is a POW in Camp Stalag IIID and may be identical with the Brady who was at Camp Stalag XXA 301 in 1941. Brady is said to have been in jail on the continent at the time of the German attack, where or for what offence is not known. Brady was friendly with Cushing and left the camp for Berlin in Dec 1941, with Cushing and 3 others. This group is said to have been moved to Berlin to be trained in radiotelegraphy. They were still in Berlin in May 1942.

While G2's belief that Brady was a POW in Stalag IIID was obviously incorrect, apparently based on Brady's intercepted POW card, the information is otherwise remarkably accurate. Apart from its links with MI5, G2 had its own source inside Friesack camp.

A POW card from a James Brady, POW 7815, Stalag IIID, to Mr [X] Co Roscommon, was noticed in censorship, thanking [X] for a parcel and asking for German grammars. [X] replied on 11.6.43 stating that he had given authorisation for parcels to be sent to Brady through Mr Trimble, Armagh sec of the Irish Fusiliers' comforts fund, and that he had asked the Red Cross to send German grammars. [X] was interviewed and said he had no personal knowledge of Brady and could not identify him. He was not a friend or relative and had not, to [X]'s knowledge, any relatives in the neighbourhood. The way in which the correspondence had begun was that about Xmas 1940 he had received notification from a records office in Edinburgh that James Brady was missing and about a week later a letter from the same address saying that Brady was a POW in Germany and had been taken prisoner in the Channel Islands. He could not remember the Edinburgh address. In August 1941 he got a communication from the British Red Cross saying that Brady was a POW at Stalag IIID giving instructions as to the sending of parcels.[16] In June 1942, NOK sent on a parcel of clothing and chocolates ... and wrote asking Brady who he was and who his people were. Brady's reply, dated 7.3.43 gives no information on this point. In January 1943, [X] got a communication from Delmege Trimble, i/c RI Fusiliers and POW comforts fund, Armagh, with a form to be signed by him as registered next of kin, authorising the sending of parcels through this fund. After receiving a reply from Mr Trimble, [X] signed the form. He did

not tell Mr Trimble he was no relation of Brady's. He was unable
to offer any explanation of why Brady had given his name as
next of kin. He had acted from charitable feeling. Nothing has
emerged to discredit [X's] story. He is described as a very decent
respectable man.

There is thus no clear connection between the Brady at Stalag
XXA 301 and the Brady at Stalag IIID. 17 men were moved
from the former camp to Stalag IIID 961 in September 1942. It
is not established, however, that Brady was one of these.[17]

Frank Ryan died on 10 June 1944, just a few days after the
D-Day landings at Normandy. His last days had been painful
and he was only able to breathe with great difficulty when he
was admitted to a sanatorium near Dresden, suffering from
pneumonia compounded by pleurisy. He is said to have been
deliriously shouting orders in Spanish as he passed away. Ryan
was buried on 14 June in a cemetery at Dresden-Loschwitz,
under a simple wooden cross which bore the name 'Francis
Richard' in English but also the name 'Proinnsias Ó Riain'
– his real name in Irish.[18]

Present at the funeral was Francis Stuart. In August 1943,
he had moved to Luxembourg with the staff of Irland-Redaktion (of whom he was now the only Irishman), but in January
1944 he ceased broadcasting propaganda for the Germans
and returned to his teaching post in Berlin. That summer,
however, he lost this position when all third-level institutions
in Germany were closed as part of the country's 'total war' effort, and subsequently moved to the Austrian town of Dornburn
where he spent several months trying unsuccessfully to move to
Switzerland. In September 1944, the remaining staff of Irland-
Redaktion, namely Dr Hans Hartmann, an interpreter and a
secretary, moved to a village near Oldenburg where Hartmann
broadcast intermittently almost until the last days of the war.[19]

Back in Friedenthal, Frank Stringer continued with his
driving course for five weeks but proved unproficient. He was,
apparently, now considered capable of undergoing combat

training, and 'learned marching, small arms drill, map and compass reading, grenade throwing, the use of machine guns and direction finding by the moon and the stars'. By their own accounts, by July 1944 Brady and Stringer were members of No. 1 Company, SS Jager Battailon 502. On 20 July, No. 1 Company was involved in an operation in the heart of Berlin.[20]

Until that date, most of the unsuccessful assassination attempts against Hitler were the work of individual opportunists, with no thought given to exploiting the possible aftermath. By July 1944, a group which included diplomats and high-ranking officers had agreed on the principles of a plan which would follow the death of Hitler with a seizure of power by the Wehrmacht. A year before, contingency plans were drawn up to allow the army to implement emergency countermeasures in case of internal disturbance or uprising, on receipt of the code word 'Valkyrie', allowing such measures as securing vital installations. The plotters were presented with a man of action in the form of Colonel Graf von Stauffenberg, the chief of staff to the commander of the Reserve Army, but it fell to this one man to both carry out the assassination of Hitler and direct the coup in Berlin, one of the main reasons for the plan's failure. Von Stauffenberg was granted access to Hitler in his 'Wolf's Lair' forward headquarters in East Prussia and succeeded in planting a bomb near him in a briefing room, leaving before the explosion. His assumption that Hitler was dead proved to be false. It took von Stauffenberg more than two hours to fly from East Prussia to Berlin, where the leaders of the Berlin coup attempt assembled in the Army High Command (OKH) headquarters in the Bendlerstrasse. The codeword 'Valkyrie' was not issued until four in the afternoon, and due to several factors, not least the news that Hitler was still alive, the coup attempt collapsed within hours.

At about six o'clock that evening Skorzeny and his adjutant, Hauptsturmführer Karl Radl, another Austrian who had accompanied him on the Gran Sasso raid, had just boarded a train to Vienna on official business when a Waffen-SS officer ran alongside the train with an urgent message for Skorzeny to contact his office immediately. Skorzeny sent Radl on to Vienna, then contacted Friedenthal and ordered von Foelkersam to place SS Jager Battailon 502 on alert and to report as soon as the first company was ready to move; the troops in Friedenthal were kept constantly on a fifteen minute alert. Skorzeny then drove to the headquarters of RSHA VI at Berkaerstrasse where he found the staff, including Schellenberg, to be armed and expecting an attack from the OKH at Bendlerstrasse. Von Foelkersam was ordered to report to the scene immediately, having already ordered No. 1 Company to Berkaerstrasse, which he did without delay. According to his own account, Skorzeny began a reconnaissance of the Panzer Inspectorate at Fehrbelliner Square, where he found that a tank unit of the German Army had received from Bendlerstrasse a warning of a 'putsch' by the Waffen-SS and orders to carry out an armed reconnaissance of the Leibstandarte barracks at Lichterfelde. The Oberst in command was too prudent to carry out the order, and when Skorzeny drove to Lichterfelde he found the Leibstandarte in a state of high alert, fully prepared to fire on any Wehrmacht panzers that might have appeared there. Both sides agreed not to move from their positions and a potentially serious situation for Nazi Germany was averted. It was becoming clear that elements in the Bendlerstrasse were attempting to carry out a coup against the Nazi regime.

By 9 p.m., No. 1 Company of SS Jager Battailon 502 arrived at the RSHA VI headquarters in a column of twenty vehicles, under the temporary command of a Hauptsturmführer who rejoiced in the wonderful name of Karl Fucker. Despite his amusing surname (at least to an English speaker) this young officer, who like Skorzeny was an Austrian and an engineer in civilian life, was to prove one of the unit's most outstanding leaders. Just before midnight Skorzeny, on the orders of Führer Headquarters, led the company across a bomb-devastated

Berlin to the Bendlerstrasse, to support the Wachtbattalion of the Grossdeutschland Division commanded by Major Remer. Remer had earlier been ordered by Army General Paul Hase to arrest propaganda minister Joseph Goebbels, but had been persuaded to telephone Hitler's headquarters, from whom he learned personally that the Führer was still alive. He remained loyal to the regime and ordered his Wachtbattalion against the conspirators. Arriving at OKH, Skorzeny observed the departure of Generaloberst Fromme, the commander-in-chief of the Reserve Army, before he contacted Major Remer. The pair quickly decided that Remer's Wachtbattalion would surround the Bendlerstrasse complex while Skorzeny led his company into the courtyard. Accompanied by von Foelkersam and three others, Skorzeny entered the building and found most of the staff officers inside in a state of shock; on learning that Hitler had survived the assassination attempt, Fromme had organised a counter-coup and ordered the execution by firing squad of Stauffenberg, General Olbricht, Oberst von Quirnheim and Stauffenberg's adjutant. The sentence had been carried out at 11.15 p.m. in the Bendlerstrasse courtyard, the bodies of the executed now lying under tarpaulins. Although not an active participant, Generaloberst Fromme had been aware of the conspiracy against Hitler and was anxious to silence any possible accusers. It was to no avail: he was replaced as commander of the Reserve Army by Reichsführer Himmler on Hitler's orders, and was executed the following March. Skorzeny occupied the Bendlerstrasse until the morning of 22 July, when he learned of Himmler's new appointment; even Skorzeny, a lifelong admirer of Hitler, was astonished, regarding Himmler as 'incapable of understanding military problems'. Himmler at least had an able deputy in Oberstgruppenführer Hans Juttner.[21]

The following morning, von Foelkersam accompanied SS-Oberführer Schellenberg as he took Admiral von Canaris, the former commander of the now defunct Abwehr, into custody for his part in the conspiracy. As von Foelkersam

was a former officer in the Brandenburg regiment, Canaris
was his former commanding officer. This episode would not
have caused any grief for von Foelkersam; since his transfer
to SS Jager Battailon 502 he often expressed his lack of trust
in Canaris and his suspicions regarding his command of the
Abwehr and the Brandenburgers in particular. Canaris was
subsequently hanged, along with 200 others convicted by a
'people's court'.[22]

Were Brady and Stringer involved in No. 1 Company's
operation in Berlin? It is a definite possibility; both omit
certain details from their accounts, but they correctly name
as their company commanders the successive Waffen-SS officers commanding No 1 Company, SS Jager Battailon 502
at that time. Their accounts, however, are uncharacteristically
vague as to the details of their activities at this time; for example, their swearing of the SS oath of allegiance is perhaps one
of those details that they thought best not mentioned.

According to Frank Stringer:

> Neither Brady nor I liked the infantry training, as it was too hard,
> and as there was a big radio station in Friedenthal we applied
> to Obersturmführer Hunke (who had taken over command of
> the company from Obersturmführer von Volkersamt [sic], who
> in turn had replaced Mensel) to work as radio operators, telling
> him we knew something about it. The only reason we applied for
> this job was because it would be an easier life. Hunke agreed and
> both Brady and I were transferred to the radio station, which
> was a military station.
>
> Although he had completed three months of the training
> regime, Brady agreed that Stringer and myself were fed up with
> infantry training so we went to see the Company Commander
> Hunke and told him that we were radio specialists and wanted a
> transfer. We then worked at the radio station in Friedenthal. We
> did more training there.[23]

Obersturmführer Werner Hunke had been one of the unit's
original officers since Skorzeny's assumption of command;
he had to endure the nickname 'Chinese' due to his birth in

that country, although he had left it as a child and had no
knowledge of the country or its language.

On 1 August, with the Red Army just across the Vistula
from Warsaw, General Bor-Komorowski ordered the Polish
resistance in the city to rise in rebellion against the Germans.
Although there were 35,000 members of the Polish Home
Army in the city, only 6,000 of them were armed, and heavy
weapons were in short supply. Since Warsaw lay on a major
German supply route to the east, the Army Chief-of-Staff,
Colonel General Guderian, requested that the German Army
deal with the matter. Hitler, however, charged Himmler with
the task, making the suppression of the Warsaw rising an SS
matter. Seizing an opportunity to carry out some significant
ethnic cleansing of the Polish population, Himmler appointed
SS-Obergruppenführer Bach-Zelewski to command the
operation and issued him orders to kill all non-combatant
civilians and level every street in the city. Among the SS units
unleashed upon the population of Warsaw was the bestial
SS Sonderkommando Dirlewanger, whose 900 troops were
reinforced by nearly 2,000 inmates of the SS penal facility of
Danzig-Marzgau. Dirlewanger's men embarked on an orgy
of violence: patients in hospital beds were massacred, babies
were spitted on bayonets, prisoners were doused in petrol and
burnt alive. Despite the fact that at one stage his men had
threatened Bach-Zelewski's headquarters with machine guns,
Dirlewanger was promoted to SS-Oberführer and awarded
the Knight's Cross. Another SS unit in Warsaw composed of
Ukrainian renegades was withdrawn having killed thousands
of civilians and collapsing into anarchy. Among the artillery
brought in to pulverise Warsaw's streets was the massive sixty-
centimetre 'Carl' mortar which weighed 132 tonnes and had
to be transported by rail. Nearly three quarters of Warsaw's
buildings and all significant landmarks were levelled. The Polish
rebels fought on for two months while the Red Army sat tight
across the river; although their supply lines were genuinely
overstretched, Stalin was happy enough to let the Germans

deal with the Polish Army, who could offer opposition to the intended communist annexation of their country. By the time of the eventual Polish capitulation on 2 October, 160,000 inhabitants of Warsaw were dead.[24]

On 24 August 1944, a Russian offensive in north-west Romania tore through the Romanian Third and Fourth Armies, allowing the Russians, in turn, to inflict heavy losses on the German Eighth Army and nearly destroy the German Sixth Army for the second time in its existence, the first having been at Stalingrad. On the same day the young King Mikhail deposed the pro-German Marshal Antonescu and ordered all German personnel to leave the country. Two days later, the new Romanian government formally declared war on Germany. While most of Germany's former European partners followed the same pattern of surrendering to the Allies and subsequently going to war against Germany, Romania performed its volte-face with astonishing speed. In a short space of time, Germany was facing nearly twenty Romanian divisions under Russian control. German military forces in Romania and many of their families who had been comfortably far from the front now found themselves hundreds of miles behind enemy lines almost overnight.

Skorzeny received an order from the Oberkommando der Wehrmacht (OKW):[25] 'Form two special platoons for immediate operation to start from Temezvar airport, Romania. The object is to bar the Carpathian mountain passes, reconnoitre behind the enemy, wreck his communications and help German civilians to safety.' The operation was codenamed 'Landfried' and was placed under the command of a young Untersturmführer called Walter Girg, who had been posted to Friedenthal only four months previously, directly after his commissioning at the Waffen-SS officer school at Bad Tolz.

Due to the Waffen-SS system, Girg was a hardened combat veteran and the holder of the Iron Cross in both classes even before commencing officer training. He was placed in charge of a team which included Russian speakers, demolition experts – and one incognito Irishman, whom it might be speculated was thought well of by his commanders. James Brady recalled: 'About August 1944, about fifty members of the battalion, including myself, but not Stringer, were posted to Romania. We were in Romania for about three weeks, during which time I helped to blow up two river bridges and one railway bridge.' At the last moment, Girg was warned that Temezar airport had fallen into Russian hands and his team instead diverted to an emergency airfield from which they commenced operations. According to Skorzeny's account: 'They operated behind the Russian lines, in Russian, Romanian and Bulgarian uniforms, according to the territory … Fifty men were committed, who operated 700 km behind the lines. They were divided into an eastern group, a western group and a central group. The first [Brady's group] obstructed three passes and located appr. 2,000 men from the Ploesti AA batteries in the vicinity of Kronstadt [Brasov], of whom 250 were brought back.' This was a German anti-aircraft regiment guarding the vital Ploesti oil fields, smartly turned out and equipped with the latest air defence artillery, who were patiently waiting to surrender to the Russians. The aforementioned 250 troops who were persuaded to stage a breakout succeeded in returning to German lines. Skorzeny recalled: 'The western group brought back German residents and collected intelligence. The central group was under the command of Girg. It placed demolitions in the Rotenturm pass, south of Herrmanstadt [Sibiu] and observed Russian preparations in that vicinity. On one occasion they marched for about fifteen km in a Russian column. They were discovered and condemned to death. Girg however managed to escape from the firing squad and reach the German lines. He submitted a report containing valuable information on Russian order of battle and was awarded the Ritterkreuz [Knights Cross].' According to Brady's all too brief account of this spectacular special operation, his first time in combat: 'There were only twenty-two of us left when we pulled out of

Romania. Some men were killed by the Russians and others by the Romanians.' Girg's central group bore the brunt of the casualties, the other two escaping with minor losses. Interestingly, apart from Girg's Knights Cross, two NCOs of the party were awarded the also prestigious German Cross in Gold. It would be reasonable to speculate that the nineteen remaining personnel received some lesser decoration.[26]

Brady returned with his group to Friedenthal, where much had occurred in his short absence. In September 1944, SS Jager Battailon 502 was dissolved and its personnel absorbed into a new battalion, Jagdverband Mitte. While the title of this unit is open to different interpretations, Skorzeny himself preferred 'Commando Group Centre'. Earlier that summer it was recognised that the expansion of the Branden-burg Regiment into a conventional unit, and the use of its irreplaceable elite troops as line infantry, was a mistake. Therefore the special elements ('zbv') were withdrawn and formed into 'Streif Korps' which were attached to army corps for use in special operations. It was proposed by Skorzeny and von Foelkersam (a former Brandenburger) that these units be used as the nucleus for four territorial 'Jagdverband' and in September 1944 permission was granted to them to recruit Brandenburg volunteers. '1,200 were in fact recruited, but only 900 remained after the unfit had been eliminated.' It is noteworthy that, despite the fact that they were now nominally in Waffen-SS units, several of the former Brandenburgers chose to retain their Wehrmacht ranks:

> The Territorial Jagd Verband were separate bns drawn from political and nationalist groups in the countries where they were to operate. Plans for their formation were made by Skorzeny and von Foelkersam in May or June 1944, and the bns were activated in September by order of O/Gruf Juttner, head of the SS Fuehrungs Haupt Amt. A Jagd Verband was to be available to the Armed Forces in each theatre to carry out special tasks in the tradition of the defunct Div Brandenburg. The final aim

was to have all units engaged in sabotage behind the enemy lines under a unified command in theatre territory, i.e. the Fuehrungs Stab [Headquarters Staff] of the Territorialen Jagd Verband.

In September 1944, the activation of the SS Jagdverband organisation was confirmed. This consisted of four units in the process of formation, namely Jagdverband Ost, Jagdverband Sued Ost, Jagdverband Sued West and Jagdverband Nord West. Based in Friedenthal was Jagdverband Mitte and the new Jagdverband Fuehrungs Stab. Haupsturmführer Fucker was named commanding officer of Jagdverband Mitte in October 1944.

Also placed under Skorzeny's command in the new organisation was the reconstituted SS Parachute battalion:

SS Fallshirmjager Btl 500 was commanded by Hauptsturmführer Milius. It had just returned from operations in Yugoslavia, including an unsuccessful parachute attack on Tito's HQ, where it had been attached to XIII (?) [actually XV] Alpen Korps. It had also been committed for a short time on the Russian front. On Himmler's orders Skorzeny was put in charge in August or September 1944 and the bn became part of the Jagd Verbande organisation. The Bn was reorganised in Neustrelitz. Its criminal elements were removed, and it was renamed SS Fallschirmjager Bn 600. After unfit personnel were eliminated it had appr. 250 men. New recruits came from the GAF.

On 25 May 1944, SS Fallschirmjager Battalion 500 carried out a combined glider and parachute assault on the headquarters of Marshal Tito, leader of the 400,000-strong Yugoslav partisan armies which by then were forcing the Germans to divert eleven badly needed divisions from the eastern front. Tito escaped capture and the SS paratroops soon found themselves surrounded by overwhelming numbers of partisans. The remnants of the battalion established a defensive position in a nearby cemetery and held out through a night of vicious fighting until reinforcements reached them the following morning. Most reliable accounts claim that the

SS Fallschirmjager battalion was all but wiped out in this operation.

Skorzeny estimated the new battalion would eventually attain a strength of 900 men organised into three companies. Some 30 per cent of these originated from the Waffen-SS, the remainder from the Luftwaffe and German Army. The loss of the Ploesti oil fields was already beginning to make itself felt: there was only enough available aircraft fuel to train one company as parachutists; the others were designated 'glider companies'.[27]

Jagdverband Mitte did not have long to wait for its first mission. After his return from Romania, Brady was to rest in Friedenthal for only two weeks 'before my company was ordered to Hungary. We went to Budapest as it was our job to get [Admiral] Horthy out before Hungary packed in.'

By October 1944 Germany's eastern front was not so much crumbling as collapsing. Like Romania, Germany's European allies began deserting her to avoid destruction. On 3 September, a new government of Bulgaria was appointed and declared neutrality. On 8 September, the Russians moved in and the new government declared war on Germany. A pro-Soviet government took power, although the Bulgarian Army took some time before it could commence operations against the Germans. On 4 September the Finnish government signed an armistice with Russia, and a Finnish delegation in Moscow soon accepted peace terms which included loss of territory, huge reparations and the internment of all German personnel in Finland. In fact, the Finns allowed the eight divisions of the German Twentieth Army to withdraw to Norway, but the withdrawing Germans adopted a stringent 'scorched earth' policy which caused serious damage to Finnish infrastructure and industry. Clashes between German and Finnish forces escalated into full-scale confrontation, and when three Soviet armies drove into Finland in October, they were supported by several Finnish divisions. The Russians took the opportunity to continue into Norway and seize the main German base at Kirkenes. Further south, a Russian offensive through the Baltic states trapped the thirty divisions of the German Army Group North in Latvia.

Germany's concerns as to the loyalty of Hungary were amply demonstrated in March 1944 when eleven Wehrmacht divisions were sent across the border to begin an effective German occupation of the country. In their wake followed over 500 SS and SD personnel under the overall command of SS-Obergruppenführer Otto Winkelmann; these included a 'Sonder Einsatzkommando' led by the infamous SS-Obersturmbannführer Adolf Eichmann. The strongly pro-German Dome Sztojay was appointed prime minister, and SS-Brigadeführer Dr Edmund Veesenmayer as Hitler's ambassador, playing a pivotal role in the implementation of the 'Final Solution' in Hungary. Eichmann quickly set about organising the eviction of the Hungarian Jews from their homes and their concentration into ghettoes, and in May began sending thousands of Jews on trains to the death camp at Auschwitz. By early July, Veesenmayer announced that 437,403 Jews had been sent to Auschwitz. By August, however, it was obvious that German victory was doubtful; Admiral Horthy, the Hungarian regent, replaced Sztojay and called a halt to the deportation of Jews.[28] Since early that summer, Niklas Horthy (Admiral Horthy's son) was secretly negotiating with the Soviets via two of Marshal Tito's agents, negotiations which came to the notice of SS-Obergruppenführer Winkelmann. The stakes for Germany were high; Hungary's defection to Russia would cut off seventy German divisions fighting in the Carpathian mountains and would bring the Red Army to the borders of Austria. At 10 a.m. on the sunny Sunday morning of 15 October, Horthy's son, accompanied by a friend, parked his car outside an office building in Budapest. A canvas-covered truck parked behind him, carrying three armed Hungarian Army officers acting as a bodyguard, while two more officers began strolling nearby. Just in case, there was a Hungarian Army battalion based nearby, with soldiers stationed in buildings around the square, including a unit in the house next door. Niklas Horthy and his friend proceeded into the office building and upstairs where Tito's agents were awaiting them on the second floor. Shortly afterwards, another civilian car pulled up in front of Horthy's, parking almost bumper to bumper. One of the Hungarian officers in the truck jerked back the canvas cover and watched as the car's owner, a particularly big man, opened the bonnet and began to fiddle with the engine. He was not challenged; had he been, he could have produced documentation identifying himself as 'Dr Wolff' from Cologne. The big man was in fact a heavily disguised Otto Skorzeny. Sitting on a park bench nearby, unobtrusively reading newspapers, were an officer and two NCOs of Jagdverband Mitte, and hiding in a nearby street were thirty more men of the unit, led by von Foelkersam. Winkelmann had taken the precaution of placing agents on the third floor of the office building above where the meeting was taking place.

The catalyst for an explosion was provided by two of Winkelmann's SS men who strolled by Skorzeny and dashed for the entrance of the office building. Niklas' bodyguard reacted like lightning; the Hungarian officers opened fire with submachine guns, killing one 'policeman' and wounding the other. Skorzeny's men on the park bench rushed to his assistance, one of them receiving a leg wound, and the little group fought their corner until von Foelkersam's unit came running to their aid. The Jagdverband Mitte assault group swept through the square, firing at doors and windows where Hungarian troops were appearing. An explosive charge was set off in the doorway of the building containing the nearest Hungarian unit, trapping them inside.

Winkelmann's agents inside the building arrested the four conspirators, rolling a carpet around Niklas Horthy in the process. The prisoners were taken from the building and placed aboard an SS truck that drew up outside, and within seconds were being driven to Budapest airport. Von Foelkersam and his men began discreetly withdrawing, leaving Skorzeny to negotiate with the commander of the Hungarian battalion which had just arrived at the scene. Having delayed the Hungarians long enough to allow von Foelkersam's men to escape, Skorzeny drove at speed to the airport and arrived in time to witness the aircraft carrying the younger Horthy and his companion taking off.[29]

Admiral Horthy's reaction was not long in coming. The seat of his administration rested in the Bergburg (Castle Hill), a fortification three kilometres long by 600 metres wide, towering above the Danube. The garrison was reinforced to over 2,000 troops, and with the news of his son's kidnapping, Horthy ordered all the Bergburg's gates to be closed and barricaded. Since the German embassy was situated in the Bergburg, this trapped several German diplomats and officials, including SS-Brigadeführer Dr Edmund Veesenmayer and SS-Gruppenführer Karl von Pfeffer-Wildenbruch, the senior Waffen-SS officer in Hungary.

At 2 p.m. Admiral Horthy made a radio broadcast in which he declared that Germany had lost the war and called for a separate peace between Hungary and Russia. It was a critical situation for the Germans, made worse by the news that Horthy's commander-in-chief had already defected to the Russians. Failure to take decisive action could result in Horthy surrendering Hungary to the Russians with disastrous consequences for Germany. Excessive force, however, could anger the Hungarians enough to take the Russian side anyway. In fact, present in Budapest at this time was a keen advocate of brute force in the form of SS-Obergruppenführer von dem Bach-Zelewski, who had brought with him the 65-centimetre mortar with which he had devastated Warsaw and was now willing to use to level the Bergburg. Skorzeny, however, had prepared his own plan (Operation Panzerfaust) as an alternative to a suicidal airborne assault that the German high command had proposed, but which he had ruled out having covertly reconnoitred the Bergburg in the guise of 'Dr Wolff'. For this operation, Skorzeny was provided with a small but high quality force, organised in Vienna and now ready for action in Budapest. This force consisted of four companies of officer cadets from the prestigious Theresian military academy in Wiener-Neustadt, 700 men in all.

Also available was a composite battalion-sized force of Fallschirmjager, originally intended for the proposed airborne assault. This comprised a reinforced company of 250 men of the SS-Fallshirmjager Battalion 600, under the temporary command of SS-Obersturmführer Marcus. The Luftwaffe's own special operations unit (KG 200) had its own battalion of Fallschirmjager, and two companies of this were placed at Skorzeny's disposal.

No. 1 Company of Jagdverband Mitte was reinforced from its normal strength of 175 to 250 men and was placed under the temporary command of Obersturmführer Manns. Hauptsturmführer 'Chinese' Hunke was also present and taking part in the operation.

At 3 a.m. on 16 October 1944, Skorzeny assembled his officers and gave his orders. The battalion of officer cadets were to attack the Bergburg from the south, blowing up an iron fence there and pinning down the Hungarian troops within. The paratroops would attack from the east through an underground tunnel that led from a quay on the Danube to the war ministry building within the fortress, breaching several armoured doors in the process. The most important part of the assault would be carried out by Jagdverband Mitte. A detachment under the command of Hunke would enter over the western wall and attack the front of Horthy's palace before the arrival of the main force. Skorzeny would lead No. 1 Company himself through the Vienna Gate, accompanied by four panzers that had been 'borrowed' on the way to the front, and a platoon of Goliaths. The latter were tiny tank-like vehicles filled with explosives and directed to their targets by remote control.

Skorzeny's column was drawn up in convoy below the Bergburg in the pre-dawn twilight at 5.30 a.m., thirty minutes before the expiration of an ultimatum in which the Germans demanded that Horthy open the Bergburg and retract his peace offer to the Russians. Waiting in the trucks, some of the Jagdverband Mitte commandos took the opportunity to catch a few minutes' sleep while others kept watch. These troops (which included James Brady) were liberally equipped with Panzerfaust rocket launchers and at least some were carrying the Sturmgewehr 44, the revolutionary new German assault rifle. Skorzeny took his place in the command vehicle at the head of the convoy, along with von Foelkersam and five NCOs who had accompanied him on the raid on the Gran Sasso. When 6 a.m. arrived with no visible compliance with the ultimatum, Skorzeny stood up in his vehicle and gave a signal. The engines of the trucks and tanks roared to life and the sleeping commandos jerked awake. As dawn broke, the convoy rumbled up the hill to the Vienna Gate; to Skorzeny's relief, the road was not mined and the barricade at the gate had been opened in an apparent show of good faith. The Hungarian sentries stared in surprise as the convoy passed, Skorzeny and the tank commanders saluting smartly as they passed. The convoy still had to cover a kilometre to Horthy's palace, during which the non-armoured vehicles were dangerously exposed to the machine guns of the garrison. Had the Hungarians received definite orders to fight the Germans, a bloodbath would have ensued. In the event, as at Gran Sasso, fortune was to favour the bold. Minutes before the expiration of the ultimatum, Admiral Horthy had travelled to the house of Gruppenführer von Pfeffer-Wildenbruch, one of the more aristocratic types of Waffen-SS officer, having sought his protection. He had not given his garrison commander any orders for the defence of the Bergburg. The convoy divided into two, Skorzeny's own group driving by the German embassy, then the war ministry, where two loud explosions announced that the Fallschirmjager were forcing their way through the tunnel.

Having reached the front of the palace, where one of his tanks smashed through a barricade, Skorzeny encountered three Hungarian tanks and six anti-tank guns which fortunately held their fire. While a small group of his NCOs took position at the front of the building with Panzerfausts pointing at the entrances, Skorzeny dashed into the palace, grabbed a Hungarian officer and demanded to see the garrison commander. As small arms fire broke out in the palace gardens and 'Chinese' Hunke reported the capture of the war ministry, radio station and the Bergburg's entrances, Skorzeny demanded and received the garrison's surrender. Liaison groups were dispatched to spread word of the ceasefire and a few Panzerfausts were fired to dissuade the last Hungarians still fighting in the palace gardens.

Peace was restored by 6.30 a.m. Operation Panzerfaust had prevented the defection of Hungary to the Russians at the cost of four German dead and twelve wounded, mostly sustained by the officer cadets. Hungarian casualties were three dead and fourteen wounded. Admiral Horthy was transported out of Hungary aboard his own special train, escorted by Jagdverband Mitte. James Brady recalled: 'We took Horthy to Munich where he was met by the Deputy of the German Foreign Minister.' Horthy was subsequently brought to the secure Hirschberg Castle in Upper Bavaria.[30]

Alone among her allies, Hungary would remain shackled to Nazi Germany and would share its death agonies. Although Skorzeny's action was a surgical operation which cost a minimum of lives, he was ultimately the servitor of an evil regime. This was amply demonstrated shortly afterwards when one of Budapest's remaining Jews encountered SS-Obersturmbannführer Adolf Eichmann who cheerfully informed him: 'I'm back again.' The following month, Eichmann sent thousands of Jews from Budapest on a death march to Germany, hundreds dying on the roadside from cold and exhaustion. After a protest by a group of senior SS officers (chiefly SS-Oberstgruppenführer Hans Juttner) who witnessed the barbaric treatment meted out to the Jews involved, the marches were suspended. Much to the discomfort of some senior SS officers who were chiefly concerned as to their culpability in the event of Germany's defeat, Eichmann ordered the death marches to continue. Budapest's stay of execution was a short one. That December, the city was devastated by the artillery of the advancing Red Army.[31]

It is rather ironic that, but for a simple twist of fate, or more precisely a drunken night in May 1939, the only two Irishmen known to have joined the Third Reich's armed forces would, almost certainly, have ended up fighting against them; both, after all, had volunteered to join the British Army at a time when war with Germany seemed imminent. It is even more ironic that, had Brady and Stringer remained with the Royal Irish Fusiliers in 1939, it is unlikely that both would have still been alive by late 1944.

In January 1942, the 1st Battalion Royal Irish Fusiliers, along with the 6th Royal Iniskillen Fusiliers and the 2nd Royal Irish Rifles, were incorporated into the 38th (Irish) Brigade, the first commander of this new formation being Brigadier The O'Donoghue, Brady and Stringer's old battalion commander. The establishment of an Irish Brigade in the British Army was the brainchild of Winston Churchill and was carried out despite the opposition of Northern Irish unionists. In December 1942 the new brigade was deployed in Tunisia, suffering heavy casualties during the six months spent there. In the month of April 1943 alone, the 1st Royal Irish Fusiliers suffered 216 casualties. In the assault of Point 622 in the Oued Zarga mountains on 25 April 1943, the battalion's A and D companies, each already reduced to thirty men, lost more than half of their remaining men in the successful assault.

The list of the 'Faughs' battle honours tell their own story. Following Tunisia, the battalion fought in Sicily after which they landed in Taranto on the Italian mainland. Subsequently they fought at Termoli, reinforcing a commando assault. At Monte Cassino, the Irish brigade's assault on the village of Piumerola was instrumental in the German withdrawal from the devastated mountain monastery which they had held for months against Allied assaults.

A deep mutual respect was to grow between the 'Faughs' and the German Fallschirmjagers who were to meet in battle on several occasions. The battalion retained an extremely strong Irish ethos; when being withdrawn through Italy for a well deserved rest from combat, one group of Irishmen flew an improvised Irish tricolour from their troop train. In early 1944, the 38th (Irish) Brigade received some recognition of its status with the authorisation of a distinctive Celtic caubeen head-dress for its three battalions.

The nature of the warfare in which the battalion was involved, a series of assaults against heavily defended German positions in mountainous terrain, was to incur a continuously high casualty rate. On one terrible night, 19 October 1944, the 'Faughs' assault on Monte Spaduro resulted in the loss of a full quarter of the battalion, 146 men being killed, wounded or missing. 'A' Company, along with 'B' Company, was again reduced to a handful of men, while 'D' Company was reduced to thirty effectives.

In all, between December 1942 and the end of the war in May 1945, over 350 men of the 1st Battalion Royal Irish Fusiliers were killed in action, with a correspondingly high number of wounded. One young veteran estimated that of the 600 men of the battalion who went to war in 1939, not more than fifty still remained by 1945.[32]

It is most ironic that the course of events that caused Brady and Stringer's decision to join the Waffen-SS proved to be the safer option for them. This state of affairs was not to last for long, however.

Throughout the war, only a handful of Irishmen attempted to serve Nazi Germany, with only Brady and Stringer being known to have served in arms. There are unsubstantiated rumours of another two: a 'Dr Patrick O'Neill' was claimed to have served with 'SS-Sturmbattalion 500' and another named

'Haye' is claimed to have lost his legs while fighting in the Ukraine with a French Waffen-SS unit in 1944. There is no reliable evidence to confirm the existence of either.

By contrast, the contribution of individual Irishmen to the Allied cause was immense. In early 1945, the British Admiralty, war office and air ministry provided statistics that indicated that over 42,000 Irish citizens were then serving in Britain's armed forces; this figure did not take into account such factors as the numbers of Irish killed, captured and invalided out, and many researchers believe the actual number to be significantly higher. Nearly all of these Irishmen (and women) had voluntarily left neutral Ireland to join the struggle against Nazism. Their motives were hardly economic: employment in Britain's war industry was plentiful and far better paid than the armed forces. Indeed, many thousands of Irish citizens worked here also. Not only did these Irish volunteers serve in large numbers, they also served well, including such men as Dubliner Brendan Finucane, Wing Commander in the RAF at the age of twenty-one, who had shot down thirty-two German aircraft before his death in 1942. Six Victoria crosses, Britain's highest military award, were awarded to Irishmen throughout the war.

Even the thousands who fought in Britain's armed forces did not number all the Irishmen who served the Allied cause. One example was famous Irish playwright Samuel Beckett, who continually risked his life in the French resistance, being awarded the Croix de Guerre after the war. In Rome, Monsignor Hugh O'Flaherty organised the concealment of thousands of escaped POWs and Jews from the Germans until the liberation of the city in June 1944.[33]

In early 1944, the Germans began gathering the Irishmen in their POW camps and, according to one such prisoner, 'for reasons best known to themselves and for motives, now perhaps best forgotten, they gathered them all together at Luckenwalde'. About 1,500 'Irishmen' soon found themselves at the huge Stalag IIIA at Luckenwalde, south of Berlin; while 1,000 of this number were genuine Irishmen, the

'Irishness' of some of the remainder was somewhat suspect. It is possible that the Germans were considering another attempt to recruit Irishmen; following the 1943 agreement between the Wehrmacht and the Waffen-SS, any foreign volunteers were diverted to the latter organisation. Perhaps this was an inevitable consequence of having the same officer, SS-Obergruppenführer Gottleib Berger, responsible for both POW administration and for recruitment to the Waffen-SS.

However, few of the Irishmen at Luckenwalde ever mentioned any serious attempt to recruit them. Apart from the Irish POWs' traditional lack of cooperation, it is doubtful that the Waffen-SS would have relaxed their racial standards enough to admit a few of the 'Irishmen' now incarcerated there. According to one former POW, these included a Navaho native American named Flaherty, a Zulu from South Africa whose long tribal name happened to begin with an 'O' and a Sierra Leonean named Barry who had been raised by Irish missionaries and who was a fine singer of Irish songs with a wonderful Cork accent. In the event, the Irish POWs remained at Luckenwalde until the Russians arrived there in April 1945.[34]

Frank Stringer transferred to the communication centre at Friedenthal in the summer of 1944. This involved him transferring his billet from the company 'lines' in the northern camp to the signallers' separate accommodation hut in the south camp. He recalled:

I remained on at the radio station, and after I had been tested in Morse transmitting and receiving I was given a job as an operator. My work consisted of operating a line called '18' which was connected by radio with a station unknown to me, but which had its call sign which, however, was changed every day according to a reference table used. The call sign of my own station was similarly changed daily. All messages which I sent or received were in code, and sometimes I coded the outgoing messages and decoded the incoming. But much of this was done by a staff of SS girls who worked in the Coding Room. I knew nothing of the contents of many of the messages but in some cases I did, and they all related to matters of military importance, dealing with the transfer of troops in the main. For this job I was paid the same wages as I had earned as an SS infantryman, which was 10 marks a week plus all found.

The officer in charge of this radio station was Untersturm-führer Mussler. His deputy was Unterscharführer Schodstedt (phonetic), and I was responsible to him. He wasn't too satisfied with me as sometimes there were delays in getting messages out. This was usually my fault as I made mistakes sometimes when I wasn't thinking what I was doing.

In October 1944, I was sent alone and unaccompanied to Neu-Strelitz, about 30 miles away, and I took a suitcase radio set with me. My instructions were to try and locate by radio my own station at Friedenthal. The place at Neu-Strelitz was an SS camp called Jagdverband Ost. I was able to find Friedenthal alright but unable to code my messages properly, and so at about the end of November 1944, I was sent back to Friedenthal.

Whilst I was at the camp at Jagdverbande Ost I found that about 100 Serbians, Frenchmen and Norwegians were there in civilian clothes and were being trained in horse-riding and ex-plosives, under the command of Hauptsturmführer Winterfeld. Some of the instructors were named Untersturmführer Bemer (deputy to Winterfeld); Oberscharführer Henn; Oberschar-führer van De Huyder; Unterscharführer Schultz.

Stringer was slightly in error here. Neustrelitz was where the staff of Codd and Colepaugh's agent school near The Hague had been transferred after the dissolution of A-Schule West. In keeping with Skorzeny's policy of militarising the 'civilian' elements of his command, the school had been designated No. 4 Company Jagdverband Northwest. Stringer's naming of staff members does tally largely with Skorzeny's account. The staff included:

Hauptsturführer Winter, CO Director of Training
Untersturmführer Henn, Deputy and Explosives expert
Untersturmführer Hein, W/T Instructor
A Flemish NCO from Flanders, Co Jagdverbande Northwest, chemical sabotage.

Sturmbannführer Radl later claimed that Jagdverbande North-west never reached an operational stage due to the non-availability of Brandenburg personnel. By November, the Kampf Schule at Neustrelitz had become a 'werewolf' training camp; throughout occupied Europe, the Nazis were forced to confront resistance groups and partisans, and the 'werewolf' movement was intended to be a Nazi version of these, performing acts of sabotage and assassination against Allied occupation forces. Skorzeny was ordered to assist SS-Gruppenführer Prutzmann in the training of civilian personnel. After the war, he claimed to have had misgivings about the whole scheme, expressing serious doubts about its viability in a densely populated country with a good infrastructure for the occupiers to make use of and with no possibility of outside help. Other individuals have expressed doubts as to suitability of the German character for guerilla warfare. Nevertheless, by the following March, over 400 'werewolves' had been trained at Neustrelitz, the standard course consisting of a week's instruction in weapons and sabotage. Skorzeny discovered, however, that Prutzmann had greatly exaggerated the efficiency of his organisation. In the event, the most notable act of resistance carried out by 'werewolves' was the assassination of the American-appointed mayor of Aachen in January 1945. Rather than local guerrillas, however, this act was actually carried out by a team parachuted into the area from a captured American bomber. It might have seemed like a suitable task for Skorzeny's Jagdverband Mitte, but at that time they were busy elsewhere.

Stringer continued: 'Also during this time I learned that Hunke had been relieved of the command of my company at Friedenthal and his place had been taken by Obersturmführer Fucker and that he had taken my company (including those who had been sent to Romania and had not returned) to a place called Gravinver [*sic*] in Germany supposedly for training, but in reality to prepare for an offensive on the western front, and they were to wear American uniforms and use American tanks. They were to be called the American Tank

Corps 150, and were to be led by Untersturmführer Girk [*sic*].'
Since Stringer spent most of 1944 on the 'sidelines' of the action at Friedenthal, some of the details in his account for this
time appear to be in error. Hauptsturmführer Fucker was in
fact the battalion commander of Jagdverband Mitte, only two
of his companies were taken to the Grafenwohr training area
to form Panzerbrigade 150, and Obersturmführer Girk was
not the brigade commander. Stringer later mentioned that
'my battalion at Friedenthal was commanded by a Dr Wolf,
who was Sturmbandführer [*sic*], but whose real name was
Skorzeny. I had seen him once or twice but had never spoken
to him.' Dr Wolf was of course the alias that Skorzeny had
used in Budapest:

> I returned from Neu-Strelitz to Friedenthal at about the end
> of November 1944. I was then told by Mussler I would have to
> give up the radio and go back to my billet. When I arrived there
> I found only 5 or 6 men of my company. The remainder of my
> company and the other companies of my battalion had gone
> to Gravinner [*sic*], as I had heard when I was at Neu-Strelitz. I
> remained at Friedenthal doing nothing until the end of January
> 1945, when the battalion returned. I then rejoined my own
> company. I then learned from them that the battalion, led by
> Girk [*sic*], had actually been used on the Western Front in the
> Ardennes offensive, as an American tank unit, but had not been
> too successful.[35]

Hitler showed his delight at the successful outcome of Operation Panzerfaust in Budapest on 20 October 1944 when Skorzeny, accompanied by von Foelkersam, received the gratitude
of his Führer at the 'Wolf's Lair' at Rastenburg where he
was promoted to SS-Obersturmbannführer and awarded the
German Cross in Gold, a prestigious but gaudy decoration
which was often nicknamed the 'fried egg'. In a private meeting, Hitler revealed to Skorzeny his plan for a massive forthcoming offensive on the western front, operation 'Wacht am
Rhein'. Two massive tank formations, the Sixth SS Panzer
Army and the Fifth Panzer Army, along with the mainly

infantry Seventh Army, were to drive through the Belgian
Ardennes across Belgium and Holland to seize the vital Allied
supply port of Antwerp, which Hitler hoped would force
the western Allies to the negotiating table. The emergence
of the Sixth SS Panzer Army, the biggest formation yet
composed principally of Waffen-SS formations, indicated
Hitler's growing confidence in this force. This was to prove
a double-edged sword – the Waffen-SS would continually
be tasked with ever more dangerous and costly missions.
Skorzeny's part in this operation was to form Panzerbrigade
150, a light brigade of three full battalions which would
utilise captured American vehicles and uniforms to seize
the vital bridges across the river Meuse in a surprise attack.
The codename for this undertaking was 'Operation Grief',
which would be carried out in conjunction with a parachute
battalion assault (Operation Stosser) and an assault by SS-
Kampfgruppe Peiper, a brigade-sized armoured formation
commanded by SS-Obersturmbannführer Jocheim Peiper, a
skilled and ruthless panzer commander who had once served
as Heinrich Himmler's adjutant.

According to Skorzeny:

> The mission of this unit [Panzerbrigade 150] was to seize the
> bridges across the Meuse, to operate as shock troops, and take
> advantage of the element of surprise. It was activated at the
> Truppen Uebungs Platz [manoeuvre area] at Grafenwohr in
> November and was composed of the following elements:
>
> Appr 1000 volunteers from the army, navy, GAF [Luftwaffe],
> and Waffen-SS of whom 120 officers and 600 men formed a
> Commando Co and the rest were divided among other units of
> the brigade.
>
> Two Cos of Jagd Verband Mitte – 360 men
> Two Cos of Fsch Jg Btl 600 – 380 men
> Two Bns of KG 200 – 600–800 men – GAF parachutists
> Two Panther tank Cos – 240 men
> Three Pz Gren Cos – 520 men
> Two AT Cos – 200 men
> One Hv Mort Co – 100 men

All figures given are approximate. The total strength of the brigade was 3,000 men, of whom 300 to 400 were dressed in American uniforms. When this unit was committed, all non-combat elements remained at Truppen Uebungs Platz Wahn, S of Cologne, reducing the brigade to a combat strength of 2,400 men. Before the offensive, in early December Skorzeny had made a tour of the various Army HQs on the Western Front in order to familiarise himself with the plan of action.[36]

Skorzeny had less than five weeks to assemble and train his brigade; it was originally intended that this would consist of 3,300 men, at least some of whom would speak English in the American fashion, and equipped with fifty armoured vehicles and over 200 trucks and jeeps. By late November, it had become obvious that this was an impossible objective. Only fifteen American trucks, thirty jeeps and four American scout cars were eventually procured for Panzerbrigade 150, and Skorzeny was left with no option but to modify German vehicles for the task. Five Panzer V (Panthers) had their appearance altered with sheet metal to resemble American M10 tank destroyers, and along with five Sturmgeschutz armoured vehicles were painted olive green with white five-pointed stars in the American pattern.

Panzerbrigade 150's strength did not exceed 2,500 men; 500 of these were from the Waffen-SS, 800 from the Luft-waffe and the balance from the Heer. Of the 400 English speakers assembled, it transpired that half had only a rudi-mentary knowledge of the language. Of the remainder, most could speak English with a proficiency ranging from good to excellent, but only ten could speak the language perfectly with a knowledge of American slang. Since there were only enough American uniforms and weapons available to equip a few of Skorzeny's men adequately, Skorzeny decided to con-centrate his 150 best linguists into a unit designated 'Enheit Stielau', who were given a hurried training in demolitions, communications and details of the US Army. It was intended that members of this unit could identify themselves to other

German units by wearing blue scarves and removing their steel helmets on contact.

The rest of the brigade were divided into three Kampf-gruppe of light battalion size, each designated X, Y and Z. The unit's officers did not learn the details of Operation Grief until 10 December, less than a week before the start of the offensive. The main assault of 'Wacht am Rhein' would be undertaken by the Sixth SS Panzer Army, spearheaded by the massive 'Leibstandarte' and 'Hitlerjugend' Panzer divisions, as well as the 12th Volksgrenadier Division; each division would be accompanied by a Kampfgruppe of Panzerbrigade 150. It was intended that when the three divisions reached the Hohes Venn in the Ardennes on the first day of the offensive, the three Kampfgruppe would move forward that night and seize at least two of the vital Amay, Huy and Andenne bridges across the Meuse.

Moving at night, Panzerbrigade 150 reached its forward assembly area near Munstereifel two days before the start of the offensive. At 5 a.m. on 16 December 1944, after a short artillery barrage, the three German armies crashed into the weakly defended American lines along a forty-mile front. The initial attack took the Americans by surprise and the salient briefly formed in the American front line caused the conflict to be known to the Americans as 'The Battle of the Bulge'. That afternoon, Panzerbrigade 150's three Kampf-gruppes moved out, each accompanying its assigned division. Hauptsturmführer Adrian von Foelkersam took command of Kampfgruppe X when its original commander was killed by a mine. Progress was slow, however, and after two days the objective of the Hohes Venn had not been reached. With the element of surprise lost, Skorzeny proposed that his three Kampfgruppe be combined to form a single conventional unit, and was ordered to assist in an assault on the Malmedy area. Here Panzerbrigade 150 encountered determined American resistance; when SS-Kampfgruppe Peiper had passed through the area a few days earlier, some of its inexperienced and trigger-happy teenage soldiers had massacred nearly 100 American prisoners. Word of the 'Malmedy massacre', the worst such incident perpetrated against American forces by the Germans, spread like lightning among American forces in Europe and did much to bolster their fighting spirit. Hitler's underestimation of the Americans' fighting ability, along with the intervention of Patton's Third Army and a break in the weather which allowed the full weight of Allied airpower to be brought to bear, were major factors in the failure of the offensive. By mid-January the Germans were back where they started, with the loss of over a 100,000 men.[37]

Skorzeny estimated that his force suffered 15 per cent casualties before being withdrawn from the line on 28 December, with Skorzeny and von Foelkersam both wounded. Panzerbrigade 150 was transported by train back to Grafenwohr where it was disbanded, and its troops returned to their own units by the end of January 1945.

'Enheit Stielau' had been assigned to behind-the-lines operations: 'At the start of the operation, three or four recon teams of three men each were sent out, dressed in American uniforms and equipped with jeeps. Two sabotage teams of five men each in American uniforms, driving three-quarter tonne trucks, were sent against enemy-held bridges. One recon and one sabotage team came back. It had been planned to commit 300 to 400 men on similar missions but this proved impossible when the offensive did not sustain itself.' In all, Skorzeny later claimed that a total of forty-four 'Enheit Stielau' personnel were sent behind American lines, of whom he claimed all but eight returned. The Americans, however, executed eighteen Germans for wearing American uniforms.

The Hollywood depiction of Skorzeny's Enheit Stielau tends to be that of American-uniformed Waffen-SS men speaking flawless American English, ruthlessly slaughtering all Americans unfortunate enough to encounter them. In fact less than ten of the unit, most of whom were Wehrmacht personnel rather than Waffen-SS, spoke English well enough to have a hope of passing as Americans. This was to prove the downfall of some of the fake Americans who did not return to German lines; one team was killed when they betrayed themselves by using the term 'company' incorrectly, while another was captured (and subsequently executed) when they asked for 'petrol' instead of 'gas'. There is no evidence that these 'Americans' killed any prisoners; although Panzerbrigade 150 fought in the Malmedy region, it had no involvement in the massacre that occurred there.

Although one of its reconnaissance teams is said to have made it all the way to the river Meuse, Enheit Stielau accomplished little of material value to the Germans. Neither did Operation Stosser, the attempted parachute drop behind enemy lines; a combination of inexperienced pilots and Fallshirmjager dropped at night resulted in a fiasco. Their enormous psychological impact, however, was a different matter, resulting in a state of near paranoia among the American forces. Strangers behind American lines were regarded with deep suspicion. General Omar Bradley, commander of 12th Army Group, was obliged to identify himself several times during the course of every journey he undertook. When one of the captured 'Americans' repeated a rumour that had been popular at Grafenwohr, namely that Panzerbrigade 150's real mission was to travel to Paris to capture the Allied high command, Allied Supreme Commander General Eisenhower was placed under effective house arrest for his own safety.[38]

Although Skorzeny was to become notorious for his use of American uniforms, there was nothing new about this ruse. SS Jager Battalion 502 used Russian and Romanian uniforms in Romania for Operation Landfried, and the Brandenburg regiment made use of Allied uniforms on several occasions. The use of enemy uniforms was a ploy that the Allied forces had not hesitated to use themselves on occasion. During the operation that encircled the German Sixth Army in Stalingrad two years earlier, the Russians used captured German panzers to seize a vital bridge. In fact, in the early stages of the battle of Aachen in October 1944, the US Army de-

ployed small units of Rangers wearing German uniform and
speaking German, who actually took part in combat while so
dressed.[39]

Could James Brady have been a member of Enheit Stein-
lau? When Stringer described spending the months of
December and January in Friedenthal, he made no specific
mention of seeing Brady there. Skorzeny was desperately
short of personnel who spoke English well enough to pass as
Americans, and Haupsturmführer Menzel's original recruitment of Brady to SS Jager Battalion 502 in March 1944 is
very likely to have been influenced by Brady's remarkable
command of the English language. It might not have been
necessary for Brady to have had any knowledge of American
slang; Irish accents were far from rare in the US Army.

It seems likely from Brady's postwar statement that his
interrogators questioned him on this very point, and he specifically claimed that he had remained at Friedenthal during this period. 'We returned to Berlin, where we stayed until
the middle of January 1945. I then met Stringer again and
we spent Christmas [1944] together. I heard that one of our
companies, the 1st, to which I was later attached, had been
engaged on the western front. I later learned that it was the
Ardennes offensive and that the unit had previously been
trained to use American equipment.' It would have been most
wise for Brady to deny being a member of Panzerbrigade 150
even if he was involved; while Brady's admissions to his activities against the Russians were serious enough, an admission
to having fought against the western Allies could have proved
ultimately fatal. However, while there were exceptions to the
rule, as for example the Dutch Waffen-SS units that fought
for the Germans at Arnhem, it was not normally the policy of
the Waffen-SS to deploy western European volunteers on the
western front. While the 'Das Reich' SS Panzer Division in
the summer of 1944 included many conscripts from occupied
Alsace, such personnel often had divided loyalties (a few

had relatives in the French resistance) and it was eventually
concluded that their conscription was a mistake. This would
probably have accounted for the five or six members of Jagdverband Mitte's No. 1 Company that remained in Friedenthal
with Frank Stringer. To be fair, James Brady may have been
among this group; while Stringer did not specifically mention
that Brady was at Friedenthal with him during Christmas
1944, neither does he deny it.[40]

Having disbanded Panzerbrigade 150, von Foelkersam
requested command of his own battalion, namely Jagdverband Ost, an 800-strong unit of which half were Germans,
the remainder comprised of Russians and Balts. Skorzeny
granted the request with some reluctance, having come to
greatly depend on von Foelkersam's skill in planning and exe-
cuting special operations.

Since July 1944, the Red Army had halted at the Vistula, until a massive buildup of forces was completed. On 12
January 1945, the Russians launched their last great winter
offensive of the war. On 18 January, Jagdverband Ost was deployed to the city of Hohensalza, one hundred miles east of
Poznan in occupied Poland and directly in the path of Marshal Zhukov's First Belorussian front. Two days later the town
was surrounded, and von Foelkersam's battalion attempted to
break out the following night. Of Jagdverband Ost's 800 men,
only a handful returned to German lines after several weeks.
Adrian von Foelkersam was not among them. Skorzeny felt
the loss keenly; von Foelkersam was a trusted comrade and a
close friend.[41]

Another of Jagdverband Mitte's officers went missing at
about this time. Obersturmführer Girg of Operation Landfried in Romania, and a group of fifty men, of whom some
were Russian volunteers, were taken by ship to Danzig where
they were 'sent on an operation in Poland without Skorzeny's
knowledge or consent'. Manning captured T-34 tanks and
wearing Russian uniform, the group were sent behind Russian
lines on a long-range reconnaissance and sabotage operation.

They continued to transmit important information until radio contact with them ceased after a few days. It would not be the last Skorzeny had heard of Girg, however.[42]

As the German forces in Poland began to collapse, and the Russians reached the eastern provinces of Germany itself, Colonel-General Guderian urged the formation of Army Group Vistula, a group of German armies to prevent the Russians from reaching the Oder river and driving into the heartland of Germany. Hitler agreed, but instead of selecting a Wehrmacht officer to command, he instead appointed 'the loyal Heinrich', Reichsführer SS Heinrich Himmler, which even Skorzeny regarded as 'a regrettable decision'. When the Germans invaded Russia in 1941 they were helped greatly by the incompetence of Marshals Vorishilov and Budyenny, appointed for their loyalty to Stalin rather than any military competence. In turn, the Russian invasion of eastern Germany was greatly facilitated by the new commander of 'Army Group Vistula'. Even a competent general would have had his work cut out here; the new 'Army Group' was originally little more than a corps of three battered panzer divisions, to which a number of 'divisions' were added that existed as such in name only. Himmler was to prove very much a part-time general, refusing to relinquish his existing appointments of Minister of the Interior, chief of the RSHA and commander of the Reserve Army. While a general could not be expected to share the living conditions of his troops, Himmler took things to an extreme – while those of the troops at the front that were lucky enough to sleep in the face of constant Russian night attacks did so in foxholes with temperatures dropping to minus ten degrees centigrade, the Reichsführer slept in a huge bedroom (compared by some officers to a 'boudoir') of red wood furniture with pale green drapes and coverlets with orders that his sleep should not be disturbed no matter the crisis. He began his morning with a bath, massage and breakfast and rarely appeared in his luxuriously appointed office before ten-thirty.[43]

By the end of January, Russian forces had reached the Oder, even establishing bridgeheads to the north and south of Kustrin, a fortress on the river just fifty miles east of Berlin. On the evening of 30 January, Skorzeny was in his office in Friedenthal when he received a telephone call from the new commander of 'Army Group Vistula', ordering him to gather all his available forces without delay and march to Schwedt, a town on the Oder about halfway between Kustrin and Stettin to the north. Himmler's original order also required Skorzeny to liberate the Russian-held city of Freienwalde along the way, the first of many such nonsensical orders that Skorzeny was to receive.

Skorzeny spent the night organising his available units, constantly interrupted by a series of irritating phone calls from the Reichsführer. In Friedenthal itself he had the Jagdverband Mitte battalion and the Scharfschutzen-Kompanie, the latter a company of seventy snipers commanded by Obersturmführer Otto Wisler. There was also the Jagdverband headquarters staff which included Hauptsturmführer Hunke (operations officer), a supply company and two signals platoons. In Neustrelitz to the east there was the SS-Fallschirmjager Battailon 600 under the command of Sturmbannführer Siegfried Milius, and Jagdverband Nord West. The latter could deploy only two operational companies which were comprised mostly of Dutchmen, Danes, Finns and Norwegians, not including the Kampf Schule there, although it had been designated 'No. 4 Company' of the unit. The SS para battalion now numbered (according to Skorzeny) 900 men, a support company having been added which was equipped with heavy machine guns and mortars. Skorzeny also claimed that Jagdverband Mitte now numbered 800 men. These figures were disputed by Sturmbannführer Karl Radl, who claimed that neither battalion exceeded 500 men; Radl's figure would appear to be the more dubious given the fact that the line company of each unit comprised 175 men, while a similar assertion by Radl that Jagdverband Mitte was a 'German only' unit was patently untrue.

Neither Himmler nor Führer Headquarters could offer any information on how far the Russians had advanced, and at 3 a.m. Skorzeny was obliged to send two reconnaissance patrols to Schwedt-on-Oder to ensure that the Russians had not already taken the city. At 5 a.m. Skorzeny's main force drove out from the barracks in driving snow and freezing darkness.

On issue to Jagdverband Mitte at this time were camouflage combat suits worn over the standard battledress. These were reversible garments, white on one side for use in snow, 'eichenlaub'(oak tree) pattern on the other side for use in more temperate conditions. Also in service was the Sturmgewehr 44: this advanced weapon pioneered the concept of the assault rifle, a fully automatic weapon firing a shortened rifle cartridge for use in close-quarters battle. The Germans were using this weapon in combat twenty years before other armies introduced similar weapons. All in all, the best equipped members of Jagdverband Mitte would not have looked out of place in a modern army.

It was the first time that Jagdverband Mitte was deployed in its entirety. Until now only a maximum of two companies were deployed on operations at any one time, always leaving a reserve of elite troops from which the unit could be reconstructed if necessary. Skorzeny's force already included several western European nationalities, including two Irishmen. According to James Brady: 'About the third week in January 1945, the whole battalion – including Stringer and myself – were taken in lorries to Schwate [sic] on the river Oder. Here we held a bridgehead on the eastern bank of the river for a month against the Russians. Stringer was in the bridgehead.'

Dawn was breaking over the icy streets of Schwedt-on-Oder when Skorzeny arrived two hours later. 'The Pearl of the Uckermark', famous for a castle and an aristocratic cavalry regiment, was a city with a population of 50,000, greatly swollen by the flood of refugees from the east. He met his reconnaissance patrols there and sent them onward to Konigs-berg-Neumark, a town ten miles east of Kustrin. Skorzeny found the city to be almost defenceless; the Oder river was frozen solid and provided no obstacle to the advancing Rus-sians, while the 'garrison' consisted only of a reserve battalion of elderly men, 150 officer cadets and their instructors who were on an engineering course, a group of pioneers who could not march, and a number of sick and wounded. It soon became obvious, however, that there was another source of manpower: a stream of retreating soldiers whose units had been destroyed in the fighting to the east. These were given orders to assem-ble in a barracks where they were fed, issued equipment and organised into new units among which the officer cadets' in-structors were distributed. Within three days Skorzeny had two new battalions, for which the army provided some staff officers. Arrangements were made to channel the flow of civil-ian refugees and to evacuate the worst cases by train.

Having established a command post at the village of Nieder-kronig on the east bank of the Oder, Skorzeny began organis-ing his perimeter defences; these were constructed by a labour service unit sent from Stettin, and a workforce composed of the remaining male civilian population of Schwedt. The de-fences consisted of three concentric lines, the outermost run-ning five miles outside the town, the innermost within a mile. Observation posts were established outside the outer line and aggressive patrols carried out to the east, some penetrating forty miles behind Russian lines and bringing back prison-ers and intelligence. The thick ice on the Oder and the canal parallel to it were dynamited, turning them both into viable obstacles. Skorzeny's supply officer (Hauptsturmführer Ger-hardt) located a depot near Frankfurt-on-Oder from which he was able to procure hundreds of MG-42s and ammunition. This machine gun, of such a superlative design that it still re-mains in service with some European armies, could fire at a rate of 1,200 rounds per minute. The noise of this weapon was likened to 'tearing lino' rather than the chatter of a normal machine gun. Given the fact that Brady's account mentions that he became a machine-gunner at this time, it is almost certain that he would have wielded one of the deadly 'Hitler sagans' (Hitler saws) as the MG-42 was nicknamed due to its lethal effectiveness against Russian infantry attacks.

About thirty miles to the south-west was a factory from which Skorzeny procured forty new 75mm anti-tank guns with ammunition. These were presumably the PAK 40 anti-tank guns, capable of knocking out any Russian tank at close range. Hermann Goering sent two battalions of anti-aircraft guns, including the superb 88mm and 105mm artillery which Skorzeny (originally an artillery officer) used as field artillery; the 88mm in particular had a proven record of being used in this role. Six of Goering's guns were mounted on heavy trucks and began firing on the Russian lines from several different positions, giving an illusion of greater strength. Another battery was mounted on the barges on the now ice-free canal west of the river, allowing them to fire and rapidly change position most effectively.

From the first day, Skorzeny sent out reconnaissance patrols to establish the extent of the Russian advance, and the first Red Army unit was encountered in Bad Schonfliess, less than fifteen miles from Schwedt. One of these reconnaissance patrols encountered an eerie sight: a column of concentration camp victims being marched to the west.

By 3 February, Skorzeny was able to deploy the two battalions he had formed from the stragglers, and used them to man the outer ring of defences. The second ring was manned by Jagdverband Mitte, while Milius' SS Fallschirmjager battalion deployed to the east of the bridgehead to take the first brunt of the Russian assault. Reinforcements continued to trickle in, including two battalions of the Volkssturm, a militia raised in the last months of the war from teenagers and elderly men. Badly armed, trained and led, they often suffered heavy casualties in combat. One of these battalions was composed from the farmers of Konigsberg-Neumarkt and led by the local district commander of the Nazi party, while the other was formed from tough Hamburg dockers who fought particularly well against the Russians despite the fact that most were former communists. Another battalion was sent by the Luftwaffe, consisting of personnel who not only had no aircraft to fly or maintain, but who had not even received any infantry training. To the dismay of their highly decorated commanding officer, Skorzeny wisely broke up the battalion and distributed the personnel among his other units, where the airmen were able to benefit from the experience of the veteran infantrymen. More exotic reinforcements were to follow, including a squadron of horse cavalry, a unit of Cossacks and a regiment of Romanian-Germans.

By 5 February, the long-range reconnaissance patrols to the east were no longer possible as the Russians brought up increasingly stronger forces. Skorzeny himself led a reconnaissance patrol to Bad Schoenfliess, comprised of veteran members of Jagdverband Mitte, to find the town was already held by the Russians. Three-man patrols stealthily made their way to the town's railway station where they observed over forty Russian tanks. Withdrawing with only a handful of civilians that they had been able to evacuate, Skorzeny gave the order for his troops to occupy Konigsberg, and this was accomplished by the two Volkssturm battalions, the SS Fallschirmjagers and an army battalion. The Russians attacked in force in the afternoon with several infantry battalions, led by the tanks that they had brought up to Bad Schoenfliess, several of which were destroyed at close range by Panzerfausts. During the course of the fierce street fighting which ensued, the leader of the Konigsberg Volkssturm fled, and his example was followed by two groups of his battalion. The resulting desperate situation was only salvaged by the Hamburg dockers and the Fallschirmjager, the latter suffering heavy losses in the process. After midnight, Skorzeny gave the order for his troops to withdraw from Konigsberg, and he himself returned to his headquarters at Schwedt-on-Oder where he met the district leader who had fled the previous day. This man was charged with cowardice and desertion and subsequently executed.

By 7 February, the Russians had begun a series of daily attacks on the bridgehead, concentrating on the same three areas, and Skorzeny abandoned his outposts in villages outside the bridgehead. Apart from T-34s, the Russians were also using American-supplied Sherman tanks. The commander of 'Army Group Vistula' was not pleased to hear of the evacuation of the villages and at 4 p.m. ordered Skorzeny to present himself at his headquarters to account for his actions. This, however, was during the outbreak of heavy fighting, and Skorzeny was only able to make an appearance four hours late and still dirty from combat, to the fury of Himmler who threatened him with court-martial and demotion. There are slightly varying versions of Skorzeny's reaction, most describing him as calm and reasonable. The outcome was that Himmler, realising that his 'generalship' was coming under increasing scrutiny, invited Skorzeny to dinner during which he promised him a battalion of armoured assault guns.

The battalion actually arrived the following day, when thirty brand new Sturmgeschutz IVs of the 210th Assault Gun battalion arrived at Schwedt under the command of Major Langel, so fresh from the factory that they had not even been painted. The Sturmgeschutz (Stug for short) assault gun was essentially an armoured fighting vehicle with a fixed turret, the Stug IV mounting a 75mm gun which would prove effective against all Russian armour. The first effective armoured support that Skorzeny had received, they arrived none too soon. They were immediately deployed across the river between Niedersaaten and Konigsberg and were in action the following day when the Russians launched a major assault on Grabow and Hausberg, one battery stopping an armoured assault by 'Joseph Stalin' heavy tanks, destroying thirteen of them in the process. Shortly afterwards, Skorzeny himself led an assault on Russian positions near Hauseberg,

involving both the 210th Stug battalion and Jagdverband
Mitte. A Russian flamethrower battalion was wiped out, and a
large quantity of artillery and heavy machine guns captured.

The Russians captured Grabow but the town was briefly
retaken following a surprise attack by a recent reinforcement
from Friedenthal. This was a light armoured company led by
Obersturmführer Otto Schwerdt which included ten veterans
of the Gran Sasso raid. Following his difficulties in procuring
tanks for Panzerbrigade 150, Skorzeny ordered the formation
of this unit to ensure the availability of armoured support for
Jagdverband Mitte. Schwerdt, soon to be promoted Hauptsturmführer, had a rather murky background; apart from his
own involvement at Gran Sasso, he was involved in terrorist activities in Denmark the previous year. Four of the Gran
Sasso veterans were killed in the assault on Grabow, and were
buried in the graveyard there with full military honours.

Hermann Goering paid a visit to Schwedt, travelling almost as far as the front line. He visited a Luftwaffe artillery
crew and Sturmbannführer Milius' command post, handing
out cigars and liquor with which Skorzeny noted he was 'very
well supplied'.

Skorzeny's command eventually rose to 15,000 troops,
which made him the commander of an ad hoc division although he did not receive the corresponding rank. James
Brady might have sympathised – he was placed in command
of a section, although he did not receive the promotion to
NCO rank that such an appointment normally merits.

Although the bridgehead continued to shrink in the face
of overwhelming Russian opposition (the Stug battalion
was withdrawn after ten days to be redeployed at Kustrin),
Skorzeny's innovative tactics kept the position intact for four
weeks, even though there was never any possibility of the
grandiose counter-attack proposed by Himmler. Skorzeny at-
tributed most of his success to his own elite troops, who had
acted as the hard core of his command. He reserved particular
praise for Obersturmführer Wilscher's company of snipers,

who operated in two-man teams from the 'no man's land' between the opposing lines. The Germans had learned the hard way from the Red Army just how effective snipers could be in warfare, and Wilscher's snipers were particularly ruthless, specialising in picking off Russian tank crews who were escaping from their stricken vehicles.

Skorzeny was called away from Schwedt-on-Oder on 28 February, and summoned to Führer Headquarters in Berlin. The bridgehead was finally abandoned on 3 March. Sturmbannführer Milius took charge of the demolition party of the last bridge over the Oder as a rearguard attempted to cross it under heavy fire. The charges were detonated and the bridge destroyed as soon as the last survivor had crossed. Milius' battalion had suffered heavy casualties during the four weeks of fighting but, along with Jagdverband Mitte, were soon to suffer even worse losses.[44]

By Brady's account: 'At the end of February 1945 we evacuated the bridgehead and were transferred to another bridgehead at Oderbridge [sic].' Within a week of the successful withdrawal of Skorzeny's force from Schwedt-on-Oder, orders were received to establish another bridgehead on the Oder south of Schwedt, east of the town of Oderburg and west of the town of Zehden. What exactly Himmler hoped to achieve by this is unclear; apparently it was hoped that the Russians would delay their final assault on Berlin until such time as the east bank of the Oder river was cleared of all German forces. Perhaps Himmler also believed that Skorzeny's successful defence of Schwedt-on-Oder vindicated his own decision to use special forces as line infantry. Skorzeny's two main battalions, Jagdverband Mitte and SS-Fallschirmjager Battailon 600, would form a battlegroup and hold their positions for as long as possible before retreating across the one bridge available to them, which would be destroyed by explosives after their withdrawal. It was a simple, if extremely risky, plan, but as the German General von Moltke once observed, plans rarely survive contact with the enemy.

The force involved was designated SS-Kampfgruppe
Solar, a slightly unusual designation: such battlegroups were
normally named after their commander, while 'Solar' was actually Skorzeny's codename. In fact, Skorzeny would not even
command the unit – he was called away to defend Germany's
western frontier when the Americans captured the Ludendorff bridge across the Rhine; Skorzeny was involved in the
desperate German attempts to destroy it. Command of SS-
Kampfgruppe Solar fell to Sturmbannführer Milius, while
Obersturmführer Fritz Leifheit took command of the de-
pleted SS-Fallschirmjager Battailon 600. Jagdverband Mitte
remained under the command of Haupsturmführer Karl
Fucker. The relatively junior ranks held by the battalion commanders are noteworthy, but were a feature of the Waffen-
SS in the final year of the war. Skorzeny was effectively a
divisional commander with the rank equivalent of a battalion
commander. SS-Kampfgruppe Solar received slight reinforcements in the shape of six armoured cars and four Panzer
IV tanks. The latter were no match for the standard Russian
T-34 tank, even on an individual basis. There was also an artillery battery comprising six 150mm howitzers under the
command of Hauptsturmführer Reiche. Only two of these
guns, however, were actually positioned in the bridgehead;
the remaining four were kept on the west bank of the Oder
and, due to extreme ammunition shortages, were under orders
not to fire at targets across the river.

On 9 March 1945, SS-Kampfgruppe Solar moved across
the Oder and relieved a battalion of naval personnel. These
men were former sailors without warships or useful infantry
training and understandably wasted no time in vacating their
positions. While Milius set up his command post in the basement of a church in the village of Alt-Kustrinchen, Fucker
and Leifheit established their battalion headquarters in the
same village, their troops 'digging in' and setting up positions
in their designated areas. Jagdverband Mitte deployed in the
north of the bridgehead, SS Fallschirmjager Battailon 600 to

the south. James Brady and Frank Stringer were now with No. 1 Company of Jagdverband Mitte, which was now under the command of Hauptsturmführer Manns who had commanded the reinforced company during Operation Panzerfaust in Budapest.

Brady and Stringer were a long way from home as they prepared to defend Hitler's crumbling Reich. The port of Berdiansk, where the pair had spent the August of 1943, had long since fallen to the Russians. The Channel Islands, where they were originally abandoned to the Germans, had been bypassed by the Allied forces and was still garrisoned by a ragged and emaciated Wehrmacht infantry divison. SS-Ausbildlager Sennheim had been burnt out and abandoned to the Americans in January. The Allies had already redrawn the borders of Europe. The small chunk of Germany that SS-Kampfgruppe Solar was attempting to defend was to be handed over to Poland and the river Oder was to form the postwar frontier between Germany and Poland.

On Saturday 10 March, Milius ordered his force onto the offensive, with the objective of pushing back the light Russian forces in the vicinity and capturing the village of Alt-Rudnitz. Although the village was not captured, the surprised Russians were pushed back and some ground was gained, providing a welcome boost to morale. The bridgehead now held by SS-Kampfgruppe Solar was four kilometres wide by four kilometres deep. Although the Russians began a desultory artillery barrage of the German positions, the SS paras and commandos had two weeks of relative respite before experiencing the full force of the Red Army's wrath. Brady, however, had been taken to the rear: 'We held [the bridgehead] for a few days and then we made an attack, forcing the Russians back a short distance. The Russians then attacked and I was slightly wounded. I went behind the lines to a training unit at Eberwarlde [sic].' This was presumably the town of Eberswalde. 'I was attached to a police unit – I was training the civilian police who had been called up. This lasted for about two weeks.'

Duo to a dearth of manpower, the Berlin civil police were armed and dispatched to the front in the last days of the battle of Berlin, causing a predictable collapse of remaining order in the shattered city.

The sturdy steel and concrete bridge over the river Oder, upon which the safe retreat of SS-Kampfgruppe Solar depended, was already being prepared for demolition by the Wehrmacht's 257th Engineer Battalion. Having had some experience of bridge demolition in Romania the previous year, it is likely that Brady would have been alarmed had he learned that the reservist officer in charge of the demolition had planted several large explosive charges without observing the basic safety precaution of disarming them until such time as they were ready to be used. It is said that, in wartime, if anything can possibly go wrong, then it will. Sure enough, an exploratory Russian artillery barrage onto the bridge found its mark, and with a loud blast the bridge was destroyed. Surrounded by Russians, SS-Kampfgruppe Solar was now trapped on the wrong side of the river.

On Friday 16 March, after an intense artillery barrage, the Russians launched a limited ground assault on the Zehden bridgehead. They initially succeeded in pushing back the Waffen-SS battlegroup for five kilometres but were halted before the village of Niederwutzen and pushed back again. The Russians were content to continue an increasingly heavier artillery barrage, which inflicted heavy casualties among Kampfgruppe Solar. For now the Russians had higher priorities. Nearly a week later, on 22 March, the trapped members of the SS-Kampfgruppe heard what appeared to be a curious humming noise in the distance, which increased in density until the air seemed to vibrate. This was the noise being generated by a stupendous thousand-gun Russian artillery barrage onto the German forces near the Kustrin salient to the south. In a well executed pincer movement, the Russian forces to the north and south of Kustrin had succeeded in linking up to the west of the fortress, trapping the 20th Panzer Division there.[45]

At 6 p.m. a small glimmer of hope for the men of Army Group Vistula presented itself when a short and rather scruffy general turned up at the headquarters of Heinrich Himmler, who had been persuaded to relinquish command. Despite outward appearances, Colonel-General Heinrici was an officer of the old school and a master of the defensive battle. The two men were a study in contrasts: to the despair of his staff officers, Heinrici tended to wear a sheepskin jacket in the field, something that marked him as someone who did not spend much of his time in comfortable offices. Often there was little to distinguish him from his soldiers other than the Knight's Cross with Oak Leaves that he wore at his throat, a decoration that Himmler was known to covet. On his Reichsführer's uniform, Himmler wore several decorations; these included the 'Blood Order' that was issued to Nazis who were involved in Hitler's abortive 'Beerhall Putsch' in 1923, a medal for service with the Waffen-SS to which he was not actually entitled, and an ornate Luftwaffe aircrew insignia. The latter was apparently a present from Hermann Goering since Himmler certainly never qualified as military aircrew.

After Heinrici's arrival, Himmler launched into a long attempt to justify his position, which was interrupted by the news that Kustrin had been cut off. Himmler took his leave with indecent haste, leaving Heinrici to acquaint himself with his new command without the benefit of even a proper briefing. Although the 'Army Group' now at least had the benefit of a capable commander, this came too late for the men trapped at Zehden and Kustrin.[46]

Ironically, the deployment of Jagdverband Mitte from Friedenthal to the Oder was to prove the safer option for the unit's members, in the short term at least. Their base at Friedenthal had been subjected to a heavy Allied air raid, although the headquarters staff were already relocated to Hof in Bavaria. Skorzeny was to claim that the BBC had triumphantly announced the destruction of his base three times.

On Sunday 25 March, the Russians were ready to turn

their full attention to the German units in the Zehden bridgehead. Having surrounded them with a force comprising a tank brigade, two infantry brigades and a cavalry division, the Russians unleashed a murderous barrage from over 500 artillery pieces. The Russian artillery included large numbers of the greatly feared 'Katyusha' multi-barrel rocket launchers, known to the Germans as the 'Stalin Organ'. Launched from rails mounted on the backs of trucks, the 100lb projectiles soared into the air with a scream like a jet engine, trailing dense plumes of black smoke that were visible for miles. It was not unknown for defective rounds to cause casualties among the crews firing them. The missiles descended with a terrifying howl before thoroughly blanketing their target; each truck was capable of covering a 200-square foot area with sixteen warheads in ten seconds.

This enormous volume of firepower was being directed into an area of less than sixteen square kilometres. The Kampfgruppe's trenches, dugouts and barbed wire obstructions dug into the sandy soil were obliterated; by that evening the heavily-cratered ground resembled a lunar landscape.

On this day, James Brady faithfully returned to Jagdverband Mitte. This cannot have been an easy task. At this time the only method of crossing the Oder near Zehden was by the few small boats belonging to the engineer battalion. The engineers were also attempting to construct an improvised footbridge above the bridge's wreckage, but it would appear that this was not finished at this time.

By the following morning (26 March) SS-Kampfgruppe Solar's ammuntion was almost exhausted. The Russians began pushing back the Waffen-SS troops toward the river, and by mid-day they had reached the village of Alt-Kustrinchen. Hundreds of howling Katyusha rockets poured onto the devastated town and its hapless defenders, the 2nd Company of the SS parachute battalion. In the basement below the village's church, Sturmbannführer Milius was sharing his command post with scores of his troops who were wounded in

the bitter fighting. The church basement was filled with the
agonised cries of the injured and the stench from their in-
fected wounds. Emergency surgery was being carried out on a
shaking old kitchen table, which orderlies had to hold steady
during operations. Conditions in this emergency aid station
were so appalling that medical staff were willing to risk near-
certain death in the hellish barrage outside just for a short
break from the hellish conditions within.

The 3rd Company of the SS paras were taking the brunt of
the Russian attack, due to the fact that they were the sub-unit
linking SS-Fallschirmjager Battailon 600 with Jagdverband
Mitte. Throughout the morning they fought off four assaults
which often culminated in vicious hand-to-hand fighting.
Bizarrely, the paras of 3rd Company almost welcomed such
assaults, since they gave the only respite from the constant
barrage of Katyusha rockets and 152mm heavy artillery. At 1
p.m., however, with their stock of Panzerfausts almost expend-
ed, they found themselves facing an attack by two full battalions of infantry, spearheaded by a company of T-34 tanks.
On the company commander's orders, the remaining Panzerfaust launchers held their fire until the T-34s were almost
upon them; when they were launched, several of the firers were
killed by the explosion of their own weapons. Although half of
the Russian tanks were stopped, the 3rd Company were overwhelmed by a force ten times the strength of their own.

Upon hearing that his two battalions had been separated,
Milius ordered the withdrawal of his forces from Alt-Kustrinchen, and also that the wounded be carried out. A platoon
volunteered to remain behind to allow their comrades to get
clear – a suicide mission if ever there was one.

Jagdverband Mitte was still holding the village of Niederwutzen which controlled the approach road of the now demolished bridge across the Oder. Had it not been for the engineer officer's blunder, it might still have been possible at this
stage to withdraw the survivors of SS-Kampfgruppe Solar
across the river at this point as originally planned.

Of 27 March, Brady bleakly recalled: 'The Russians attacked again and just about wiped us out.' On that morning,
the Russians concentrated a comprehensive creeping barrage
onto the shrinking German position, starting by pouring a
rain of shells and rockets onto a line before the German front
line, then slowly working their way back. It was incredible that
any of the Waffen-SS troops survived at all, far less enough
to continue fighting. The front line of SS-Kampfgruppe Solar was now pushed back to within 500 metres of the Oder,
while even Milius' command post was now based in a bunker
within 200 metres of the river. Row upon row of wounded
men were lying upon the river bank, Russian shells exploding
among them. More than a year later, Brady would recall: 'The
last time I saw Stringer was in the bridgehead at Oderbridge
[*sic*], before I was wounded. He was then a lance-corporal.'
Shortly afterwards, Brady was 'slightly wounded in the head'.
Although he claims that this wound was slight, it was to keep
him in hospital for over a month.

Milius was faced with no other option but to withdraw
his remaining troops across the river, but the impossibility of
such a move during daylight meant that they had to continue
to hold off the Russians until after nightfall.

That day, at Hitler's insistence, three divisions of the German Ninth Army attempted to relieve Kustrin. Although
some of the force almost reached Kustrin, the attack was defeated with the cost of 8,000 dead.

It was not until after 10 p.m. that Milius was able to give
the order for each individual company to withdraw to the
riverbank. Again, a group of men volunteered to form a rearguard to allow their comrades to escape. The most seriously wounded cases were carried to small boats to be ferried
across, while the less seriously wounded (which would have
included Brady) were laid upon barn doors. It is difficult not
to be struck by the fierce loyalty to each other displayed by
the men of Jagdverband Mitte and the SS paratroops; it is
not difficult to imagine Brady and Stringer contrasting this

with their apparent abandonment by the British in Guernsey. Those lucky enough not to have been wounded had to fend for themselves. Some brought wooden planks and rubber tyres to help them float, but most had no option but to strip to their shorts and plunge into the freezing river upon which chunks of ice had floated only three weeks earlier. Although it was a bright moonlit night, the worst conditions possible, the men of Kampfgruppe Solar began their river crossing in a highly disciplined manner. It was not long before the Russians noticed the men in the water, and soon artillery and tank shells began plunging into the river. Over eighty men are thought to have died crossing the Oder that night, some by Russian gunfire, others exhausted by three days' unrelenting combat succumbing to the strong current and freezing water. It took the fittest men over an hour to cross; those lucky enough to do so received hot drinks and woollen blankets. The surviving wounded were soon receiving treatment and being evacuated to hospitals around Berlin. Brady was brought to Grunau, a district of eastern Berlin. While the remainder of Kampfgruppe Solar were crossing the Oder, the Russians threw in a final ground assault to clear the eastern bank of the Waffen-SS who had volunteered to stay behind. It was not until dawn that the last gunfire ceased and their comrades on the west bank knew that the rearguard was no more.

Hauptsturmführer Karl Fucker began organising the survivors of his battalion into formation. According to Stringer: 'During this time about 60 per cent of my company were killed and the other companies in the battalion suffered as badly.' The dead included Hauptsturmführer Manns, officer commanding No. 1 Company. It would be safe to assume that a high proportion of the survivors were wounded. When a convoy of vehicles arrived to transport the survivors of SS Fallschirmjager Battalion 600 back to base it soon transpired that there were only 36 of the SS paratroops left unscathed. Even these remaining able-bodied men were at the last limits of their endurance. At this moment a telegram was delivered

to Sturmbannführer Milius, sent by no less a personage than
Colonel-General Heinrici. Calling his remaining men to attention, Milius read the telegram in full:

> The combat group commanded by Sturmbannführer Milius
> showed great bravery in the Zehden bridgehead and performed
> its mission unswervingly, inasmuch as the circumstances per-
> mitted this. I would like to be able to express my special admir-
> ation of the bold officers and troops.

Heinrici's recognition of SS-Kampfgruppe Solar's battle provided a visible morale boost for its survivors. It was a good
example of his style of leadership; it is rare for an officer of his
rank to personally express such admiration to an officer with
the equivalent rank of major.

Most of the survivors of Jagdverband Mitte were clad
only in shorts and woollen blankets. Replacement uniforms
were in short supply due to the destruction of their base at
Friedenthal. At least one member of the Jagdverband found
himself wearing the 'Brownshirt' uniform of the Sturm
Abteilung (SA), while some, including Frank Stringer, were
clad in tropical uniforms originally intended for issue to the
Afrika Korps!

In his postwar interrogation by the British Army, Frank
Stringer claimed: 'I kept away from the front line by 'swinging
the lead' and stayed in the cookhouse.' Although the British
accepted his story, this version of events is dubious in the extreme. This, after all, was in a time and place where even Wehrmacht units were routinely hanging men for such offences as
'malingering'. Brady's later version of events places Stringer
not only in the bridgehead at Schwedt-on-Oder, but also
squarely in the Zehden bridgehead, where the possibilities of
maintaining a non-combatant status were slim indeed. Furthermore, according to Brady, Stringer had even received a
promotion to 'lance-corporal', something which Stringer himself did not allude to in his own account.

Even in the best known published accounts of the last days

of Nazi Germany, a conflict in which whole divisions were being wiped out, the destruction of SS-Kampfgruppe Solar merits not a mention. Indeed it is only due to the impressive research carried out by Antonio J Munoz for his work, *Forgotten Legions,* that it is recorded at all. Curiously, this loss does not feature in any of Skorzeny's accounts of his wartime career. He himself spent most of the month of March on 'official business' in Berlin; it should be noted that this was hardly a safe posting in the rear since Berlin was under constant and heavy air attack. By any standards, the courage displayed by Milius' Kampfgruppe in the Zehden bridgehead was of the highest order, worthy of a cause far more deserving than that of the defence of Nazi Germany. Even in this, however, the sacrifice of SS-Kampfgruppe Solar achieved little. Himmler had squandered the lives of hundreds of elite soldiers to temporarily deny the Russians four kilometres of river bank.[47]

On the night of 19 March, the remaining garrison of Kustrin broke out of their position, most reaching German lines. Their commander was placed under arrest, on Hitler's orders.

SS-Fallschirmjager Battailon 600 spent the next two weeks attempting to return to full strength. A trickle of the less seriously wounded returned to the unit after treatment, and appeals were made to Waffen-SS officer and NCO schools for volunteers. Many of these high quality personnel came forward, but not enough, and Milius was obliged to accept Kriegsmarine and Luftwaffe personnel to make up numbers.

At the end of March 1945, Skorzeny met his Führer in the Reich Chancellory and was informed that he had been awarded the Oak Leaves to his Knight's Cross for his defence of Schwedt-on-Oder. Skorzeny was shocked by Hitler's physical condition; the Nazi dictator was bent and aged, with hands that trembled. It was the last time that Skorzeny would meet Hitler. On 30 March, he received orders from OKW to transfer his headquarters from Hof in Bavaria to an area west of Salzburg. There, he was to assist Field Marshal Schorner in establishing the 'Alpine Fortress' in the Austrian Alps. In theory over twenty divisions would defend a fortified area running fifty miles from Bregenz to Bad Aussee in the east, and over 200 miles from Fussen, Traunstein and Salzburg in the north to Glurns, Bozen and Lienz in the south. The realisation of this plan was to prove another matter.

In early April, Skorzeny established his headquarters in Achtal near Teisendorf. On the morning of 10 April he was informed that the Russians were advancing on his native city of Vienna. Concerned for his family, he set out for the city and arrived by nightfall to find the city darkened and defenceless. Establishing that his family had already left the city, Skorzeny returned to the mountains, despondently signalling Führer Headquarters that he expected the city to fall that day. He was joined at his headquarters by fellow Austrian Sturmbannführer Karl Radl, and shortly afterwards a courier arrived with his Oak Leaves decoration.[48]

In early May, John Codd, still residing in Lehnitz, was in a meeting with a man from the 'Deutsches Nachrichtenburo' (German news bureau) and told to remain ready for a possible mission involving Britain or Northern Ireland. Codd had no real choice in the matter since civilians were not permitted to leave the Berlin area without permission. He evidently enquired about Brady and Stringer and was informed that Stringer 'was engaged on the Eberswalde section on the Berlin front on ammunition supply and was alive on 16.4.1945', while Brady 'was known to be alive on 16.4.1945, when he was fighting in the Eberswalde section of the Berlin front against the Russian forces'. Brady, in fact, was still hospitalised at this time. The date, however, was significant: on this day the Red Army launched its final offensive on Berlin. While Zhukov's First Belorussian Front broke west from its bridgehead at Kustrin, encountering determined German opposition from the Seelow Heights, Marshal Koniev's First Ukrainian Front crossed the Neisse river to the south and began its own advance on the German capital.[49]

Another significant date proved to be 21 April 1945. On that morning the US Eighth Air Force carried out the last air raid of the war on Berlin. The previous day (Hitler's birthday) the German government had announced the issue of 'crisis rations', which consisted principally of a pound of meat, a can of vegetables, rice, sugar and coffee. John Codd and his wife had another source of rations, having travelled to Steglitz that day to collect Red Cross parcels from the huge Stalag for French POWs there. The air raids had stopped for a reason: on that day, for the first time, Russian artillery shells began to fall on the city as the Red Army closed in. The Codds made their way to the railway station under increasingly heavy bombardment to catch the train back to Lehnitz. The Deutsche Reichsbahn had performed miracles to keep the train services going, but it beggars the imagination that they would continue this service in the face of a Russian bombardment. Shells actually passed over the train as it continued northwards. The town of Oranienburg was soon under attack from the First Polish Army, a formation raised by the Russians during their advance through Poland. To counter this offensive, SS-Hauptsturmführer Frischessky called up the local Hitler Youth and assembled them in the Totenkopf Caserne; since even boys of sixteen had already been committed to combat, this 'force' consisted mostly of thirteen-year-olds in short trousers, who were armed and attached to Volkssturm and SS units. Frischessky himself escaped to the west shortly afterwards. In two days of savage combat, Oranienburg changed hands four times. One Hitler Youth unit was reduced from 120 to 8 boys, its fifteen-year-old commander being hanged by the SS.[50]

At 9 p.m. the wail of an air raid siren announced that the fighting had reached Lehnitz, and Codd and his wife went into the air raid shelter in their garden. Soon fighting was raging in their own neighbourhood. Bullets cracked overhead, combining with the 'thwump' of Panzerfausts and the sucking 'whoosh' of Panzerschrecks being fired close by. Suddenly, there was a calm. A Russian soldier was standing in the doorway of the bunker. Having apparently satisfied himself that the bunker contained only civilians, he left. After a night spent in the shelter, Codd and his wife went quietly back into their house and stayed in the cellar. 'All during the day Russian soldiers came in, looked around and took any valuables they could find and raped the young women.' Codd and his wife spent the next three days in Lehnitz, and contacted a Polish officer who 'advised them to leave while the Polish soldiers were there'. This was good advice.

Sachsenhausen concentration camp was liberated by the Red Army on 23 April. Estimates of the total to have died in this camp vary between 50,000 and 100,000, but in recent years over 40 tonnes of human ashes were found on the site. There were only 3,000 emaciated prisoners left in the camp; thousands of others had been marched to the west by the SS in the face of the approaching Red Army. Those unable to keep marching were shot dead on the roadside, while those who survived this death march were liberated by the US Army near Schwerin. Despite the fact that 11,000 Russian POWs were murdered in Sachsenhausen, the Russian NKVD continued its use as a prison camp for several years after the war.[51]

Also picked up by US forces in Schwerin were a group of Britons who had been involved in the 'British Free Corps'. With this group was an Irishman named 'Dillon', who claimed to be a broadcaster. However, there is no record of any Irish member of Irland-Redaktion with this name. Could this perhaps have been the mysterious O'Duffy, who had been earmarked for Operation Taube II in 1942 as a trusted worker for the SD?[52]

With a small hand cart and just a few personal belongings, John Codd and his wife left Lehnitz in the company of a female neighbour and her mother, reaching Wandlitz by about 8 o'clock that night. 'Passing through the Russian lines there were a good number of Polish soldiers who were coming up behind the Russians.' At Wandlitz, the couple met a group of freed French POWs and decided to remain with them until the end of hostilities.

The inhabitants of the special compound at Sachsenhausen, including 'Red' Cushing and the other three Irishmen near Friesack, had been transferred in early April to the concentration camp at Flossenburg, and then to Dachau a fortnight later. There they witnessed horrific sights, including starving prisoners and piles of corpses. From Dachau, the important prisoners were transported in a small fleet of vehicles to Innsbruck in Austria, apparently part of a German scheme to gather 'prominente' POWs in the 'Alpine Fortress' as a bargaining chip. The Sachsenhausen group, however, were soon sent through the Brenner Pass into northern Italy where they were liberated by the Americans. Another group of 130 prominent prisoners from the Dachau camp, including a skeletal Lieutenant Colonel John McGrath, were sent by road to Innsbruck in western Austria where they were freed by the US Third Army. Cushing's group were transported back to London where they were thoroughly interrogated. While Cushing admitted to the betrayal of Lieutenant Bissell in Friesack in 1941, there may have been more to this than met the eye. Far from being punished, Cushing continued to serve in the British Army for nearly twenty more years, retiring as a senior NCO.[53]

Among the many foreign volunteers of the Waffen-SS involved in the bitter street combat now raging in Berlin was James Brady. He was still in hospital when 'the Russians arrived there, and then everybody who could fight, including myself, was brought into Berlin'. By now Brady was a corporal (SS-Rottenführer). Brady's account can be frustratingly brief with regard to many interesting details, but nowhere more so than his lack of an account of the part played by the only Irishman known to have fought in the Battle of Berlin. He mentions only that he 'was wounded in the legs and taken to a hospital in Berlin'.

According to John Codd, Frank Stringer was based near Eberswalde on the day that the Russians launched their final offensive on Berlin. Luckily for him and the remaining 250 men of Jagdverband Mitte, Skorzeny had succeeded in organising a transfer of the unit to his command. According to Stringer: 'The remnants of the battalion withdrew to Weildorf, near Salzburg, where we remained for about ten days doing nothing.' Milius' reconstituted SS-Fallschirmjager Battailon 600 was not so lucky. They were committed to the fighting outside Berlin and were annihilated for a third and final time.⁵⁴

Among the members of Jagdverband Mitte that Skorzeny was able to gather was an old friend, Walther Girg, who had last been heard of behind Russian lines south of Danzig in January. While crossing the frozen Vistula, the truck carrying Girg's radio operator had fallen through the ice, along with the codes and frequencies essential for contact with Friedenthal. In early March, at the isolated coastal fortress of Kolberg, Girg's group presented themselves and were naturally regarded with deep suspicion by the garrison commander, even when Girg displayed the Knight's Cross under his scarf. Unable to contact Friedenthal (which had been bombed out anyway) and facing a possible firing squad, Girg persuaded Oberst Fullriede to radio Oberstgruppenführer Juttner at the Bendlerstrasse and obtain contact details from him; Sturmbannführer Karl Radl was informed and quickly confirmed Girg's identity. Girg's party was a welcome reinforcement for Oberst Fullriede, who was responsible for defending Kolberg and 68,000 refugees with a force of only 3,000 men. Ironically, the 1806 siege of this town was the subject of a major Nazi propaganda film, which was completed in January but due to actual events in 1945 was destined to be shown to very few. Girg's group carried out patrols to delay the Russians while German warships slowly evacuated the civilians, and were with Fullriede on the last day of the siege (18 March) when the last of the garrison were evacuated from the coast. Oberst Fullriede received the Knight's Cross for his defence of Kolberg, while Girg receieved the Oak Leaves for his own medal and promotion to Hauptsturmführer.[55]

It soon became apparent that the Alpine Redoubt existed only in the minds of the Nazi hierarchy and, ironically, Allied intelligence officers. Far from the twenty divisions envisaged for its defence, there were only Skorzeny's troops and the shattered remnants of German divisions retreating from the Russians. The Allies, however, took the threat very seriously; in Eisenhower's map room hung a carefully prepared intelligence chart of the area covered with symbols denoting non-existent ammunition dumps, troop concentration points and even chemical weapons facilities.[56]

On 25 April, Skorzeny reduced his headquarters staff in size: apart from Skorzeny and Radl, the staff now included Obersturmbannführer Walter, Hauptsturmführers Besekow and Schmiel, Obersturmführers Schrotter and Graf, as well as signals staff, guards and three female secretaries. Skorzeny's new headquarters was now based in a special train at Puch near Salzburg which he had obtained from Berlin with some difficulty. This was equipped with telephones, radios and telex machines.

On the afternoon of 28 April, Skorzeny, who still wore an ornate wristwatch that had been presented to him by Benito Mussolini after his rescue, learned of the death of the former Duce, who had been captured and executed by Italian partisans, along with his mistress. The bodies were subsequently mistreated by an angry crowd. Two days later Skorzeny heard the first rumours of the death of Adolf Hitler, whom he was still hoping would flee Berlin for Austria. The next day (1 May) Admiral Doenitz, as Hitler's successor, officially announced the news of Hitler's death on German radio. Skorzeny had all the remaining men of Jagdverband Mitte fall in alongside his command train and announced simply: 'The Führer is dead! Long live Germany!' Together, the Germans of the unit sang the German national anthem, 'Deutschland Uber Alles'. Then, along with the European volunteers (which would have

included Frank Stringer), all Skorzeny's troops sang 'I Had a
Comrade', the haunting German soldier's song of comradeship and duty. The Waffen-SS men had little time to mourn
their Führer. On the same day High Command South gave
orders for 'Schutz Korps Alpenland' (Alpine Guard Corps),
as it had grandly designated Skorzeny's command, to organise the defence of the South Tyrolean passes to facilitate the
withdrawal of the German forces remaining in Italy. The 250-
strong 'corps' had already set out for the Italian border before
it was learned that the German troops in Italy had already
surrendered to the Allies, but it quickly returned when its officers learned of the new situation. Skorzeny received no further orders from High Command South and was left to his
own devices.[57]

According to Frank Stringer's recollection:

> In May – about two days after Hitler was reported killed
> – Fucker told us that the Unit would be broken up into small
> parties and would take to the hills in the Tyrol. The unit was
> divided into two units and Fucker took charge of one and his
> deputy, Obersturmführer Ludwig, took command of the other.
> I was in Ludwig's party, which consisted of about thirty–forty
> men. He broke the unit up into parties of five or six men each,
> and each was called by the name of its leader. I became one of
> a party of five men of which the leader was Oberscharführer
> Haan. My party and the other parties under the command of
> Ludwig were then taken to a village in the Tyrol called Hals,
> near the town of St Johan. We went there in lorries and took
> with us foodstuffs, explosives, machine guns, small arms, and
> two radio transmitting sets. These were about 18" high, 18"
> wide and about 6" broad. They were battery sets and were fitted
> into tin cases. On our arrival in Hals all these materials were
> unloaded off the lorries, taken up into the hills and were buried.
> The explosives were buried in a shed underneath the floor, at the
> back of a house. The machine guns and small arms were buried
> in the face of a cliff about a mile from the house.[58]

On 6 May, Admiral Doenitz issued the order that all remaining German forces would lay down arms at midnight on

8 May. Skorzeny withdrew his force into the mountains grouped in small units as follows:

> *Fuehrungs Gruppe* near Annaberg (Austria). This group included:
> Skorzeny
> Radl
> Obersturmbannführer Walter
> Hauptsturmführer Hunke
> Obersturmführer Dr Graf
> Untersturmführer Koenig
> Oberscharführer Boenning
> Oberscharführer Behr

> *Gruppe Hauptsturmführer Fugger 59*, vic Steinernes Meer (Austria), 40–50 men organised in two or three squads. One squad was probably commanded by Obersturmführer Ludwig.[59]
>   *Gruppe Hauptsturmführer Girg*, vic Lofer (Austria), 40–50 men organised in two or three squads.
>   *Gruppe Hauptsturmführer Streckfuss*, nr Altenmarkt, 40–50 men.
>   *Gruppe Obersturmführer Wilscher*, nr Bischofshoren (Austria). Appr 30 men.
>   *Gruppe Hauptsturmführer Winter*, nr Mauterndorf (Austria). Appr 20 men.
>   *Gruppe Untersturmführer Schuermann*, nr Altaussee (Austria). Appr 30 men.

Stringer remembered: 'Two of our men tried with our radio sets to locate Fucker's men but were unsuccessful. All of us in Ludwig's command stayed around in the Hals area for about three weeks.'

Although not involved in any hostile actions, Skorzeny's force was not to officially surrender until 20 May.[60]

5

AFTERMATH

Germany surrendered to the Allies on 8 May 1945. On that date, John Codd and his wife were still staying with the French POWs at Wandlitz, where they were soon joined by ten British soldiers who had recently left another POW camp. This assorted group made their way shortly afterwards to Basdorf where the Russians had organised a repatriation centre. All across Europe a vast movement of humanity was taking place. Apart from former POWs, millions of slave workers drawn from across occupied Europe and forced to work in Germany were trying to return to their own countries. Sixteen million ethnic Germans were driven from their homes in East Prussia and eastern Europe and sent across the Oder-Neisse line where the eastern border of Germany had been redrawn. It was a good time for an anonymous civilian couple to make their escape from Germany.

At Basdorf, Codd was interrogated by a Russian officer and offered a plausible cover story – he and his wife were English and had been guests in Le Toquet before the German invasion in 1940, after which they were interned by the Germans and forcibly relocated to Germany. The Russian accepted Codd's story and introduced him to the camp commandant, a 'sympathetic and helpful' Frenchman. While the French POWs were happy to remain at Basdorf until their eventual repatriation, Codd was understandably 'not keen' to do so. Basdorf was only a short distance south of Oranienburg. Codd's original plan had been to make for Dresden, where his German neighbours owned a second home. However, at Wandlitz a relationship sprang up between the younger woman and one of the British soldiers, a man from Derry. It was then decided to leave this woman's mother 'in a place of safety' while she posed as the Derryman's war bride. The two couples, along with three of the British soldiers and 'an Englishman who had lived in Vienna and who had been released from Sachsenhausen internment camp' made their way to another repatriation camp at Birkenwerder. While the others were happy to remain here, the Codds continued on to Velten where they stayed for a short time. They then continued on to Nauen, on the way falling in with a group of eleven Belgians and two Frenchmen. After a week of travelling, during which Codd successfully bluffed his way through several Russian controls, the group reached Schoenhausen on the Elbe river. Outside the town they encountered a fork in the road with two notices – one directed 'all British POWs' to the left, the other directed all French citizens to the right and into the town.

The group, including Codd and wife, continued into the town where they found a repatriation centre for French and Belgians. After some deliberation, Codd entered the camp where he told 'his story' to a Russian officer (presumably the same story he had told to the Russian officer at Basdorf.) The officer at Schoenhausen took kindly to the couple and arranged for them to be driven in a Russian truck to a big camp at Belzig where they stayed overnight, again meeting the British ex-POWs and the 'Englishman from Vienna'. The following day they were driven to Magdeburg where Codd bluffed his way through yet another Russian interrogation. Given the volume of civilian refugees on the move it is unlikely that any of these interrogations could have been lengthy or detailed. The Codds were then transferred to an island in the Elbe where they were handed over to the Americans, giving a statement to an officer of the American Military Government after what, again, was unlikely to have been a long

interrogation. They were to remain in Hildesheim for another
week, living in a partially occupied hospital.[1]

At about this time SS-Obersturmbannführer Otto Skorzeny marched into a building near Annaberg in Austria and
announced to the American soldiers there his name, rank
and his intention to surrender his unit. Despite the fact that
he was the subject of several 'wanted' posters in the area, he
was unrecognised and it was with some difficulty that he
eventually arranged the provision of a jeep to transfer himself,
Radl, Hunke and an interpreter to Salzburg. The Americans
were rather suspicious as to why Skorzeny had waited over
a week to surrender himself and his unit. They subsequently
observed: 'Skorzeny stuck to the following account of the
Schutzkorps. When he observed the conditions in upper
Austria, where desertions were out of hand and entire units
were withdrawing without proper authority, he suggested
the organisation of a 'stragglers' patrol to Gauleiter Eigruber.
For this purpose Schutz Korps Alpenland was formed. It
consisted of ... seven groups with a total strength of appr 250
men.'[2]

     There were very good reasons why a Waffen-SS unit in
Austria would hesitate before surrendering to the Americans.
In the last days of the war, the Americans' worst fears regarding the 'Alpine Fortress' appeared to be confirmed when
several of the most formidable Waffen-SS panzer divisions
began appearing in the region. These 'divisions', however,
were mere shadows of their former selves, often no more
than a tenth of their establishment, who were desperately
retreating from the Russians in an attempt to surrender to
the western Allies. Any Waffen-SS captured by the Russians
could expect little more than a quick execution or long years
as a slave worker. In the event, the Hohenstaufen (9th) SS
Division's previous chivalry (on the western front at least)
stood to its credit. When the divisional commander, Sylvester
Stadler, presented himself at the headquarters of the Ameri-

can 71st Division, he found himself greeted by an American officer whom he had treated well when the roles had been reversed in the Ardennes the previous winter. The surrender of the Hohenstaufen was accepted, as were most of the other Waffen-SS units. An exception was made for the remnants of the notorious Totenkopf Division who were handed back to the Russians.[3]

Skorzeny and his three companions met the jeep near Annaberg; the driver was a cheerful Texan who allowed his passengers to purchase a bottle of wine for the journey. Having been dropped outside a hotel in Salzburg, they were in turn driven to an American battalion headquarters at Werfen, while Hunke was taken to St-Johann. Skorzeny was taken to a comfortable villa and led to the dining hall where he claimed to have been in the act of indicating his unit's positions on a map when the doors and windows were flung open and he found himself covered by several submachine guns. His pistol was taken from him and, having been strip-searched, he was ordered into another jeep with a military policeman's pistol pushed into his side. In a convoy of three jeeps, escorted by two armoured cars, Skorzeny was taken back to Salzburg, where he found himself accused not only of attempting to assassinate Eisenhower the previous winter but also of smuggling Hitler out of Berlin. He was to face a series of interrogations over the next few months, including one conducted by Colonel Henry Sheen, Eisenhower's chief of counter-intelligence.

He was presumably satisfied with Skorzeny's answers, as the press were presently notified that the assassination threat to the Allied Supreme Commander had been a red herring.[4] At least one of the interrogations concerned a very interesting bullet that was taken from the pistol seized from Skorzeny at Werfen, marked by a cross on its nose. According to slightly varying accounts by Skorzeny, earlier in the war the Germans had captured two Russian agents on an assassination mission. Their pistols were found to contain a lethal poison; an animal

shot with one (according to one version a stray dog shot by
Skorzeny) died within seconds:

> At Skorzeny's request the Kriminal Technisches Instut der
> Sipo, Berlin, manufactured special 7.65 caliber pistol bullets
> containing poison. The poison was an aconite compound and
> escaped through slits in the sides of the bullets. The bullets
> were supplied to Skorzeny at Friedenthal. He issued appr six
> each to Hauptmann Hellmers, CO of LSt II West fuer Front
> Aufklaerung in Oct 44 and to Obersturmführer Hardieck of
> 150th Panzer Brigade in November 44. Skorzeny at first tried to
> persuade the interrogators that these bullets were manufactured
> and issued solely for suicide purposes. He readily agreed,
> however, that Hellmers was most unlikely to have wanted them
> for such a reason. He finally admitted that they were intended
> for assassinations. He claims that they were not to be used
> without special orders.[5]

Subsequently the Americans rounded up and took prisoner
some of Skorzeny's commandos. These men, however, evidently made no mention of the large arms dump near Hals
and in fact the Americans missed at least two small units, one
of them Frank Stringer's. Given the standard of radio technology of the time, not to mention the mountainous terrain,
it is not surprising that the two groups lost contact with their
parent unit and were apparently not informed of the surrender
of the 'Schutz Corps'. By about 23 May, according to Stringer's
account:

> All the men wanted to go home, Ludwig sent a runner to find
> Fucker and get some passes from him for the men to use. We
> heard that this man had been successful but on his way back
> had been captured by the Americans. Owing to this Ludwig
> decided to split us all up. I then adopted the name of Willy
> Oswald; as Lepage was a French name and if I was picked up by
> the Americans it would appear suspicious.
>   Before we split, Ludwig told us that he would put an adver-
> tisement in all the big German newspapers, which would read:
> 'Solar. Ladies underwear found at railway station. Owner please

apply to Box no. –.' When the men saw this advertisement they were to get in touch with the number given and they would then get further instructions from Ludwig.

We then broke up and I went off with two men named Witt and Pohan to Stefischkirschen where all the groups were to meet. We were the first there and met only one other group which was in charge of [sic] Untersturmführer Bierer. He said that as he had no SS blood grouping mark under his arm he would go into a German prisoners' camp in the American area with Pohan (who also had no markings) and obtain their discharge. He would then make copies of the discharge papers and give them to us. Accordingly Bierer and Pohan left us, but we never saw them again.

Witt, Haan and I then went to Ulm with the object of going to Bierer's father's mill to await Bierer. But when we got near to Ulm we found that the French were there and as we feared they would capture us as we were partly in German Africa Corps uniform we decided to split up. I went off on my own after we had all got to Nuremburg, and contacted an American officer in that town. I told him I was an English prisoner of war and as I was wearing khaki shorts and no hat he accepted that and directed me to Frankfurt.[6]

Having spent a week at Hildesheim, John and Irma Codd were transported by aircraft to Brussels with twenty others. There they were accommodated in a repatriation camp at the Artillery Barracks for two weeks, by which time they were claiming 'southern Irish' nationality. Here, they were interrogated by a British intelligence officer who sent them to the British consul, who in turn suggested that they be sent to Paris to contact the Irish legation there. It would appear that Codd did not feature prominently on any Allied 'wanted' lists. Instead they were sent to the 'Mission Francaise en Belgique du Ministere des PGDR' where they were again interrogated by a sergeant of British military intelligence. At the Mission they met an Irishman named Flanagan who had lived on the Channel Islands. All three were sent by train to Lille where they stayed overnight and were interrogated again the next day; the Codds were classified as 'déportées politiques' and were sent by train to Paris. Flanagan received another classification and stayed in Lille.

On arrival in Paris the Codds were interrogated yet again by French security officers, the couple evidently being well practiced by now. Having been photographed and fingerprinted, they were given repatriation cards and allowed to proceed to the Irish legation. While the staff there helped them to obtain hotel accommodation, they were not able to provide documentation without first contacting Dublin. Instead of waiting, the Codds went to the British consulate (apparently claiming to be British again) and were issued with air tickets to London, which they flew into on 15 June. They proceeded to the Reception Centre in Cannon's Park, and having been questioned by military and civilian staff (who obviously could not have known Codd's true background) they were given a travel voucher to Ireland and directed to Euston station. There they discovered (having missed the train) that the voucher had not been signed properly, and with what must have taken some considerable coolness, returned to Cannon's Park to get the voucher signed. Having spent the whole weekend in London, the pair boarded the Monday morning train for Holyhead and caught the ferry across the Irish Sea, arriving in Dun Laoghaire on the evening of 18 June.

The couple then made their way to Codd's mother's house, but the homecoming was not a happy one. Mrs Codd, the widow of a British soldier and the mother of two more, was not pleased with the circumstances in which her son had returned home, not least with the German war bride he brought with him. Codd was to spend his first night at 'home' sleeping on the roadside. Soon afterwards, he was taken into custody by the Irish authorities, alerted to his intended return by the Irish legation in Paris and notified of his arrival at Dun Laoghaire harbour. While Codd may not have appeared on any British 'wanted' list, he featured prominently on that of Irish military intelligence (G2). He and his wife were interrogated again, but this time by a garda and an army officer who, to Codd's evident dismay, knew all about his activities in Friesack camp and at the SS radio school in Lehnitz. Codd was questioned at length not only about his own activities but those of the other Irish POWs recruited by the Germans. After the interrogation, it was decided to release the couple; although they would certainly have been interned had they arrived during wartime, the only other Irishmen working for the Sicherheitsdienst (SD) to have arrived in Ireland, John O'Reilly and John Kenny, had already been released from Arbour Hill prison since the German surrender. John Codd's personal documents were confiscated; these included a 'Fremdenpass' (German internal 'passport for foreigners') issued in October 1943 in Codd's own name and which gave his occupation as 'Sportlehrer' (sports instructor). Shortly afterwards, the couple took up residence in 59 Montpelier Hill in Dublin, a grim tenement building which, conveniently for G2, was only a short distance from their headquarters. A copy of Codd's statement was forwarded to MI5, but although the British noted ruefully that 'John Codd and his wife Irma Codd of German origin arrived in this country as civilians and managed to reach Éire where they now are', they displayed no further interest in the matter.[7]

On 5 June 1945, the *Irish Times* noted: 'Colonel John Mc-Grath is back in Dublin, two stone lighter than when he left, after five years in German prison camps, and long spells of solitary confinement in total darkness ... In August Colonel McGrath hopes to return to Dublin for good to resume his old job as manager of the Theatre Royal.'[8]

On 18 June 1945, the same day that John Codd returned to Ireland, the suspicions of an American military police patrol in the eastern German city of Leipzig were aroused by one young man of military appearance whose only documentation was a paper issued in a German military hospital indicating that he was a German soldier returning home to Hamburg. The young soldier was arrested and sent to an American

prison camp at Weissenfels where he was interrogated by the
Intelligence Corps. Despite their evident suspicions, he continued to insist that he was a German.

After the German surrender, the wounded James Brady
(for it was he) had been moved on a stretcher from Berlin
to the military hospital at Eberswalde where he was to stay
for a week. 'Several of us then left the hospital; I was still using crutches and I travelled to Bercheseble [*sic*], sometimes
by lorry and sometimes by train and at times helped by the
Russians.' While the excesses of the Red Army in Berlin are a
matter of record, there were also recorded instances of Russian
frontline soldiers displaying such kindness to captured Germans. Having spent a further week in a hospital here, a young
female interpreter born in Russia of German parents provided
Brady with the paper he was carrying when arrested in Leipzig. Brady 'left Bercheseble about the end of May 1945, and
was tramping about the country in company with two or three
Germans, being undecided what to do'. In the middle of June,
Brady and another German soldier slipped from the Russian
to the American zone by swimming across the river Mulde
near the town of Grimma. Soon afterwards he travelled to
Leipzig where he was arrested. Despite further interrogations,
Brady did not reveal his true identity or background.[9]

On 22 June Frank Stringer turned up at the Artillery
Barracks in Brussels, a week after John and Irma Codd had
left. Although he had been directed to the railway station at
Nuremburg to catch a train to Frankfurt, he instead caught
a train to Belgium and made his way to Brussels, where he
was directed to the POW repatriation facility. Coinciden-
tally, one of the officers running the camp was Brigadier
The O'Donoghue, Stringer's former commanding officer in
Guernsey, although there is no record of them ever meeting.

It is possible that Stringer was considering the type of
escape that Codd had carried out, but the Leitrim man
possessed no civilian clothing, and neither Codd's language
skills nor his guile.

Apparently having considered his options, Stringer related: 'The next day I asked to see a British intelligence officer as I wanted to tell him where the explosives and other things were hidden at Hals. Later the same day I saw a Sergeant who had come to see me and told him about it.' This was Sergeant Gonty of the 50th Field Security Section to whom Stringer claimed he had 'been trained by the Germans in radio transmission and receiving in order that he might be sent to the United Kingdom for the purposes of Espionage and Sabotage with another man named Brady ... with the sole intention of reporting the matter to the British Intelligence Authorities once he had arrived in England or Ireland'. Stringer admitted unconvincingly: 'I didn't tell him at first about my association with the SS, as I forgot and it didn't come to my brain at the time.' Gonty was not satisfied with Stringer's story and brought him to Sergeant Adeleine of the intelligence corps, who 'found Stringer hesitant and evasive in his answers which aroused my suspicions as to the truth of his story'. Ordering Stringer to strip to the waist, Adeleine 'observed under his left arm the tattoo mark 'A' which from my experience I knew to be an indication that Stringer had been either a member of the Waffen SS or some similar military or peace organisation. I asked Stringer when he joined the SS and he then told me of his membership and activities with the Waffen SS.' Although Stringer was taken into custody and faced further interrogation, he was later flown to Salzburg and was escorted by a British intelligence officer to the arms dump near Hals. At Stringer's subsequent trial this officer spoke on his behalf, describing his action as 'very helpful', and observing that 'it was necessary to locate these explosives, which amounted to two tonnes, in order to neutralise them and in order to save them from coming into the hands of any enemy that might be in the locality.' The latter remark was indicative of the concern with which the Allied forces viewed the 'Werewolf' movement.[10]

In August 1945 Stringer was interviewed over two days

by Captain Reginald Spooner of the intelligence corps. Stringer did not attempt to offer any justification for his actions, claiming only that 'the reason I joined the SS was because I thought I would learn more about what was happening all over Germany than I would on a farm. I realise the position I am in and that I may be charged with treason, but there is nothing I can say about it.' It is doubtful that Spooner would have been impressed by any proffered excuses in any case. Captain Spooner was in fact a Detective Inspector from Scotland Yard who had been commissioned into the British Army in April 1945 and was one of a team of officers investigating British Army personnel who had turned traitor. Throughout his lengthy statement, Stringer astutely played down the part he played in Jagdverband Mitte, claiming to have played no part in combat operations.[11]

Having spent ten days in the American camp at Weissenfels, James Brady was transferred to another camp at Naunberg, and in July 1945 was moved to a POW camp at Siershan in the Rhineland. This was one of the 'Rheinwiesenlager' (Rhine meadow camps), one of the heavily populated POW camps set up by the Allies to contain the millions of German soldiers taken prisoner after the German surrender. Conditions in these camps were harsh due mostly to a desperate shortage of adequate supplies, particularly food and shelter. Over 3,000 German POWs are thought to have died as a result, but this represented a far lower ratio than the 4 per cent of the 260,000 British and American POWs estimated to have died in German camps. Both figures are eclipsed by that of over three million Russian POWs known to have died in German captivity.

The 25,000 Germans in Siershan camp were taken over by the French in late July 1945, and in late September Brady was transferred to a POW camp in Epinal in France. In October he was moved to Camp No. 2004 at Luneville. The French took charge of thousands of German POWs in 1945 as a workforce to re-establish their shattered economy. Former Waffen-SS soldiers could expect to be put to work in coalmines and freezing rivers, and it would appear that Brady finally made a partial admission to his past in a possible attempt to curry favour. At Luneville he 'was registered as an Irish POW because I told the French that I was Irish, but was living in Germany when the war broke out'. This appears to have been of some benefit to him: Brady was put to work in 'canals and minefields' but was informed that he would be repatriated (to Germany) in January 1946.[12]

In October 1945, Lieutenant Colonel John McGrath (retired), now decorated with the Order of the British Empire (OBE) and again manager of the Theatre Royal in Dublin, made an address to the Dublin Rotary Club. Paying tribute to the Irish POWs in Friesack, he noted: 'The Irishmen under me were magnificent; they took my advice and instructions, nobody did anything to be ashamed of, at any time in any country. We played the Germans at their own game. They worked on us with their best brains, but with all our handicaps we won the game and the camp was broken up as a hopeless effort, and I was arrested by the Gestapo and landed in jail.' While displaying commendable loyalty to the vast majority of the men at Friesack of which these remarks were true, this still ignored the very few of which they were not. Rather nationalistically, McGrath concluded: 'Maybe in many and various circumstances the Irish are best left alone. It is surely time it was appreciated.' Sadly the years in Sachsenhausen and Dachau had taken their toll; a short time later McGrath had to resign his post at the Theatre Royal due to 'nervous disorder'.[13]

In the same month in Dublin, the Hotel Esplanade on Parkgate Street was sold at auction for a little over £7,000. The buyer was one John Francis O'Reilly, who had parachuted from a German bomber into west Clare in 1943. One newspaper observed: 'Where O'Reilly got the money to buy his hotel (reportedly to be renamed the Parachute Hotel) is a mystery. Since his release he has been living in Dublin, apparently without a job.' O'Reilly was in fact living in a flat at Montpelier Hill, which would have made him a neighbour of John Codd, although the two men never mentioned having met. O'Reilly had actually bought a share in the hotel with both the £500 his father had received for turning him in and an undisclosed amount of the money supplied to him by the Sicherheitsdienst in 1943. There were, however, many people in Dublin who did not approve of his good fortune nor the means by which he had come by it. 'On 11 November that year two incidents occurred which caused him some apprehension. On that day - Remembrance Day -there was a commotion in his hotel. A party of Irishmen, ex-members of the British Army, wearing emblems and poppies, marched right through the hotel in a body without stopping and went out the back door.' Later O'Reilly was attacked by 'a man home on leave from the British Army (who) accused him of being a Nazi and said he should have been shot'. O'Reilly later illegally obtained a pistol and ammunition for his own protection, claiming that he was 'in the same position in this country as Joyce was in England'. This was a reference to William Joyce, better known in England as 'Lord Haw-Haw', who was executed after the war for the propaganda broadcasts he had made for the Germans. The pistol was subsequently seized by the gardaí and O'Reilly fined for its illegal possession. In early 1947 O'Reilly disposed of his interest in the hotel at a profit of £100. He did not immediately seek anonymity; in 1952 the British magazine, the *Daily Sketch*, published his version of his wartime activities in a serialisation. It is noteworthy that Joseph Lenihan, who was also parachuted into Ireland by the Germans but who worked for the Allies instead, made no attempt to profit from his own experience. Shortly afterwards O'Reilly effectively abandoned his young family and left the country.[14]

In January 1946, Brady escaped from Luneville camp 'with the assistance of some friends', despite the fact that he was due to be returned to Germany in that month. Some 170,000

Germans are known to have escaped from the French camps during this period, over half being recaptured, but Brady remained at large: 'I arrived in Germany in March 1946, and stayed at Heilbren [Heilbronn], in the American zone, where I had connections, until May 1946.' He was unusually reticent about his activities during this period, claiming that 'I do not wish to say anything further as to how I got out of the camp or who assisted me', and later adding that 'I wish to say nothing further about my activities or friends during the period from January 1946 to September 1946.' Remarkably, the British showed no interest in further investigating Brady's mysterious activities during this time.[15]

What was James Brady doing in the town of Heilbronn, less than 100 miles from the city of Nuremburg, between March and May 1946? Otto Skorzeny's accounts offer a fascinating possibility. After his surrender, Skorzeny was charged with war crimes and in September 1945 was flown to Nuremburg to be imprisoned there; he shared an aircraft with Field Marshals Keitel and Jodl, Colonel-General Guderian and Admiral Doenitz, Hitler's successor as Führer of Germany. In March 1946, the American officer commanding the prison suddenly ordered a state of alert – the guard was tripled, anti-tank barricades were erected and machine guns placed around the prison. Fr Sixtus O'Connor, the Irish chaplain at the prison, later confided to Skorzeny that a 'motorised German guerrilla unit' had been sighted near the city, which the Americans believed intended to storm the prison and release the prisoners. Fr O'Connor was amused to note that this unit was allegedly led by Skorzeny, despite the fact that he was actually incarcerated in the prison! It would not be the last wild allegation to be made about him. Later, Skorzeny discovered that in fact several of his former commandos had indeed been preparing a raid on the prison to rescue him and Doenitz. They were led by a former signals officer of 'Schutz Korps Alpenland', who, like Frank Stringer, had discharged himself in May 1945 and made his own way to Nuremburg.

Still staying there in September, he was incensed to discover that his former commander was being tried as a war criminal and gathered together some former members of the Jagdverband. Skorzeny later expressed relief that the rescue was abandoned, claiming that the plan was 'totally impracticable'. Any such assault on the prison at Nuremburg, successful or not, would have had massive and dire repercussions; Skorzeny's Jagdverband was known to have been heavily involved in training 'werewolf' units to resist the Allied occupation of Germany, and the spectacle of his former commandos carrying out such an act nearly a year after the German surrender would have confirmed the Allies' worst fears about a Nazi resistance movement, possibly prolonging the eventual foundation of the Federal Republic of Germany by several years.

In May, Skorzeny was transferred from Nuremburg to Dachau, and in the same month Brady left Heilbronn. He received discharge papers from the Americans in the name of 'Charles Lacy', whose home town was indicated as Nauen in the Russian zone, where he now proceeded.[16]

Frank Stringer's court-martial took place at St Anne's Barracks in Brussels on 9 April 1946, commencing at 10.30 a.m. Stringer had been incarcerated for the ten months since he gave himself up, the last six weeks of which he spent in solitary confinement. The charge laid against him was that 'having been made a prisoner of war, voluntarily serving with the enemy in that he between 1st August 1943 and 8th May 1945, having been made a Prisoner of War, voluntarily served with the Waffen-SS, a portion of the German armed forces in Germany, and on the Russian front and elsewhere'. The court could award the death penalty on conviction of this offence.

The trial was a formality; in fact Stringer's defending officer advised him to plead guilty, but only found out at the commencement of proceedings that this was not possible in cases where the charge could warrant a death sentence. The odds were against Stringer in any case. The prosecuting officer was a qualified barrister and a member of the Judge Advocate General's branch, while the officer appointed to defend him was a solicitor in civilian life with a self-professed 'ignorance of military law'. The latter was poorly briefed for his task, only having been detailed for the duty very recently and evidently not having any advisor on military law made available to him.

The prosecuting officer made his case essentially by reading out the statement that Stringer had made to Captain Spooner the previous August. In Stringer's defence, his defending officer offered an unsworn statement which was read by the judge advocate and attached to the proceedings:

Statement by 7043206, Fus F.S. Stringer:

I am an Éire citizen and I voluntarily joined the British Army in 1938. After I joined my Battalion I got drunk and was sent to Prison for assault. When the War started I applied to the Prison Governor to rejoin my unit but permission was refused. Later when the Germans broke through into France and we could hear the guns at Cherbourg I again applied to rejoin my unit and fight but permission was again refused. I was still in prison when the Germans came to Guernsey and I was taken from there and made a Prisoner of War. In 1943, I and other Irishmen were asked if we would join the German Army. At this time the War with Russia was being fought and being a Catholic I hate the Russians so I joined the German Army in order to fight them. At no time did I intend to fight against England. I knew that Russia had attacked Finland and that she had made a pact with Germany. If I had wished to fight on the Western Front I could have done so for a part of my unit fought in the Ardennes offensive but I only wanted to fight against the Russians. As soon as I returned to British hands I asked to see a British Intelligence Officer as I wanted to tell him about the explosives and radio apparatus hidden in the mountains. I made a full statement of what I had done to Sjt. Gonty and Sjt Adeleine and later I went with Major Croome by aeroplane to Salzburg where I showed them the hidden material.

I ask the court to believe me when I say that I did not intend to
fight against England.

9th April '46

F.S. Stringer

Having observed that he had originally advised Stringer to
plead guilty (and had evidently not had a defence prepared),
the defending officer made a strong protest against the fact
that Stringer had been held for ten months without any charge
being made against him or offered any legal advice. Having
been advised that this was permissible under military law,
Stringer's defending officer observed that 'if this prosecuting
officer was appearing before a High Court in England ... all
I can say is that those sort of tactics would be the subject of
investigation.'

The Judge Advocate then began his summing-up, which
was also based largely on Stringer's statement made the previous September, and which admirably satisfied the onus on
the prosecution to prove the allegations against him beyond
all reasonable doubt. It was noted that this statement's 'ad-
missibility in evidence has not been challenged by the defence'. At 11.50 a.m. the court closed to consider, re-open-
ing at 12.15 p.m. Major Croome, the intelligence officer who
had escorted Stringer to St Johann in Austria, testified as to
Stringer's good behaviour in prison and the aid he had rendered in locating the explosives dump there.

Stringer's defending officer then spoke in mitigation:
'From the first moment I came into this room I have been
under no illusion about the accused's guilt and, as I said earlier, I advised him to plead guilty. He was prepared to plead
guilty and I came into this court prepared to plead guilty but,
according to the manual of Military Law I was unable to
do so.' Despite this unpromising start, the officer went on to
speak earnestly on Stringer's behalf:

Stringer joined the Army in 1938. He was a Southern Irishman. He volunteered for the Army. By the time he was nineteen he was in prison in respect of the offence on Army Form B296. From then onwards he was divorced from all the normal sources of information which you and I have had throughout the war. Newspapers and radio and things like that do not reach people in prison. He only heard rumours. He says in that statement that Russia had made a pact with Germany. He says that Russia attacked Finland and at a later date after Germany attacked Poland, Russia had as well. All those points do have a distinct bearing on the case. The accused hated Russia. I am not denying that and as I say, he is a Southern Irishmen. If any members have any knowledge of education, particularly religious education, in Southern Ireland, it is a matter of common knowledge what part that education plays in Southern Ireland. The Russians are hated. When he went to prison he knew certain things against Russia and I suggest when he had the opportunity he fought against them. Certainly it is a matter of history, but the last time he was able to get information it was to the effect that there was a pact between Russia and Germany.

Having already noted that 'the prosecution's case depends entirely upon the accused's statements; their case stands or falls by this long statement', the defence made use of Stringer's own statement on his behalf, asking the question, 'was Germany's war effort helped in the slightest by the inglorious efforts of Fusilier Stringer?' Stringer's failures were emphasised, his incompetence as a radio operator in Berdiansk and Friedenthal, his failure in a driving course, and his account of his service on the eastern front which 'consists mainly of an inglorious performance in the cookhouse'.

Stringer was found guilty; he escaped the death sentence, but was sentenced to fourteen years' imprisonment. After consideration, two years of the sentence were remitted. Stringer was sent to Wormwood Scrubs prison, where in August he was informed that the British Army Council had decided to remit a further four years of the sentence. This left Stringer with eight years to serve, and in the event he was to serve only half of them.[17]

James Brady reached Nauen in July. Since his account mentions that he received civilian clothing at Nauen, this would appear to indicate that he wore military uniform in the interim. Could this be a clue to Brady's state of mind? It might have been possible, although very difficult, to adopt his real identity again and claim to be an Irish national in an attempt to get home, had he chosen to do so. Did James Brady really regard himself as a German soldier rather than an Irishman?

August 1946 found James Brady wandering the ruins of Dresden. At 10.15 on the night of 13 February 1945, this beautiful city, popularly known as the 'Florence of the Elbe' due to its distinctive baroque architecture, was subjected to an air raid by 244 RAF Lancaster bombers. This first wave dropped their entire payload within two minutes, a mixture of high explosive bombs to cause structural damage to buildings and incendiary bombs to set them on fire. The fires in the city reached temperatures of over 1,000 degrees centigrade, creating the terrifying phenomenon known as a 'firestorm'; the intense heat above the fires causing a violent updraft which sucked in the surrounding air at ground level with enough force to drag people into the flames. Three hours later, a second wave of over 500 more Lancasters dropped over 1,800 tonnes of bombs, deliberately targeting areas of the city that were not already ablaze. The bomber crews in the second wave were able to clearly see the blazing city from forty miles away. Just after noon, 300 American B-17s dropped another 800 tonnes of bombs in a daylight raid.

The bombing of Dresden was to become a fiercely controversial event even before the end of the war. Over 80 per cent of the city's houses were demolished or damaged, with official figures citing over 35,000 fatalities. For years after the bombing, entire city blocks were reduced to blackened walls with carbonised window frames. The city's streets were choked with eighteen million cubic metres of rubble. It was small wonder that some observers compared the ruins to Hiroshima. The once-beautiful Old Town was annihilated;

the famous Frauenkirche, the Lutheran Church of our Lady, whose 314-foot sandstone dome had dominated the Dresden skyline, now lay in a pile of blackened rubble, its statue of Martin Luther blasted from its plinth. The copper dome of the city's castle was blackened and melted, the heat of the firestorm having caused molten copper to pour onto the civilians sheltering within. The castle's clock was frozen in time at twenty past two, and along its roof stood rows of decapitated statues. The market square presented a particularly eerie sight: nearly 7,000 corpses had been gathered there and destroyed by fire to prevent an epidemic.[18]

Having spent a few days in Dresden, Brady moved to Halle, where he stayed for two weeks. At Halle, he met a man who he wrongly took to be a former British soldier. This individual 'had an English accent and said he was staying in Germany as he had married a German girl. He was living at Halle but wouldn't tell me his name or any particulars concerning himself.' This was in fact Eric Pleasants, a former member of the British Free Corps. As a civilian, he was trapped on the Channel Islands by the German invasion, and having been imprisoned for his part in an escape attempt was sent to a German internment camp for civilians. Having successfully obtained a transfer to Marlag-Milag camp for merchant seamen, he volunteered for the British Free Corps in 1944. While based in Dresden, he married a young German woman in early 1945, and while visiting her parents' house outside Dresden, actually witnessed the destruction of the city by Allied bombers. He and his wife were in Berlin when the city fell to the Russians, and were forced to escape through the sewers back to Dresden. The couple stayed near the city for several months and remained when the American occupation troops withdrew and the Russians moved in. The couple were arrested by the Russians in 1946 and separated; Pleasants was sent to a labour camp in the Arctic Circle for seven years, after which he returned to England. He never saw his wife again.

Having left Halle, Brady moved to Wittenburg. 'All this

time I was able to live with the assistance of connections and with money made easily in the Black Market.' On 10 September 1945, Brady travelled to Berlin and wandered about the city, where he had lived for the early part of 1942 and had been stationed nearby (in Friedenthal) for most of 1944. Most of Berlin still lay in ruins, and was divided into zones controlled by the British, Russians, Americans and French. As yet it was still possible to wander freely between the zones. In 1948, the Russians began restricting access to their area as part of increasing cold war tensions.

The following day Brady reported to the British POW department, where he was interrogated, but did not tell the truth about his prior activities. After nine days (during which he was evidently being investigated), he was brought to Hamburg and flown to England, arriving in London on 21 September; there he was accommodated in the Great Central Hotel, the designated 'transit area' for former POWs. Three days later, Brady entered a hotel room to be confronted by Sergeant Cash and Sergeant Skelton of the Special Investigation Branch of the British Army's military police. At 10.30 a.m. Brady began to dictate a lengthy statement, the first part of which took until six in the afternoon. He was at something of a disadvantage: his interrogators had a copy of Frank Stringer's statement, which covered Brady's activities in some detail, greatly restricting any possibility for playing down his own role in the Waffen-SS, as Stringer had done. At ten o'clock the following morning, the trio continued with Brady's account and finished at noon. After this, Brady was taken into custody.

On 2 December 1946, Fusilier James Brady was tried by court-martial in London. The first charge against him was that, 'Having been made a prisoner of war voluntarily serving with the enemy in that he in Germany and elsewhere between 3rd December 1945 and 8th May 1945 having been made a prisoner of war voluntarily served with the enemy that is to say in the Waffen SS, part of the German armed

forces'. The second charge against him was that of 'Deserting his Majesty's service in that he in the field on 10th June
1945 absented himself from the Royal Irish Fusiliers until
surrendering himself to the British authorities in Berlin on
11th September 1946'. The trial commenced at 11.45 a.m.,
Brady pleading 'not guilty' to the first charge but 'guilty' to
the second. Major Evans, a solicitor and member of the Judge
Advocate General's office, opened the case for the prosecution by emphasising the seriousness of the charge, 'one of the
comparatively few offences under the Army Act which may
be punished by Courts-Martial ... by the maximum penalty
known to the English law. That is the death sentence'. He noted that the prosecution against Brady essentially consisted of
the statement that he had made in September. Sergeant Cash
was called to the witness box, and Major Evans read aloud
James Brady's long statement in its entirety. Mr Hazell, the
civilian solicitor representing Brady, then questioned Cash,
and later Sergeant Skelton, after which the court adjourned
at 12.50 p.m.

The court reformed at two o'clock, and Brady's solicitor
submitted that the prosecution had failed to make a *prima
facie* case, having 'failed to produce anything which calls upon
the accused to make an answer to this charge'. Throughout
the trial, Brady's lawyer made a number of observations that
would have raised eyebrows in a more politically correct era,
among them: 'You do not expect wise decisions from young
people, especially an Irishman.' Later he noted that 'he was
not a man subjected wholly to British influence and line of
thought', and that 'this native of Southern Ireland' had spent
only a few months 'with ordinary wholesome British influ-
ences'. It should be noted that the officers of the court martial
were mainly members of the old British ascendancy in Ireland; Colonel Vandeleur, the president of the court, who had
led the Irish Guards in the ill-fated attempt to reach Arnhem
in 1944, was the scion of one of the landlord families of pre-
independence Ireland.

Mr Hazell's speech for the defence lasted nearly ninety minutes, after which the court closed for a brief recess. It reconvened after fifteen minutes and Colonel Vandeleur arbitrarily announced that the submission for the defence had been 'over-ruled'. Brady was offered, but declined, his options to give evidence, make a statement or call a witness. The case for the prosecution was summed up, in which it was submitted by reference to Brady's statement that he had admitted beyond reasonable doubt that he had been made a POW and had subsequently served with the enemy, some points of which were contended by the defence. At 4.45 p.m. the court closed for twenty minutes. Brady's 'guilty' plea to the second charge was briefly covered, after which his solicitor made a final speech with regard to mitigating factors. Mr Hazell claimed that 'this man is a native of Southern Ireland. He is a man who does not regard Great Britain as his country any more than any of us regard France as ours … this country is not his country. He regarded himself as a mercenary and he sold his services where they were best paid, and that happened to be in the British Army.' Having emphasised Brady's youth at the time of his transgressions, his solicitor drew attention to the eighteen-month sentence in Guernsey in 1939, being obviously unaware of the full facts of the matter since Brady in his statement had only admitted that 'we assaulted a civilian policeman'. As it was, Brady's lawyer contended that 'never in these days would such a sentence be allowed to stand. It might be passed, but it would be reduced on appeal. It was a savage sentence passed upon a drunken young fool.' It was Hazell's submission on the subject of Brady's abandonment to the Germans, however, that would eventually benefit him most. Hazell observed that:

The next matter is the fact of his betrayal to the Germans. He was in that jail in Guernsey when his battalion left. Representations were made: 'Cannot I be let out to rejoin my unit?' and answered: 'No'. In 1940 when it is known that the Germans were going to land in Guernsey, he says: 'Cannot I be let out? Cannot I be evacuated?' which was again answered by 'no', and there he is left like a rat in the trap until the Germans arrived on the island. It is not difficult to realise the bitterness that this boy of 20, as he then was, must have felt towards those people who could easily have evacuated him, but who left him in jail to be handed over to the Germans. He felt, and I think we all might have felt in those circumstances, 'If that is all the interest they take in me, why should I care?' I put it forward as an explanation.

James Brady was found guilty as charged and sentenced 'to suffer penal servitude for the term of fifteen years'. Subsequently the Judge Advocate General, the British Army's senior legal officer, noted in a letter to the General Officer Commanding London District: 'Regarding the sentence of 15 years' penal servitude ... In mitigation comment was made by defending council on the matter in which the accused (then a youth of 19) is alleged to have been practically abandoned to the enemy in Guernsey, and this does seem to me to be a matter that might well have influenced a southern Irishman to regard himself as a 'mercenary'. If the facts are correctly stated, although there can be no doubt that the accused voluntarily served in the enemy forces, you may think that the sentence is severe and should receive consideration.' In view of this, the GOC London District confirmed the finding and sentence of Brady's court martial, but decided to remit three years of the sentence. The trial was covered by the press and reported in Irish and British newspapers. Back in Dublin, Irish military intelligence noted the trial and sentence and took no further interest in Brady's case.[19]

On 18 August 1947, Skorzeny and nine former officers of Panzerbrigade 150 were placed on trial at the former concentration camp at Dachau. They were facing various charges including allegedly fighting while in US Army uniform and the killing of American prisoners. Chief prosecuter Colonel Rosenfeld stunned Skorzeny by producing two of his most trusted officers as the first witnesses for the

prosecution, but Karl Radl gave only monosyllabic answers
that confirmed the message that Wehrmacht headquarters
had circulated the previous year – that Skorzeny was seeking
English-speaking volunteers. 'Chinese' Hunke remained
absolutely silent in the witness box.

Another of Skorzeny's officers, however, offered far more
damaging evidence. His former supply officer testified that
before 'Operation Grief' Skorzeny had distributed poisoned
ammunition, which he claimed was marked by a red ring between the round and the casing. This evidence was given at
the end of the day, after which the court adjourned until the
following morning. By then Skorzeny had amply proved that
he had contacts on the outside, probably even with former
members of his Jagdverband. When proceedings opened the
following morning, Skorzeny's defending officer presented
the witness with a bullet marked with a red ring which he
identified as one of the poisoned bullets. The defence then
triumphantly identified the bullet as waterproof ammunition for use by troops operating in wet conditions; it had
been smuggled into Dachau and delivered to Skorzeny in
his breakfast that morning. The charge was withdrawn, but it
would not be the last that Skorzeny would hear of the 'poison
pistols'. A crucial part of the Americans' unwillingness to
pursue the matter appears to be the fact that there was no
record of the poisoned ammunition having been used. If a
dead American soldier had been found in the Ardennes with
one of Skorzeny's special bullets in him, the court-martial at
Dachau may have taken the matter more seriously.

The charge of killing American prisoners, evidently the
'Malmedy Massacre' carried out by SS-Kampfgruppe Peiper,
was withdrawn. Skorzeny's Panzerbrigade 150 had no involvement in this incident.

Eventually, the only charge remaining against Skorzeny
was that of fighting in American uniform. This charge was
demolished by a surprise witness: RAF Wing Commander
Yeo-Thomas. This officer, who had escaped from Buchenwald

concentration camp, gave evidence that while on special operations with the French resistance he and his colleagues often wore German uniform and were fully prepared to fight while so dressed. As Yeo-Thomas stepped down, Skorzeny called his fellow defendants to attention in a gesture of appreciation. The defence offered testimony from three American officers who were prepared to give similar evidence, but this was deemed unnecessary.

On 9 September 1947, Skorzeny and his co-defendants were acquitted on all charges. He was, however, to be incarcerated for nearly another year. The Danish requested Skorzeny to face charges relating to the 'Peter Group' terrorist campaign in early 1944, but eventually decided to proffer charges against SS operative Alfred Naujocks instead. This individual had surrendered himself to the Americans in October 1944 but subsequently escaped from Allied captivity, dying in 1966 without ever having faced trial. Czechoslovakia also demanded Skorzeny but on dubious grounds, and the Americans refused to extradite him. 'Scarface', as he was christened by the American press, put his time to good use by working with the US Army Historical Division, and learning English. Skorzeny and Radl cooperated on a lengthy account of the rescue of Mussolini for which they requested copyright! This account makes a lively read, switching to present tense to describe the actual assault on the Gran Sasso.

Skorzeny was given a fortnight's parole at Christmas to visit his wife and daughter in Munich, from which he returned punctually. In the new year, he and Radl volunteered to go before a de-nazification tribunal and were transferred to a German-administered internment camp at Darmstadt, being assigned to clear up bomb damage in the nearby town. By July 1948 Skorzeny was still awaiting word of any hearing, and on the 27th of that month he slipped out of the lightly guarded camp with his huge frame squashed into the boot of a civilian car. He may have been influenced in his decision by the experience of acquaintance Hjalmar Schacht, former Reichsbank president and minister in Hitler's government; despite being acquitted by the International Military Tribunal at Nuremburg, he later received an eight-year sentence from a German de-nazification court (he was actually released in 1948). The day after his escape, Skorzeny was in Hitler's former retreat of Berchtesgaden, where he would remain for some months, occasionally visited by his young daughter.[20]

Frank Stringer's sentence came up for review in 1950, and he was released in that year. Since the final note in James Brady's court martial file (dated 1949) notes that this was 'required for review due 29 December', it is likely that Brady may also have been released early in the same year. A very interesting note in John Codd's G2 file (dated August 1951) noted that '[Codd] had met few of his Friesach companions since his return to Ireland (Lee, Stringer and Brady were amongst them)', from which it is apparent that both James Brady and Frank Stringer had returned to Ireland by that time. The outlook for both men would have been grim, no better than that facing them in 1938. Ireland in the 1950s was a time of poverty, high unemployment and massive levels of emigration; half a million Irish citizens are thought to have emigrated between 1945 and 1960. John Codd had been desperately struggling to find work since his arrival in Dublin. It is likely that he talked rather too freely about his past. His G2 file noted that: 'He has been endeavouring for some time to emigrate to South America. For obvious reasons he does not wish to travel to Britain or USA. Accordingly he has contacted various refugee ships which called here.'[21]

'James Brady' had at least one great advantage over the other two men. He had lived the previous twelve years of his life under a pseudonym and now, still a young man, was presumably free to adopt his real identity again and live out the rest of his life under it.

Brady, Stringer and Codd all seem to disappear from

history in 1951. Perhaps it is best that they be allowed to do so. Several Irish families had no idea that a father or an uncle had served with Eoin O'Duffy's Bandera in the Spanish Civil War, it being thought best that any such 'fascists' be left as a skeleton in the family cupboard. Likewise, although there is no evidence that any of the three were involved in the commission of anything that could be described as a war crime during their SS service, few Irish families would welcome the knowledge that an ancestor had served in a cause so unworthy.[22]

Also in 1951, republican sympathisers raised a statue at Dublin docks of Seán Russell, the IRA leader who had died aboard a German U-boat in 1940. It was subsequently vandalised, and after repairs was relocated to Fairview Park. In Germany, Edmund Veesenmayer was released from prison having served less than three years of a twenty-year sentence.[23]

In June 1957 a reception was held at the exclusive country club in Portmarnock in Dublin which was attended by many representatives of the higher echelons of Irish society. One of the guests was a young politician named Charles Haughey. The celebrity guest of honour, a wealthy industrialist, happily signed autographs, and at one stage in the proceedings a Westland Widgeon helicopter landed on the lawn. This aircraft had been performing at an airshow near Dublin and its arrival at Portmarnock caused no small excitement among the guests; helicopters were a very rare sight in Ireland at the time. The guest of honour was nonchalant, having had long experience of such aircraft; the Germans had deployed early versions of the helicopter in Sicily in 1943 where they were used to transport Field Marshal Kesselring, and in the planning phase for the rescue of Mussolini it had been suggested that these could be used to carry out the raid on the Gran Sasso. In the event, Skorzeny, now signing autographs at Portmarnock, had used gliders.

A reporter from the *Evening Press* found Skorzeny to be

'a large and amicable man', and was informed by him that 'I never had any interest in Ireland during the war years. We looked to the east quite often ... such things as the oil pipe lines of Arabia held my militant interest for a while, but as you can well realise, there was no reason why a commando operation should be planned on Ireland.' In fact, in early 1942 SS-Sonder Lehrgang Oranienberg had been earmarked for a possible deployment in Ireland in the event of an Allied invasion, but this was some time before Skorzeny had taken command of the unit. 'Now I am a salesman for an engineering concern in Madrid. I live on a Nansen passport.' This was a passport for stateless persons; despite his acquittal at Dachau, Skorzeny was forbidden to land in France, Britain or America. The reporter noted that Skorzeny, accompanied by 'Frau Skorzeny, a very attractive Prussian', spent some time in conversation with a prominent French banker, known to have past links with espionage, who had evidently flown in from France for the meeting.[24]

Skorzeny's application three weeks earlier for a visa to visit Ireland had caused some consternation at the Irish embassy in Madrid, and subsequently at Iveagh House, the home of the Irish Department of External Affairs. The Irish Chargé d'Affaires in Madrid noted that:

Applicant was a member of the special German Paratroop Corps in last war and became famous for his part in releasing Mussolini from captivity in the later stages of the Italian campaign.

He is featured in the British 'Stop List' as of an 'unsatisfactory character' with the instruction 'refuse to land'.

He is now an engineer in Madrid and holds a Spanish *Special* passport indicating that he is 'without nationality'. He told me that at present his claim to either German or Austrian citizenship is being investigated. His wife, who intends to accompany him, has (he said) a Federal German Passport.

His Spanish Special Passport is valid for three months at a time. His present one will have to be superseded by another before he travels. It bears a Federal German visa.

The Irish embassy official added that Skorzeny 'wishes to visit Ireland purely on holiday and would be staying at the Portmarnock Country Club Hotel as a guest'. He also noted that 'Applicant has an agreeable manner and is well-dressed. He is a very big man and his face bears quite a few scars.'[25]

Skorzeny received approval for his brief visit and he and his wife spent about a week in Ireland in June 1957. The known facts of Skorzeny's postwar activities are as follows: in October 1949 he was photographed walking down the Champs Elysées in Paris; it was later alleged that he was shadowing French communists although Skorzeny himself hinted that his benefactor, Yeo-Thomas, had offered him a sanctuary in France. In 1950 he was refused a German work permit and took up residence as a stateless person in Spain. In that year he also divorced his first wife, and his first book, *Geheimkommando Skorzeny,* was published in Hamburg, subsequently becoming a bestseller in several languages. In 1951 he set up an engineering agency in a small office in Madrid. The following year he was declared 'denazified in absentia' by a German court in Hesse. In 1953 he negotiated a multi-million dollar contract between Spain and Germany for railway stock and machine tools, and was soon acting as the Spanish agent for several German firms, including Klockner AG, the Wolff Trust, Messerschmitt and Krupps. This was the time of the postwar German economic miracle, due to the West's need for a strong German economy after the outbreak of the Korean War. In 1954 Skorzeny married the Countess Ilse von Finkenstein, the niece of Hjalmar Schacht and a formidable businesswoman in her own right. Also in that year British writer Charles Foley published *Commando Extraordinary,* a laudatory biography of Skorzeny which did much to help his reputation. He is known to have travelled to Argentina where he associated with dictator Juan Peron, and to Egypt where he was a guest of Abdul Nasser, who had seized power from the decadent King Farouk in 1952.[26]

Skorzeny became the subject of a great deal of speculation in the international press. The most popular allegation
against him was that he was the leader of a shadowy organisation called 'ODESSA'. Since the end of the war it had become apparent that many wanted SS men had successfully
escaped from Europe to Argentina via well-organised 'ratlines' through Scandanavia, Belgium and Italy. The popular
press speculated on the existence of an organisation sheltering former SS men and pointed fingers at Skorzeny, a wealthy
figure who regularly travelled between Spain, Argentina and
Egypt, all countries that openly sheltered former SS men.

It might be noted that Skorzeny did himself no favours
in this regard. To the end of his days he remained an unre-
pentant Nazi and an open admirer of Adolf Hitler. He did
refrain, however, from overt anti-Semitism and Holocaust
denial in stark contrast to some former Waffen-SS officers,
notably Leon Degrelle.

Specific allegations against Skorzeny in this regard tend
not to stand up to examination. It was reliably claimed for
example that he had supplied Nasser with the services of the
notorious Oskar Dirlewanger and Adolf Eichmann. In 1960,
Dirlewanger's corpse was exhumed in southern Germany, establishing that he had died in captivity in July 1945, while in
the same year the Israelis established that Eichmann had not
visited Egypt since before the war.[27]

In recent years, courageous Argentinian journalist Uki
Goni revealed the extent of the hithero unsuspected organi-
sation of the 'ratlines' by the government of pro-Nazi dictator
Juan Peron.[28]

In late July 1958, Skorzeny presented himself at the Irish
legation in Bonn, West Germany, and filled out an application
to visit Ireland the following month. The Irish Department
of Justice approved the visa with the following stipulation:

As previously stated Skorzeny's name appears in the British
Home Office Suspect Index and the instruction in the Suspect

Circular is that he is not to be allowed to land in Britain for any purpose including transit to any destination. In view of this the grant of a visa is authorised on the understanding that Skorzeny undertakes not to enter Britain while here and that he will return direct to the Continent at the end of the visit to this country. The Legation should be asked to report the date on which Skorzeny proposes to travel here and the route.

As indicated in a subsequent report from the legation in Bonn to the Department of External Affairs:

Herr Skorzeny visited the Legation in person to apply for the visa and it was explained to him that it would be granted only on his undertaking not to enter Britain and to return direct to the continent at the end of his visit to Ireland. He gave me this undertaking and stated that he was considering flying by private plane direct to Dublin on the following day, 23rd August. Alternatively he might decide to return first to Spain and fly from Barcelona to Dublin by Aer Lingus.

Herr Skorzeny expressed his indignation at the continued refusal of the British authorities to permit him to land there. There was no reason for them to persist in this attitude and he resented being treated like a gangster. Indeed even American gangsters were allowed to land in Britain. He mentioned that he had been invited by the BBC Television authorities to participate in a forthcoming series dealing with famous fighting men and when he indicated that he would be prepared to do so and asked them to arrange with the British authorities for permission for him to go to London they replied that they would arrange to send a team to make the recordings with him in Spain.

He expressed great admiration for the Spanish and Irish peoples who, he felt, had a lot in common. It was important that their point of view, in keeping with their independent spirit, should be made known without distortion such as took place when British news agencies were relied on. In this connection he mentioned that he was arranging to act as Irish correspondent in Spain for the *Irish Press*.[29]

Referring to the Middle Eastern situation Herr Skorzeny considered that the root of the troubles there was the attempt of the British and French to perpetuate the temporary foothold they had gained during World War I regardless of the rights and interests of the Arab people. He expressed particular dislike for King Hussein of Jordan as a mere creature of the British. He had little confidence in the ability of the United Nations to bring about a satisfactory solution.

The ideal of a United Europe was one which appealed to him but he considered that it had little chance of realisation in face of the 'resistance of the politicians'. The proper way to begin to go about it would be to internationalise under European control small and disputed territories such as the Saar, the Tyrol etc, but this view did not seem to be finding favour. He summed up his views of the main source of much of the present international discords as deriving from the continued refusal of the British and French to admit that they had in effect lost the war in 1945. They attempted to cover up the real situation by identifying opposition to their own interests everywhere with Communist intrigue, as in the Middle East.

Herr Skorzeny's passport was issued in Madrid on 11 July 1958 valid for three months with re-entry. It bears an endorsement of the same date extending its validity for a further six months up to 11 April 1959. The number of the passport is 071391 C, Registration number 34574/58 and it is stamped 'Especial'. It is valid for Cuba, Germany and Ireland and the bearer is described as 'sin nacionalidad'. The fee charged for the visa was that for stateless persons, namely DM 17.70.

This visit passed off without event. Skorzeny's circumstances improved in late 1958 when an Austrian court acquitted him of charges of 'murder, robbery and arson' allegedly carried out in Czechoslovakia during the war, and Skorzeny became eligible for an Austrian passport which did not require a visa for visits to Ireland. In May 1959, when Skorzeny paid what was apparently a courtesy call to the Irish Embassy in Madrid, the Ambassador there was reluctant to shake hands with him but did so 'on the principle that an Ambassador ought to be reasonably approachable'. According to Ambassador Michael Rynne's subsequent report, classified 'secret':

The Colonel told me he was about to travel via Ireland to Canada where, he said, he was invited to do a Television broadcast.[30] He said that the BBC had already televised him this year. I made no comment on this statement except to say that I presumed Skorzeny could get a plane direct to Shannon from Madrid. Skorzeny said that his intention was to fly to London and thence to Dublin. I suggested that if he travelled that way he might be 'delayed' in Dublin and that he could just as well take a perfectly good Aer Lingus plane from Barcelona. The Colonel looked grim at this suggestion; he said he was going to London and did not expect to be delayed there. He had just come from the British Embassy where he had been nicely received. I said that, so far as I was concerned he could travel as he liked, but that, unless he wished to 'twist the British lion's tail', he could easily by-pass England. I added, rather unkindly, that, no doubt, 'personal publicity' was useful in the TV business! Skorzeny replied that he objected strongly to publicity which had always meant the newspapers telling lies about himself.

Skorzeny 'looked disgusted' when shown a recent Irish newspaper with his photograph and a report that he intended to buy a farm in Ireland; the article, however, proved to be correct.

Having ascertained Skorzeny's possession of an Austrian passport, Ambassador Rynne contacted the Canadian Chargé d'Affaires to check on Skorzeny's story, 'who told me some days later that Canada had not the least intention of admitting Skorzeny because "he is still too pro-Hitler in his outlook"'.

Despite the Irish Ambassador's advice, Skorzeny flew from Madrid to London on 28 May 1959 but was denied entry there. According to the London *Times*, Skorzeny:

> ... was refused permission to enter Britain when he arrived at London airport last night from Madrid, on his way to Ireland where it is believed he plans to settle. Immigration officers questioned him for more than an hour. His aircraft for Dublin was due to leave in four hours, but contrary to usual practice Skorzeny was taken to a transit lounge after talking with immigration officers. An official at the airport said last night: 'We were told that immigration officials would not allow him to clear controls.' A Home Office spokesman confirmed this. From the transit lounge he was escorted direct to the aircraft shortly before the other passengers went aboard.

During this visit to Ireland (but not Canada) Skorzeny evidently made arrangements to purchase a large house and farm in Co. Kildare:

'Some weeks after all this,' according to Michael Rynne, 'the Embassy was phoned by Skorzeny to ask if he might call on me on a certain day and hour, which he named, to discuss a business matter. Being rather annoyed at his not taking my friendly advice about London, and having seen that there were recent questions in the Dáil regarding the purchase of Irish land by foreigners (and because Skorzeny is a foreigner anyway for whom I am not in the least responsible!) I declined his request for an interview and asked him to write to me.' Some days later Skorzeny and his wife turned up at the Irish Embassy with 'Householders Effects Importation Forms' for production to the Irish Revenue Commissioners, with a request that Mrs Skorzeny's signature for these forms be witnessed.

Although the ambassador advised them that this procedure was not actually necessary, he assented and 'bade the two emigrants "Godspeed"'.

Before leaving, however, the Colonel insisted on telling me that he had not really been 'delayed' in London. The press reports were pure fabrications. In fact he was treated to coffee and whiskey by the London Airport people, and had refused to speak to pressmen there. He added that he 'could have gone up to London, if he wished to'. I made no comment on this. Mrs Skorzeny in saying goodbye explained to me that the Colonel had close contacts with German firms (DKW and Stinnes) who might be prevailed upon by him to set up concerns in Ireland in accordance with our new policy of seeking foreign capital etc. I also refrained from commenting on this, nor did I show the Skorzenys that day's *Irish Press* which reported that he had been refused permission to travel to Canada!

This report noted that Skorzeny had been declared 'undesirable' by the Canadian immigration authorities and had been refused entry to participate in the Canadian Broadcasting Corporation (CBC) production. The *Irish Times* noted that the CBC were instead featuring one of Skorzeny's former commandos, a 'communications expert' who now lived in Montreal.

In June 1959, it was announced that Skorzeny had purchased Martinstown House in Co. Kildare with 165 acres of surrounding land. This substantial building was built in 1830 as a shooting lodge by the third duke of Leinster and was bought for £7,500 from Major Turner, a former British Army officer and a handicapper with the Curragh Turf Club. Skorzeny visited his new property in July and stayed throughout August. In September, Skorzeny, through his solicitor, made an application for permanent residency in Ireland. The application (to which Skorzeny never received a reply) was not greeted with any enthusiasm in Irish government circles. An official in the Department of External Affairs advised against recommending the application, noting allegations (later disproved) that Skorzeny was trafficking arms to Arab countries, and that he had been refused entry to the United States and Canada for his 'pro-Nazi' viewpoint. This official also noted the further consideration that Skorzeny's name still featured on the British Home Office Suspect Index, summing up by noting that: 'I think to grant the application in this case would be to yield to pressure in that the applicant has attempted to force our hand by acquiring property here, in other words a permanent residence, before the question of his application for a visa had been disposed of. In all the circumstances, therefore, I think his application should be refused.' Skorzeny paid another visit to Ireland at the end of 1959, when he and his wife spent Christmas at Martinstown House.

By February 1960, discussion of Skorzeny's application had reached the level of the Secretary of the government departments concerned. A letter marked 'Confidential' from Con Cremin (External Affairs) to Peter Berry (Justice) made the following observation:

Having once more discussed the matter with my Minister, I can now say that his view is that we would be reluctant to authorise permanent residence. In formulating this view, the Minister is influenced by the fact that Skorzeny is a rather controversial character of some notoriety, and that circumstances could arise in which the fact of our accepting him for permanent residence could be used against us. Your department will be well aware of the tendency in some quarters abroad, when occasion offers, to use any stick to beat us, and my Minister does not see why we should provide an additional implement for that purpose. He regards it as quite probable that Skorzeny will continue to be 'mentioned in dispatches' and he does not see, on the other hand, that we owe anything to Skorzeny. Furthermore, it is not as if there were in his request to reside permanently here an element of asylum, as he holds a valid Austrian passport and seems to be able to live freely in Spain. Against this background my Minister is not disposed at the present time to recommend that the request be accorded.[31]

Only a week later (on 17 February 1960) Peter Berry's Minister for Justice was questioned in the Dáil in relation to Skorzeny's application by Dr Noel Browne. Both were formidable individuals: Oscar Traynor was one the last of de Valera's 'old guard', having fought in the 1916 Rising, Ireland's War of Independence and the Irish Civil War before serving as neutral Ireland's Minister for Defence during the war years. The temperamental Dr Browne, in his brief career as Minister for Health, had spearheaded a scheme that had largely eradicated tuberculosis in Ireland. The exchange went as follows:

Dr Browne asked the Minister for Justice whether Mr Skorzeny has asked for permission to reside permanently in Ireland.
    Minister for Justice (Mr Traynor): The person referred to in the Deputy's question has informed my Department that it is his intention, if permitted, to take up permanent residence in Ireland at some time in the future – probably not for several years – and he has formally applied for permission to do so.
    Dr Browne: Before the Minister grants this man a permit to reside in this country, may I take it he will make certain that this man does not intend to use Ireland as a base for furthering

any Nazi or neo-Nazi resurgent movements in Germany or anywhere else? It is generally understood that this man plays some part and, if so, he should not be allowed to use Ireland for that purpose.

Mr Traynor: As far as I am concerned, there is no evidence of any activities on the part of this individual such as suggested by the Deputy. Naturally, all these things will be taken into consideration on the granting of such a permit.[32]

This exchange in the Dáil caused an internal memorandum to be prepared within the Department of Justice which summarised Skorzeny's prior visits to Ireland and his purchase of Martinstown House. It noted that:

In September 1959, Skorzeny's solicitor made formal application for him to take up permanent residence in Ireland and to engage in farming. The application stated that it is not the intention of the Skorzenys 'for some considerable number of years to reside permanently throughout the entire year in Ireland and their visits for a number of years to come will be of duration of approximately 1–6 weeks at a time'. No reply was given to that communication. In the meantime investigations were being made into an allegation that Skorzeny was being expelled from Spain because he was trafficking in arms with the Algerians; it is now established that there is no truth in the suggestion that Skorzeny has become persona non grata in Spain and there is no confirmation of the story that Skorzeny was trafficking in arms with the Algerians. The person who made the allegation had not substantiated it when invited to do so.

The Minister for Justice is the authority in law for the control of aliens. From time to time we have informed enquirers, including the Governments of Member States of the Council of Europe, that nationals of the Member States are freely admitted to Ireland when they are of good character, are in a position to maintain themselves and do not intend to engage in business or take up employment without permission. We have also told them that permanent residence is granted as a matter of course to aliens fulfilling these requirements to the satisfaction of the Minister for Justice.

On the basis of our general attitude, there is no good reason which we could put forward publicly at the present time for refusing Skorzeny permission to reside here, particularly as he has been here on five occasions since 1957 without contravening our laws.[33]

The memorandum also noted that 'Skorzeny's visits attracted a fair amount of attention in the Irish and British newspapers, most of it not unfavourable'. One example of this was an article in the *Daily Express* of 16 August 1960 titled 'Scarface the quiet farmer', which included photographs of Skorzeny taking in the hay and posing with his wife and daughter outside his house at Martinstown. The text noted that 'The scar on his cheek – a sabre duel relic of his student days – burned fiercely as he denied any link with present day Nazi activities. Dr Noel Browne of the Irish Progressive Democrat Party questioned the minister for justice in the Dáil six months ago about Skorzeny's intention of settling in Ireland. The Colonel said: "Dr Browne's suggestions were completely untrue. When I become an Irish citizen I intend to have a chat with him. It is unfair to attack a man when you don't know him. I want Dr Browne to get to know me."'

Elements of the international press preferred more sensationalist fare. Skorzeny would sarcastically note elsewhere that while he was breeding sheep in the Curragh, he was also allegedly raising armies in India and the Congo as well as supplying and advising the Algerian FLN, the French OAS and the IRA.[34]

By all accounts, Skorzeny was well enough regarded locally, displaying little of the arrogance that was a hallmark of several of the Germans and Dutch that became landowners in Ireland after the war. He became a familiar sight about Kildare in his distinctive white Mercedes while his wife, a woman of considerable beauty and charm, was fondly remembered subsequently. Both dined regularly in a local hostelry 'The Hideout', an establishment famous for displaying the 150-year-old arm of a famous Irish boxer. Through Major Turner, from whom they had purchased Martinstown House, the

Skorzenys were introduced to several former British officers among whom they made many friends. Several such men lived in the Curragh area, largely due to its well-established reputation for breeding and training race horses. One ex-captain, however, who had spent two years in German POW camps, was furious to discover Skorzeny living nearby and made a complaint to the Irish government. Through 1960 Skorzeny, who demonstrated a fondness for manual labour, and his staff of six local men were engaged in clearing the farm of oak trees as a precursor to populating it with sheep, despite the warning of a local vet that the damp soil would support liver fluke.[35]

In May 1960, agents of the Israeli intelligence service (Mossad) kidnapped Nazi war criminal Adolf Eichmann from Argentina and brought him to Israel to face trial, in which he was found guilty and sentenced to death. The *Irish Times* printed an article headlined 'Movements of wanted Nazi exposed in Austria', which was based on a Arbeiter Zeitung report received from the Reuters and UPI press agencies. This alleged that Eichmann was hiding in Austria in 1949 and went on to claim that Eichmann's wife was visited by first Frau Skorzeny and later by Skorzeny himself, travelling under a Spanish passport under the name of 'Skorba', when he brought false papers for Eichmann whom he accompanied to Spain. In July 1960, the *Irish Times* printed the following letter from Skorzeny:

> I, Otto Skorzeny, have never seen or known Mr Eichmann and therefore I could never help him to escape from Austria. Also, my wife, Mrs Ilse Skorzeny, has never seen or known Mrs Eichmann. I have never had a Spanish, or other, passport with the name of Skorba, or any other assumed name. I always travelled under my proper name. Furthermore, it is of course not true that I took Mr Eichmann to Spain. Luckily enough, just when all the silly and untrue rumours started in Vienna and Germany I was on a visit in Germany and have given the following statement to the DPA (Deutsche Presse-Agenteur). I would be very grateful to you if you would print the complete statement also in your newpaper.

The statement read:

> In the last days German newspapers and … the German radio spread out false notices concerning myself. These notices I want to deny herewith energetically.
>
> 1.It was reported that I have met Eichmann in Austria in 1949 and helped him to escape. These two assertions are untrue.
>
> 2.It was reported, as coming from sources in Israel, that I have set fire to five synagogues in Vienna. That also is not true.
>
> 3.In conformity with a declaration from Tel Aviv a certain Friedmann has said that he would find me as he found Eichmann. Since 1945 my whereabouts are officially known, and if Friedmann would come to see me I will receive him duly.
>
> 4.I never had anything to do with the persecution of Jews.
>
> 5.Every publication of this kind, now and in the future, in the press, in the newspapers, in radio or television will be prosecuted by all means and with all possibilities the law gives me. I have instructed my lawyers to follow all these cases of slander.[36]

Tuvia Friedmann was a Polish Jew and concentration camp survivor who worked closely with Simon Wiesenthal to bring Adolf Eichmann to justice. In fact, Skorzeny's addresses in Spain and Ireland were routinely reported in the international press. With regard to the persecution of Jews, Skorzeny's many critics have never produced conclusive proof that he was so involved. Since the end of the war, Eichmann actually hid in Germany, until his escape to Argentina in 1950, although his wife lived in Altaussee until she followed Eichmann two years later.

It is interesting that Skorzeny would claim that his *current* wife never met Eichmann, since this allegation related to his first wife whom he divorced in 1950.

Although Skorzeny might claim that he never met Eichmann, Eichmann himself was not willing to return the compliment. On trial in Jerusalem, Eichmann claimed that he met Skorzeny on at least two occasions during the war;

at an SS-organised police conference in Berlin in 1945, Skorzeny spoke of his rescue of Mussolini while Eichmann spoke of his own dark speciality. In the final days of the war when Eichmann arrived in the 'Alpine Redoubt' and was tasked with organising a motley group of 'partisans', he met Skorzeny in Altaussee; there Skorzeny helped provide him with weapons and vehicles. In Argentina in the mid-1950s, Eichmann claimed that Skorzeny had introduced him to local publisher Willem Sassen, a former Dutch SS man, to whom he had given a lengthy and detailed account of his part in the Holocaust. Sassen subsequently sold these accounts to German and Israeli newspapers and they were used as evidence at Eichmann's trial.[37]

In January 1961 the Irish Embassy in Madrid drew the attention of the Department of External Affairs to an article in the Madrid newspaper *Pueblo* which featured a brief interview with Skorzeny. A journalist, calling on Skorzeny in his office in the Calle de Montera, asked him about his purchase of a residence in Ireland and was told, 'That's a fact. It has been said that I am living in Ireland, and all my friends greet me with great surprise on meeting me in Madrid. I continue to live in Spain. What has happened, actually, is that I have bought a property in Ireland, in order to spend the summers there. I have now also bought a property in (Majorca).'When asked how he had come to buy the property in Ireland, Skorzeny replied: 'My wife had capital there. And I also. My book, *Secret Missions*, translated into English, had a good sale in Ireland. As well, money was owed to me for my journalistic contributions to the press in Ireland. We decided to invest the money in a property. Do you know, that to take capital out of Ireland taxes of almost fifty per cent have to be paid?' Skorzeny enjoyed his stays in Ireland, observing that 'up until two years ago it was very cheap'. The Embassy official noted that 'it is obvious that Skorzeny is at pains to make himself agreeable in both Spain and Ireland, thus keeping a foot in either door.'

A secret G2 memorandum dated February 1961 noted that:

> Information – unconfirmed at this stage – from a delicate but very reliable source indicates that international arms dealers have been in touch with Otto Skorzeny with a view to setting up an arms dump in this country for later transshipment to Africa for sale to dissident elements in that continent. Cork Harbour is mentioned as the port of entry and dispatch of the arms. At present, however, the scheme is only at the planning stage and no arms have yet been landed here.
>
> It must be stressed that the source is delicate and needs *maximum* protection; and until such time as information can be confirmed no action should be taken to compromise the source, or to place Skorzeny under any embarrassment or disadvantage.

In July 1961, G2 further noted:

> Since then we have had no further information connecting [Skorzeny] with trafficking in arms, but we have recently received a report from a source whose reliability we cannot judge containing the following information.
>
> Skorzeny is reported to have had in the last few months meetings with:
>
> (a) Ex-Colonel Hans Ulrich Rudel, believed to be the well-known wartime German air force Officer, and an associate of Sir Oswald Mosley. The English edition of Rudel's book *Stuka Pilot* was published by Euphorion Books, Dublin in 1952.
>
> (b) Sir Oswald Mosley
>
> (c) Leon Degrelle – may be identical with a person of that name who was active in the German interests in Belgium during the last war.
>
> (d) One of Eichmann's sons, and others unnamed in Spain and Germany.
>
> The subject of their deliberations is reported to have been plans to liberate, or failing this, to kill Eichmann in Israel. In this connection it might not be without significance that we have information which suggests that Skorzeny had visited Egypt several times since June, 1960.
>
> Although I am unable, at present, to assess the reliability of

this information, and although some of it sounds improbable, nevertheless, I thought I should pass it on to you just in case there might be some substance to it.[38]

Skorzeny was known to have associated with both Rudel and Degrelle after the war. Rudel was an insanely courageous dive-bomber pilot, who had destroyed over 500 Russian tanks and became the most highly decorated officer in the Luftwaffe. After the war, he prospered in Argentina. He remained a devout Nazi and one of the few lifelong friends of the infamous Josef Mengele. Leon Degrelle, a Belgian officer of the Waffen-SS, escaped to Spain at the end of the war and remained in exile there, having been sentenced to death in absentia by the Belgian government. He also remained a devout Nazi and outspoken Holocaust denier. There is no evidence that any of Eichmann's sons were in Europe at the time, or that Skorzeny met with Sir Oswald Mosley, the leader of the British Union of Fascists.

The Israelis were taking most seriously the possibility of any attempt to kill or liberate Eichmann, who was being held under heavy armed guard in a compound near Haifa, which was even equipped with anti-aircraft weaponry.

Skorzeny paid another visit to Ireland in January 1963 and returned to Madrid thereafter. In February serious allegations were made against him; it was claimed that during the war he helped to develop a 'poison pistol'. These did not, however, involve the poisoned 7.65mm bullets that Skorzeny had admitted to procuring but not using. These claims alleged that Skorzeny had developed a poison *gas* pistol and it was also insinuated that this weapon was tested on human victims in a concentration camp. A warrant for Skorzeny's arrest was issued by the Austrian Ministry of Justice. Speaking to journalists in his luxury apartment in Castellon de la Plana, Skorzeny angrily remarked 'if they find their stupid accusations don't stand up they should shut up. These so-called charges are complete rubbish. I am a pretty good engineer, but as far as a poison gas pistol, that's ridiculous. Surely that was a Russian invention. I was a soldier and an honourable one.' Skorzeny refused to return to Vienna to answer the charges and Austria was unable to extradite him from Spain.[39]

Skorzeny's comment that the poison gas pistol was a Russian invention might well be the heart of the matter. In October 1957 Lev Rebert, a prominent Ukrainian nationalist, was found dead in Munich, where he had been living in exile. An autopsy indicated that he had died of a heart attack. Almost exactly two years later Stefan Bandera, another famous Ukrainian nationalist who had led guerilla forces against the Red Army from 1944 to 1947, was also found dead in Munich. This time a careful autopsy discovered fragments of glass on his face and traces of prussic acid in his stomach. Soon afterwards, the communist press launched a well-orchestrated smear campaign accusing prominent anti-communist and German government minister Dr Oberlander of responsibility. On 12 August 1961, the day before the East Germans laid barbed wire across Berlin as a preliminary to raising the Berlin Wall, a young Russian defected to the west with his German wife and a shocking tale to tell. Bogdan Stashinsky revealed himself to be a member of Department 13, a branch of the KGB dedicated to political assassination, and had been trained to use a device which sprayed prussic acid into the face of such unsuspecting victims as Rebert and Bandera. After death, the blood vessels would relax, creating the impression of a cardiac arrest. These revelations, for which Stashinsky received an eight-year sentence as an accomplice to murder, caused a worldwide wave of revulsion and the Soviet Union desperately embarked on a damage limitation exercise. Just as Oberlander had been accused of complicity in war crimes of which Bandera allegedly had knowledge, Otto Skorzeny was accused by the communist press of having developed the weapon and testing it on concentration camp victims.[40] It might be noted that such a weapon would be of limited use militarily, being useful only in enclosed spaces and against unusually unwary sentries. Whatever the truth of the

matter, the allegations did lasting damage to Skorzeny's standing in Ireland. On 13 March 1963, Dr Noel Browne again
raised the question of Skorzeny's possible residency. By now
the Minister for Justice was one Charles Haughey, who had
succeeded Traynor in 1961:

> Dr Browne and Mr McQuillan asked the Minister for Justice
> whether Mr Otto Skorzeny has sought to obtain Irish citizenship
> papers.
>
> Minister for Justice (Mr Haughey): Under the Irish Nationa-
> lity and Citizenship Act, 1956, the person concerned would be
> eligible to be considered for naturalisation only if he had resided in
> the State for five years. Since he is not residing here at all, and never
> has done so, the question of his naturalisation does not arise.
>
> Dr Browne: In the circumstances that this man has refused
> to answer an Austrian Government warrant on charges of
> serious crimes against humanity in the Nazi internment camps,
> would the Minister say whether he would be permitted into
> this country?
>
> Mr Haughey: I deal with facts and situations as they arise,
> not hypothetical questions.
>
> Dr Browne: Is it a fact that this man has property in this
> country and has the right to come into the country at present?
>
> Mr Haughey: He has no right to come to reside in this
> country.[41]

Although Mrs Skorzeny continued to visit Martinstown
House on a regular basis, Skorzeny himself rarely visited
after 1963, and paid his final visit in 1969. In 1970, he
was diagnosed with a malignant tumour on the spine, and
opted to travel discreetly to Germany to undergo life-saving
surgery there. When British writer Charles Whiting visited
the incapacitated Skorzeny in Germany that year, he found
him surrounded by several of his former commandos, tough
middle-aged men who had travelled from all over western
Europe to stand guard over their former leader. Although the
German surgeons predicted that Skorzeny would never walk
again, within days of the operation he was already beginning
a hard programme of physical rehabilitation, overseen by a

physiotherapist who had been another of his commandos. In three months he was walking again.[42] In 1971 Martinstown House was sold, together with its 165 acres for £80,000, more than ten times its purchase price. The new owner was an American named Tom Long, who ironically had served as a captain in the US Army during the Battle of the Bulge.[43]

Skorzeny died in Madrid in July 1975. His remains were cremated and the ashes returned to his family plot in his native Vienna.

Skorzeny was still capable of inspiring press speculation after his death. In 1989 it was revealed in the Israeli media that he had briefly worked for the Mossad! In 1963, Egypt had been undertaking an ambitious programme for ballistic missiles to be used against Israel, which involved certain former Nazis. After Mossad agents secured an invitation to Skorzeny's residence in Madrid and an all-night dinner, the former Waffen-SS man agreed to persuade the Germans to cease working on the missile project. Subsequent to this, he arranged with a former subordinate to supply details of the project to Mossad, which enabled them to put a halt to it. A Mossad insider stressed that Skorzeny had been an 'agent' rather than an employee.[44]

Following the postwar partition of Germany, Frank Ryan's grave near Dresden ended up in communist East Germany, where it ironically became a place of pilgrimage for the minuscule Irish Communist Party. In 1979, Ryan's remains were exhumed with full military honours and transferred to Dublin, where they were interned in Glasnevin cemetery in a ceremony attended by a diverse group of Irish republicans. Just a short distance from Ryan's new resting place was the neglected grave of Eoin O'Duffy. A figure of ridicule in his last years, O'Duffy also died in 1944 but was granted a state funeral by de Valera, not normally the most magnanimous of people.

Francis Stuart returned to Ireland in the 1950s and proved

himself capable of exciting controversy almost to his last years. When in 1997 he was honoured for his literary work by the cultural organisation 'Aosdána', a prominent member opposed the award and resigned in protest, initiating a lively debate on Stuart's wartime activity in the Irish media.

On the penultimate night of 2004, the statue of Seán Russell in Dublin's Fairview Park was again vandalised. This time the perpetrators were more thorough; by breaking off the head and arm and taking them away, they rendered the damage irreparable. A statement subsequently released by the group responsible read in part: 'Citizens of the state can no longer tolerate the shameful presence of a memorial to the Nazi collaborator Seán Russell in a public park in our nation's capital city.' Further referring to Russell as a 'traitor' and a 'nationalist fanatic who looked to Adolf Hitler for political and military support', the statement accused the IRA of being prepared to implement the 'Final Solution' in Ireland. The statement also referred to a recent homage to Russell at the statue by republican political party Sinn Féin and concluded: 'Luckily for the honour and welfare of the Irish people, Russell died on a German U-boat in August 1940 on his way home to carry out the orders of his Nazi masters.'

The group responsible for maintaining the statue considered a replacement to be protected by bullet-proof glass, for which Dublin Corporation pointed out public funds would not be made available. A representative of the Simon Wiesenthal Centre called for the statue to remain unrepaired 'as a lesson of what Irish neutrality was all about'. Something of a furore erupted as to the context of his use of the word 'shame' and the same individual later stressed that 'debating the complexities of Irish neutrality is a cathartic process to be undertaken by the Irish people alone'.[45]

APPENDIX 1

COMPARATIVE RANKS

WAFFEN-SS	WEHRMACHT	BRITISH ARMY (1939)
SS-Schütze	Schütze	Private
SS-Sturmmann	Gefreiter	Lance Corporal
SS-Rottenführer	Obergefreiter	Corporal
SS-Unterscharführer	Unteroffizier	Lance-Sergeant
SS-Scharführer	Unterfeldwebel	Sergeant
SS-Oberscharführer	Feldwebel	PlatoonSergeant Major
SS-Hauptscharführer	Oberfeldwebel	Company Sergeant Major
SS-Stabsscharführer	Stabsoberfeldwebel	Regimental Sergeant Major
SS-Untersturmführer	Leutnant	2nd Lieutenant
SS-Obersturmführer	Oberleutnant	Lieutenant
SS-Hauptsturmführer	Hauptmann	Captain
SS-Sturmbannführer	Major	Major
SS-Obersturmbannführer	Oberstleutnant	Lieutenant Colonel
SS-Standartenführer	Oberst	Colonel
SS-Oberführer	(no equivalent)	(no equivalent)
SS-Brigadeführer	Generalmajor	Major General
SS-Gruppenführer	Generalleutnant	Lieutenant General
SS-Obergruppenführer	General	General
SS-Oberstgruppenführer	Generaloberst	(no equivalent)
Reichsführer-SS	Generalfeldmarschall	Field Marshal

Note:

Waffen-SS ranks, particularly those of non-commissioned ranks, did not lend themselves to easy equivalence with other armies: the nearest British equivalent for example for SS-Unterscharführer would be 'Lance-Sergeant' used only in Guards Regiments, while 'Platoon Sergeant Major' was discontinued in 1940.

APPENDIX 2

MILITARY UNITS

A *section* is about ten men and is usually commanded by a corporal.

A *platoon* consists of three sections and a headquarters element and is usually commanded by a lieutenant. (30 men, 55 in some Waffen-SS units.)

A *company* consists of three platoons and a HQ and is usually commanded by a major. (120 men, 175 in some Waffen-SS units.)

A *battalion* consists of three line companies and a HQ company and is usually commanded by a lieutenant colonel. (500 to 900 men.)

A *brigade* (called a regiment in Germany) consists mainly of three battalions and is usually commanded by a colonel.

A *division* usually consists of three brigades and a HQ and is usually commanded by a major general. (10,000 to 22,000 men.)

Notes

UKNA = UK National Archives (WO = War Office, KV = MI5)

IMA = Irish Military Archives (G2 = Irish Military Intelligence, X = Secret)

INA = Irish National Archives

PROLOGUE

1 UKNA WO 71/1149 (Brady).
2 Mueller, F.H., 'Kirkland and MacDoll – Prussian Grenadier Guards under Frederick William', *The Irish Sword*, Vol. XVI, Issue 65.
3 Duffy, C., *In the Army of Frederick the Great* (Hippocrene Books, New York, 1974), p. 240.
4 O'Donnell, R., *The Rebellion in Wicklow 1798* (Irish Academic Press, Dublin, 1998), pp. 274–6.
5 *The Irish Sword*, Vol. XII, Issue 49.
6 Forde, F., 'Irish Rebels for Prussian Service', *An Cosantóir*, (Volume 35, No. 7).
7 *The Irish Sword*, Vol. XII, Issue 47.
8 Weale, A., *Patriot Traitors* (Viking, London, 2001), pp. 81–9; *Sunday Independent*, 28 December 1924; Hogan, J.J., *Badges: Medals: Insignia – Oglaigh na hEireann* (Irish Military Archives, Dublin, 1987), p. 13; Inglis, B., *Roger Casement* (Hodder and Stoughton, London, 1973), pp. 288–9, 303–7.
9 Coogan, T.P., *Michael Collins* (Arrow Books, London, 1990), pp. 131–2.
10 Lumsden, R., *Himmler's Black Order* (Sutton Publishing, Gloucestershire, 1997); Ailsby, C., *Waffen-SS: Hitler's Black Guard at War* (Sienna, Bristol 1998); Keegan, J., *Waffen-SS: The Asphalt Soldiers* (MacDonald & Co., London, 1970); Hohne, H., *The Order of the Death's Head* (Penguin, London, 2000).
11 Stradling, R.A., *The Irish and the Spanish Civil War 1936-1939* (Mandolin, Manchester, 1999), pp. 23–58.
12 Ennis, V., 'Some Catholic Moors', *An Cosantóir* (Vol. 44, Issue 2); MacGall, R., 'A Mi La Legion', *An Cosantóir* (Vol 9, Issue 12).
13 Stradling, *The Irish and the Spanish Civil War*, pp. 59–105.
14 *Irish Times*, 'The Irish Brigade Arrives Home', 22 June 1937.
15 UKNA KV 2/769 (Haller).
16 Stradling, *The Irish and the Spanish Civil War*, pp. 147–59, 166–7; MacGarry, F., *Frank Ryan* (Historical Association of Ireland, Dundalk, 2002), pp. 50–2.
17 Stradling, *The Irish and the Spanish Civil War*, pp. 171, 178–85.
18 MacGarry, *Frank Ryan*, pp. 57–62.

1 GUERNSEY

1 UKNA WO 71/1149; IMA G2/4949 (Codd).
2 Hull, M.M., *Irish Secrets* (Irish Academic Press, Dublin, 2003), p. 219.
3 Moreno, A., *A Short History of the Royal Irish Fusiliers* (Royal Irish Fusiliers Museum, Armagh, 2001).
4 *RUSI Journal* (February 1939); Aldershot Military Museum; Cunliffe, M., *The Royal Irish Fusiliers 1793-1968* (Oxford University Press, Oxford, 1970).
5 Shirer, W.L., *The Rise and Fall of the Third Reich* (Pan Books, London, 1964), p. 319.
6 Doherty, R., *Clear the Way! A History of the 38th (Irish) Brigade 1941–47* (Irish Academic Press, Dublin, 1993), p. 290.
7 Bell, W., *I Beg to Report – Policing in Guernsey during the German Occupation* (The Guernsey Press, Guernsey, 1995), p. 20.
8 UKNA WO 71/1149 (Brady), WO 71/1132 (Stringer).
9 *Ibid.*
10 Bell, *I Beg to Report*, pp. 20–1.
11 Brooke, J., *Talvisodan kanarialinnut: Brittivapaaehtoiset Suomessa 1940–41* (Soderstrom, Helsinki, 1984).
12 UKNA KV 2/769 (Haller).
13 UKNA KV 2/769 (Haller).
14 *Irish Independent*, 'A German Airborne Attack in the North', 25 and 26 April 1949, articles by General Student.
15 Stephan, E., *Spies in Ireland* (MacDonald, London, 1962), pp. 113–15; Hull, *Irish Secrets*, pp. 87–8; UKNA KV 2/769 (Haller).
16 *Ibid.*
17 Lucas, J., *Kommando* (Grafton Books, London, 1986), pp. 64–7.
18 Cunliffe, *The Royal Irish Fusiliers*. pp. 382-389.
19 *Ibid.* pp. 389-392.
20 Wood, A. and M., *Islands in Danger: The Story of the Occupation of the Channel Islands 1940-1945* (The Elmfield Press, Yorkshire, 1975), pp. 17–22.
21 UKNA WO 71/1149 (Brady), WO 71/1132 (Stringer).
22 Wood, *Islands in Danger*, pp. 33–42.
23 *Ibid.*, pp. 49, 46; IMA G2/X/1263 (Kenny); IMA G2/3824 (O'Reilly).
24 UKNA WO 71/1149 (Brady), WO 71/1132 (Stringer).

2 FRIESACK

1 Stephan, *Spies in Ireland*, pp. 170–5.
2 Hull, *Irish Secrets*, pp. 110–12.
3 Stephan, *Spies in Ireland*, pp. 149–53; Hull, *Irish Secrets*, pp. 147–54.
4 UKNA KV 2/769 (Haller).

5 Hull, *Irish Secrets*, p. 47.

6 Stephan, *Spies in Ireland*, pp. 155–62.

7 UKNA KV 2/769 (Haller).

8 UKNA KV 2/769 (Haller); Hanley, B., 'O Here's to Adolf Hitler' – The IRA and the Nazis', *History Ireland* (Vol. 13, Issue 3).

9 UKNA KV 2/769 (Haller); Hull, *Irish Secrets*, pp. 53–4.

10 Chancellor, H., *Colditz* (Coronet Books, London, 2001), pp. 3–4; Wheeldon, J., 'Bygones', *Derby Evening Telegraph*, 23 May 2000.

11 UKNA KV 2/769 (Haller).

12 IMA G2/X/947 (Brady).

13 IMA G2/4949 (Codd).

14 IMA G2/4949 (Codd); UKNA KV 2/769 (Haller); Cushing, R., *Soldier for Hire* (John Calder, London, 1962).

15 'Irish Colonel's Story of Life in German Camps', *Irish Times*, 13 October 1945.

16 IMA G2/X/947 (Brady); UKNA WO 71/1149 (Brady), KV 2/769 (Haller). UKNA WO 71/1169 (Stringer).

17 UKNA WO 71/1132 (Stringer), KV 2/769; IMA G2/4949 (Codd); Stephan, *Spies in Ireland*, p. 237.

18 IMA G2/X/0805 (Lenihan); Hull, *Irish Secrets*, pp. 179–83.

19 IMA G2/4949 (Codd); UKNA KV 2/769, WO 71/1132 (Stringer).

20 Speer, A., *Inside the Third Reich* (Sphere, London 1970), pp. 197–205; Channel 4 documentary, *Secret History – Television in the Third Reich* (Channel 4 Television, London, 2002); *Signal* Magazine, various issues, 1941.

21 O'Reilly, J., 'I was a Spy in Ireland', *Sunday Dispatch*, 13 July 1952.

22 IMA G2/4949 (Codd); UKNA KV 2/769 (Haller), WO 71/1132 (Stringer).

23 Stephan, *Spies in Ireland*, p. 237.

24 UKNA KV 2/769 (Haller), WO 71/1132 (Stringer); IMA G2/4949 (Codd). Abella, A. and Gordon S., *Shadow Enemies* (Lyons Press, Connecticut, 2002), p.20.

25 UKNA KV 2/769 (Haller); Cushing, *Soldier for Hire*, pp. 248–50; UKNA WO 71/1149 (Brady); 'Back from the Camps', *Irish Times*, 14 June 1945.

26 UKNA WO 71/1149 (Brady), KV 2/769 (Haller); IMA G2/4949 (Codd).

27 UKNA WO 71/149 (Brady).

28 UKNA KV 2/769 (Haller).

29 UKNA KV 2/769 (Haller), WO 71/1132 (Stringer); IMA G2/4949 (Codd).

30 UKNA KV 2/769 (Haller), WO 71/1132 (Stringer); Abella, A. and Gordon, S., *Shadow Enemies* (Lyons Press, Connecticut, 2002).

31 WO 71/1132 (Stringer); G2/4949 (Codd). UKNA KV 2/769 (Haller)

32 WO 71/1132 (Stringer); WO 71/1149 (Brady); UKNA KV 2/769 (Haller).

33 UKNA KV 2/769 (Haller).

34 Sweetman, J., *The Dambusters* (Time Warner, London, 2003); Brickhill, P.,

The Dam Busters (Pan Books, London, 1983).

35 Stephan, *Spies in Ireland,* p. 239; UKNA WO 71/1149 (Brady).

36 UKNA WO 71/1132 (Stringer); See also *Shadow Enemies.*

37 UKNA KV 2/769 (Haller), WO 71/1132 (Stringer); IMA G2/4949 (Codd).

38 UKNA KV 2/769, WO 71/1149 (Brady).

39 Bekker, C., *The Luftwaffe War Diaries* (Ballantine Books, New York, 1972), pp. 374–5; *War Monthly* (Issue 30: September 1976).

40 UKNA KV 2/769 (Haller).

41 Foot, M.R.D., *SOE in France* (HMSO, London, 1966), pp. 54–9.

42 Masterman, J.C., *The Double-Cross System in the War of 1939 to 1945* (Yale University Press, Yale, 1972); Hull, *Irish Secrets,* pp. 226–7.

43 UKNA KV 2/769 (Haller); Tarrant, V.E., *The Red Orchestra* (Arms and Armour Press, London, 1995), pp. 83–8, 97, 103.

44 Stephan, *Spies in Ireland,* pp. 239–40; UKNA WO 71/1149 (Brady), KV 2/769 (Haller), WO 71/1149 (Brady), WO 71/1132 (Stringer); IMA G2/4949 (Codd).

45 'Tim Ronan Remembers', *Evening Echo,* 30 May 1979; 'Back from the Camps', *Irish Times,* 14 June 1945.

46 'Irish Colonel's Story of Life in German Camps', *Irish Times,* 13 October 1945; UKNA KV 2/769 (Haller).

47 Cushing, *Soldier for Hire,* pp. 255–6; UKNA KV 2/769 (Haller).

48 UKNA KV 2/769 (Haller).

49 Cushing, *Soldier for Hire,* pp. 256–7; Simpson, C. and Shirley, J. 'The Last Days of Lieutenant Jakov Stalin', *Sunday Times,* 24 January 1980; Shulman, S., *Kings of the Kremlin* (Brassey, London, 2002), pp. 139–40.

50 'Irish Colonel's Story of Life in German Camps', *Irish Times,* 13 October 1945.

3 THE SS

1 IMA G2/3824 (O'Reilly).

2 O'Donoghue, D., *Hitler's Irish Voices* (Beyond the Pale Publications, Belfast, 1998), pp. 210–11.

3 Stuart, F., 'Frank Ryan in Germany', *The Bell* (Volume 16 No. 2 November 1950).

4 O'Donoghue, *Hitler's Irish Voices,* pp. 51–2, 56.

5 UKNA WO 71/1149 (Brady), KV 2/769 (Haller); IMA G2/4949 (Codd).

6 IMA G2/4949 (Codd).

7 WO 71/1132 (Stringer); UKNA WO 71/1149 (Brady), KV 2/769 (Haller).

8 *Author's note: for ease of narration, I will continue to refer to Brady by his given name.*

9 IMA G2/X/947 (Brady); Ó Drisceoil, D., *Censorship in Ireland 1939–1945* (Cork University Press, Cork, 1996), pp. 61–6.

10 UKNA KV 2/403 (Skorzeny).

11 Higgins, A., 'The Day We Almost Invaded Ireland', *Washington Post,* 15 March 1992.

12 UKNA KV 2/769 (Haller); Stephan, *Spies in Ireland,* pp. 234–5.

13 *Ibid.*

14 Skorzeny, O., *My Commando Operations* (Schiffer Military History, Pennsylvania, 1995), pp. 201–3; UKNA KV 2/769 (Haller).

15 IMA G2/ 4949 (Codd); UKNA KV 2/769 (Haller).

16 Skorzeny, *My Commando Operations,* pp. 126–7; Foley, C., *Commando Extraordinary* (Cassell, London, 1998), pp. 138–9.

17 MacLean, F., *The Cruel Hunters* (Schiffer Military History, Pennsylvania, 1998).

18 UKNA KV 2 /403 (Skorzeny); Skorzeny, *My Commando Operations,* pp. 141–5.

19 Stephan, *Spies in Ireland,* pp. 237–8; IMA G2/4949 (Codd).

20 'Militar Geographische Angaben uber Irland', *An Cosantóir* (Volume 35 No 3); O'Donoghue, *Hitler's Irish Voices,* pp. 12–18.

21 IMA G2/4949 (Codd); IMA G2/3824 (O'Reilly); Kahn, D., *Hitler's Spies* (Hodder and Stoughton, London, 1978), p. 266.

22 Mulvaney, P., 'Victims of War', *An Cosantóir* (Volume 61 No 6); Doherty, R., *Irish Men and Women in the Second World War* (Four Courts Press, Dublin, 1999), pp. 290–2.

23 UKNA WO 71/1149 (Brady), WO 71/1132 (Stringer), KV 2/769 (Haller).

24 IMA G2/4949 (Codd).

25 UKNA WO 71/1149 (Brady), WO 71/1132 (Stringer), KV 2/769 (Haller).

26 Skorzeny, O. and Radl, E., *The Rescue of Mussolini,* (Historical Division, US War Department, 1947); Skorzeny, *My Commando Operations,* pp. 265–73.

27 Williamson, G., *The SS: Hitler's Instrument of Terror* (Sidgwick and Jackson, London, 1994) pp. 109–17, 132.

28 Lumsden, R., *Himmler's Black Order* pp. 202, 207; Ailsby, C., *Waffen-SS: Hitler's Black Guard at War* pp. 52–97; Keegan, J., *Waffen-SS: The Asphalt Soldiers* pp. 93–6.

29 Hohne, H., *The Order of the Death's Head* p. 473; Reynolds, M., *Steel Inferno* (Dell Publishing, New York, 1997), pp. 18–19; Reynolds, M., *Sons of the Reich* (Spellmount, Kent, 2002), pp. 1–3.

30 Degrelle, L., *Epic: The Story of the Waffen-SS* (SOF Publications, Wales, undated), p. 33; Williamson, *The SS: Hitler's Instrument of Terror,* p. 132.

31 Williamson, *The SS: Hitler's Instrument of Terror,* pp. 122–3.

32 Mounine, H., *Cernay 40–45: Le SS-Ausbildungslager de Sennheim* (Editions du Polygone, Ostwald, 1999), pp. 237, 381, 466.

33 Quarrie, B. and Burn, J. *Waffen-SS Soldier 1940-1945* (Osprey, London, 1993), pp. 10–32.

34 Weale, A., *Renegades – Hitler's Englishmen* (Pimlico, London, 2002), pp. 120-121

35 Mounine, *Cernay 40–45,* pp. 177–9, 186–7, 196–9.

36 *Ibid.,* pp. 196–7.

37 *Ibid.*, pp. 197–8.

38 Lumsden, *Himmler's Black Order.*

39 Mounine, *Cernay 40–45,* pp. 186, 270.

40 Mounine, *Cernay 40–45,* pp. 149, 259, 296.

41 UKNA WO 71/1149 (Brady).

42 O'Farrell, P., *Tales for the Telling* (The Collins Press, Cork, 1990), pp. 41–57.

43 Mounine, *Cernay 40–45,* pp. 417–21.

44 IMA G2/4949 (Codd), WO 71/1132 (Stringer); KV 2/769 (Haller).

45 Himmler, H., Speech to SS-Gruppenführers at Posen, Poland, 4 October 1943 (US National Archives document 242.256, reel 2 of 3).

46 Mounine, *Cernay 40–45,* pp. 272–5, 290.

47 IMA G2/4949 (Codd); IMA G2/3824 (O'Reilly).

48 Actually Canada.

49 IMA G2/X/1263 (Kenny); IMA G2/3824 (O'Reilly)

50 IMA G2/4949 (Codd); Neillands, R., *The Bomber War* (John Murray, London, 2001), pp. 281–6.

51 IMA G2/3824 (O'Reilly); Hull, *Irish Secrets,* pp. 264–5.

52 Stephan, *Spies in Ireland,* pp. 272–5, 290.

53 IMA G2/X/1263 (Kenny); IMA G2/3824 (O'Reilly).

4 JAGDVERBAND MITTE

1 UKNA WO 71/1149 (Brady), WO 71/1132 (Stringer), KV 2/403 (Skorzeny).

2 Parker, D.S., *Battle of the Bulge* (Greenhill Books, London, 1991), pp. 116–21.

3 UKNA WO 71/1149 (Brady), WO 71/1132 (Stringer).

4 UKNA KV 2/403 (Skorzeny). This is a copy of the extensive interrogation of Skorzeny carried out by the US Army in July 1945; Released by British Public Record Office (now named National Archives) in 2001.

5 UKNA KV 2 /403 (Skorzeny); Infield, G.B., *Skorzeny: Hitler's Commando* (St Martin's Press, New York, 1981), pp. 45–53.

6 UKNA WO 71/1149 (Brady).

7 IMA G2/4949 (Codd).

8 WO 71/1132 (Stringer).

9 Foley, *Commando Extraordinary,* pp. 80–1; Skorzeny, *My Commando Operations,* pp. 398–406.

10 IMA G2/4949 (Codd): Kahn D., *Hitler's Spies* (Hodder and Stoughton, London, 1979) pp. 7–9.

11 UKNA KV 2/403 (Skorzeny).

12 IMA G2/4949 (Codd).

13 IMA G2/4949 (Codd); UKNA KV 2/403 (Skorzeny).

14 Kahn, *Hitler's Spies,* pp. 9–26; IMA G2/4949 (Codd).

15 IMA G2/4949 (Codd); UKNA KV 2/403 (Skorzeny).

16 *Actually Brady was then at the secret Friesack camp.*

17 IMA G2/X/947 (Brady),

18 MacGarry, *Frank Ryan*, pp. 72–3; Fisk, R., *In Time of War* (Paladin, London, 1985), p. 533.

19 O'Donoghue, *Hitler's Irish Voices*, pp. 137–41, 160–3.

20 UKNA WO 71/1149 (Brady), WO 71/1132 (Stringer).

21 Foley, *Commando Extraordinary*, pp. 88–100; Skorzeny, *My Commando Operations*, pp. 285–302.

22 Schellenberg, W., *The Schellenberg Memoirs* (Andre Deutsch, London, 1956), pp. 409–10.

23 UKNA WO71/1149 (Brady), WO 71/1132 (Stringer).

24 MacLean, *The Cruel Hunters*, pp. 175–98.

25 Wehrmacht High Command

26 UKNA KV 2/403 (Skorzeny), WO 71/1149 (Brady); Foley, *Commando Extraordinary*, pp. 154-156

27 UKNA KV 2/403 (Skorzeny).

28 Cesarani, D., *Eichmann – His Life and Crimes* (William Heinemann, London, 2004), pp. 162–83.

29 Skorzeny, *My Commando Operations*, pp. 312–14; Foley, *Commando Extraordinary*, pp. 106–10.

30 Skorzeny, *My Commando Operations*, pp. 314–23; Foley, *Commando Extraordinary*, pp. 104–17; UKNA KV 2/403 (Skorzeny), WO /1149 (Brady).

31 Cesarani, *Eichmann*, pp. 190–2.

32 Cunliffe, *The Royal Irish Fusiliers* pp400-433 ; Horsfall, J., *The Wild Geese are Flighting* (Roundwood Press, Warwick, 1976), pp. 162–4; Horsfall, J., *Fling our Banner to the Wind* (Roundwood Press, Warwick, 1978), pp. 210–11; Gunner, C.J., *Front of the Line* (Greystone Books, Belfast, 1991), pp. 98, 116, 138.

33 Doherty, *Irishmen and Women in the Second World War.*

34 Doherty, R., *Irish Volunteers in the Second World War* (Four Courts Press, Dublin, 2002), pp. 286–8; O'Donovan S., 'Moryah my girl!' *An Cosantóir* (Volume 53 Issue 6).

35 WO 71/1132 (Stringer).

36 UKNA KV 2/403 (Skorzeny).

37 Parker, D. and Volstad, R., *Ardennes 1944: Peiper and Skorzeny* (Osprey, London, 1987), pp. 3–15.

38 UKNA KV 2/403 (Skorzeny).

39 WO 71/1132 (Stringer); UKNA WO 71/1149 (Brady); Hastings, M., *Das Reich* (Pan Books, London, 1981).

40 Beevor, A., *Stalingrad* (Penguin, London, 1998), Pp255 ; Gott, K.D., *Breaking the Mold – Tanks in the Cities* (Combat Studies Institute Press, Kansas, 2006), p. 14.

41 UKNA KV 2/403 (Skorzeny); Foley, *Commando Extraordinary*, pp. 147–9; Skorzeny, *My Commando Operations*, pp. 396–8,406–7.

42 UKNA KV 2/403 (Skorzeny); Foley, *Commando Extraordinary*, p. 155; Skorzeny, *My Commando Operations*, pp. 407–8.

43 Ryan, C., *The Last Battle* (Collins, London, 1966), pp. 74–5; Beevor, A.,

Berlin – The Downfall 1945 (Viking, London, 2002), p. 130.

44 Foley, *Commando Extraordinary*, pp. 158–65; Skorzeny, *My Commando Operations*, pp. 412–24; Munoz, A.J., *Forgotten Legions – Obscure Combat Formations of the Waffen-SS* (Axis Europa Books, Georgia, 1991), pp. 71–95; UKNA KV 2/403 (Skorzeny), WO 71/1149 (Brady).

45 UKNA WO 71/1149 (Brady); Munoz, *Forgotten Legions*, pp. 97–9; Ryan, *The Last Battle*, p. 84; Beevor, *Berlin – The Downfall 1945*, p. 132.

46 Ryan, *The Last Battle*, pp. 82–5.

47 UKNA WO 71/1149 (Brady), WO 71/1132 (Stringer); Munoz, *Forgotten Legions*, pp. 99–108.

48 Skorzeny, *My Commando Operations*, pp. 426, 428–33; UKNA KV 2/403 (Skorzeny).

49 IMA G2/4949 (Codd).

50 Altner, H., *Berlin, Dance of Death* (Spellmount, Kent, 2002), pp. 118–19; IMA G2/4949 (Codd)

51 IMA G2/4949 (Codd); Sachsenhausen Memorial and Museum.

52 *Renegades – Hitler's Englishmen*, pp. 169–70.

53 IMA G2/4949 (Codd); Cushing, *Soldier for Hire*. pp. 261–2; 'Irish Colonel's Story of Life in German Camps', *Irish Times*, 13 October 1945. p260-262

54 UKNA WO 71/1149 (Brady), WO 71/1132 (Stringer).

55 Skorzeny, *My Commando Operations*, pp. 408–11, Foley, *Commando Extraordinary*, pp. 155–6; Hastings, M., *Armageddon* (Pan Books, London, 2004), pp. 525–6.

56 Ryan, *The Last Battle*, pp. 159–61.

57 UKNA KV 2/403 (Skorzeny); Skorzeny, *My Commando Operations*, pp. 432–5.

58 WO 71/1132 (Stringer).

59 *The Americans' prim rendition of Fucker's name!*

60 UKNA KV 2/403 (Skorzeny), WO 71/1132 (Stringer)

5 AFTERMATH

1 IMA G2/4949 (Codd)

2 UKNA KV 2/403 (Skorzeny)

3 Whiting, C., *Warriors of Death* (Arrow Books, London, 1991), p. 193.

4 Skorzeny, *My Commando Operations*, pp. 436–9; Foley, *Commando Extraordinary*, pp. 172–6.

5 UKNA KV 2/403 (Skorzeny).

6 WO 71/1132 (Stringer).

7 IMA G2/4949 (Codd); UKNA KV 2/769 (Haller).

8 'Back from the Camps', *Irish Times*, 14 June 1945

9 UKNA WO 71/1149 (Brady).

10 WO 71/1132 (Stringer).

11 Weale, *Renegades- Hitler's Englishmen*, pp. 176–7; WO 71/1132 (Stringer).

12 UKNA WO 71/1149 (Brady).
13 'Irish Colonel's Story of Life in German Camps', *Irish Times*, 13 October 1945
14 IMA G2/3824 (O'Reilly).
15 UKNA WO 71/1149 (Brady).
16 Skorzeny, *My Commando Operations*, pp. 445–6; Foley, *Commando Extraordinary*, p. 179; UKNA WO 71/1149 (Brady).
17 WO 71/1132 (Stringer).
18 McKee, A., Dresden 1945 – *The Devil's Tinderbox* (Souvenir, London, 1982); UKNA WO 71/1149 (Brady).
19 UKNA WO 71/1149 (Brady); Weale, *Renegades- Hitler's Englishmen*, p. 171; UKNA WO 71/1149 (Brady); IMA G2/X/947 (Brady).
20 Skorzeny, *My Commando Operations*, pp. 449–53, 377–8; Foley, *Commando Extraordinary*, pp. 181–200; Infield, *Skorzeny: Hitler's Commando*, pp. 133–43
21 UKNA KV 2/1951, WO 71/1149 (Brady); IMA G2/4949 (Codd).
22 *Ibid*.
23 Stephan, *Spies in Ireland*, p. 113.
24 *Evening Press*, 'Commando – A Salesman Now', 10 June 1957.
25 Irish National Archives; Department of Foreign Affairs (DFA) file P316.
26 Skorzeny, *My Commando Operations*, pp. 455–6.
27 MacLean, *The Cruel Hunters*, pp. 250–4; Cesarani, *Eichmann*, Chapter 8.
28 Goni, U., *The Real Odessa* (Granta Books, London, 2002).
29 *One of a few occasions that Skorzeny would untruthfully claim to be working for an Irish newspaper.*
30 *The Canadian Broadcasting Corporation had proposed to feature Skorzeny in a television programme called 'Front Page Challenge' in relation to the rescue of Mussolini. Most transatlantic airlines at that time were routed through Shannon airport in the west of Ireland.*
31 INA DFA P316.
32 *Dáil Éireann Reports*, Vol 179, 17 February 1960.
33 INA DFA P316.
34 Skorzeny, *My Commando Operations*, p. 461.
35 Curragh Local History Group, *The Curragh Revisited* (Curragh Local History Group, Kildare, 2002), pp. 59–60; Timmins, E, 'How a Top Nazi was at Home in Kildare', *Kildare Nationalist*, 7 November 2003.
36 *Irish Times*, 'Skorzeny denies report about Eichmann's post war escape', 9 July 1960.
37 Goni, *The Real Odessa*, pp. 304–6; Cesarani, *Eichmann*, pp. 198–9.
38 INA DFA P316.
39 *Daily Express*, 4 June 1963; *Irish Press*, 4 February 1963; *Sunday Press*, 17 February 1963.
40 Barron, J, *KGB* (Hodder and Stoughton, London, 1974), pp. 311–20.
41 *Dáil Éireann Reports*, volume 200, 12 March 1963.
42 Whiting, C., *The Most Dangerous Man in Europe* (Leo Cooper, London, 1998), pp. 1–3.
43 Curragh Local History Group, *The Curragh Revisited* (Curragh Local History Group, Kildare, 2002), p. 60.

44 'Ex-SS Man Worked for Mossad against Egyptian Rocket Project', *Jerusalem Post*, 20 September 1989.

45 *Sunday Independent*, 'Anti-Fascists Behead Statue of Russell', 2 January 2005, *Irish Independent*, 'Jewish Group Says Beheaded "Nazi" Statue Should be Left as Symbol of Irish Shame', 13 January 2005, *Sunday Times*, 'Nazi Russell Statue to be Vandal-Proof', 9 January 2005, *Sunday Independent*, 'Anti-Nazi Group Says Let Vandalised Statue Remain', 16 January 2005, *Irish Independent*, 'Letter to Editor', 28 January 2005.

Acknowledgements

I would like to gratefully acknowledge the assistance of the many people who directly and indirectly assisted in the production of this book.

The staff of the Defence Forces Library for technical assistance and advice on matters military.

The staff of the Defence Forces Archives, whose professional assistance and knowledge opened up new aspects in my research.

The Irish National Archives, the British National Archives and the German National Archives (Bundesarchiv) whose professionalism was matched only by their courtesy.

Colonel Desmond Travers and Commandant Pat Graham for reviewing the finished manuscript and advising on it.

Such historians as Antonio J Munoz and Henri Mounine, for their diligence in chronicling an obscure if fascinating area of history for the benefit of future historians.

Marcus Wendel's Axis History Forum (http://forum. axishistory.com/) and its many members for providing so many lines of enquiry.

The staff of the Aldershot Military Museum, the Royal Irish Fusiliers Museum and the Sachsenhausen Memorial and Museum.

Eoin Purcell and Brian Ronan of the Mercier Press for their patience and assistance.

Lastly my former history teacher, Des Cowman, for first providing the skills that eventually bore fruit.

Index